IMPACT

the battle story of the

TENTH ARMORED DIVISION

LESTER M. NICHOLS

BRADBURY · SAYLES · O'NEILL
CO., INC. · NEW YORK
PUBLISHERS

Dedicated to the battle dead who lie stilled forever in lands they helped liberate while fighting to crush Nazi oppression; and to the late Paul W. Newgarden, beloved first commanding general of the Tenth Armored Division.

IMPACT —
clash, collision, bump, crash,
shock, smash, charge.

— WEBSTER

"With terrific force of IMPACT, the Tenth Armored Division burst through enemy lines . . . smashed to his rear installations . . . wrecked communications and in an average day of combat, fired more than 700 tons of ammunition to help defeat the German military machine."

FOREWORD

The research and subsequent writing of IMPACT began in the Spring of 1946 as a result of a telephone call. In Washington, D. C., at the other end of the line was Lieut. Gen. William H. H. Morris, Jr., wartime commander of the Tenth Armored Division. "For some time now," he said, "I have been concerned that there is no written record of the magnificent achievements of the men of the Tiger Division." After a brief pause, he continued, "Now for the $64 question. Will you write it?" The answer, of course, is this battle account. During the years that followed, the almost impossible task of assembling factual material from countless sources was undertaken. By early summer of 1947, the first draft was completed. But the continued flow of new and important information necessitated eight successive, completely revised manuscripts during the past seven years. Thanks to the resourcefulness of Tenth Armored men from private to general, IMPACT has grown steadily in breadth and depth. It is my belief, and hope, that it is a faithful and accurate narration of the courage and achievements of one of America's truly outstanding fighting divisions in the Second World War.

The preparation of this documentation has been a daily—or, more precisely, a nightly and weekend preoccupation of the author ever since Labor Day of 1952, when the Tenth Armored Division staged its first national convention in New York City. Interest among the Tigers in this History of the Division, the many efforts to help in providing information, and the availability of names and addresses for circularization all provided the goal towards which the author has earnestly striven. This goal has been to produce a completely accurate and carefully documented account of the Tenth Armored Division. More than 2,000 hours of research and writing have been funnelled into this story in the last thirty months. But mine has been a relatively simple contribution to the recording of the Tigers' story. The long hours of research and writing have been softened by the knowledge and remembrance of the tremendous sacrifices made by these men and their families in wartime.

From more than fifty officers and men of the Tenth Armored has come significant material for IMPACT. Maximum use was made of the Fifth Avenue Library in New York City in the search for facts. In addition, both the City College of New York and the United States Military Academy Libraries provided a substantial fund of new information. Fortunately, too, the author had at his disposal three footlockers crammed with pictures, Division press clippings, war communiques, orders, complete sets of the Division newspaper, "The Tigers' Tale", staff and unit commander lists and reams of other information relating to the Tenth Armored. These sources were fully exploited to help make IMPACT a final and fitting tribute to the fighting Tigers. With the exception of that material which would not add to the readers' interest, all available information has been written into the History. Many difficult problems were encountered by the author in the preparation of the story. Consider the fantastic amount of detail that is involved in just one battle. Add to this the fact that, in the years that have elapsed since the end of the war, memories have faded, important battle records have been lost, conflicting versions of the same battle have been received and, often, rumors have come to be accepted as fact. Most of these handicaps have been overcome. The tiny pieces of an extremely difficult jigsaw puzzle of battle have been fitted, one by one, into place over the years.

The author is deeply grateful to Lieut. Col. John W. Sheffield, who contributed so much to the documentation of the story. His willingness to spend hours reviewing each chapter has resulted in substantial improvement of the final manuscript. Very much appreciated too, are the helpful suggestions of Lieut. Gen. William H. H. Morris, Jr. Without his support, the History could not have become a reality. The author is indebted to Brig. Gen. Williams L. Roberts, who provided many pages of factual information and insisted on absolute perfection, especially with regard to the Bastogne chapter. Appreciation is extended also to Lieut. Col. Willis D. Crittenberger, Jr., who offered many valuable suggestions and added many facts for the improvement of the History. Others who contributed much to IMPACT are Brig. Gen. Edwin W. Piburn, Major Cortland A. Bassett, Major Floyd Walters, Lieut. Col. Curtiss L. Hankins, Lieut. Col. George Seignious, Colonel Joseph A. McChristian, Colonel Ned Norris, Lieut. Col. John F. Laudig, Colonel Wade C. Gatchell, Sergeant James Gallagher, Corporal Harold C. Barnett, Sergeant Don Jerge, Pfc. Delmer D. Hildoer, Major Jack Madison, Captain John R. Walker, Lieut. James Swauger, Lieut. Col. William W. Beverly and many others.

Andrew Quin and Edwin Grace, President and Secretary of the Tenth Armored Division Veterans' Association, along with other hard-working members of the Boston and New York Chapters, worked diligently to supply much-needed lists of Tiger addresses. Larry Davidson, president of the 796th AAA Battalion Association also provided address lists. Richard S. Henry toiled long hours in helping to complete the first draft of the manuscript. Ray Lutz's excellent pictures are to be found everywhere in IMPACT, Dan Davidoff drew the fine maps and charts and Lieut. I. E. Levine and John J. McCarthy offered expert suggestions for the improvement of the narrative. The reader's attention is directed to the many outstanding publications which include, in part, details of the Tenth Armored's combat activities. They are: "Patton and His Third Army" by Colonel Brenton G. Wallace; "The U. S. Army in World War II, The Lorraine Campaign", by H. V. Cole; "History of The XX Corps"; "Dark December", by Robert E. Merriam; "Third Army, A Brief History of Operations in Europe"; "War As I Knew It", by General George S. Patton; "Bastogne, The First Eight Days", by Colonel S. L. A. Marshall; "The Tenth Armored Division in The Crailsheim Operation" and "The Tenth Armored Division in The

Saar-Moselle Triangle", both Armored School Studies, Fort Knox, Kentucky; "The U. S. Seventh Army In The European Theater of Operations"; and "Battle History, Combat Command A, Tenth Armored Division".

The author's appreciation is offered also to Hugh Schuck, assistant telegraph editor and former war correspondent of The New York Daily News; H. V. Kaltenborn, distinguished commentator for the National Broadcasting Company; and Hal Boyle, Associated Press columnist and former war correspondent. C. E. Dornbusch, special assistant in government documents; The New York Public Library; and leading authority on military publications, provided much-needed information relating to the preparation of IMPACT.

Finally, it is hoped that IMPACT will measure up to the high standards of achievement set by the Tenth Armored Division's 37,000 men, who served so well the cause of peace, as members of one of America's outstanding combat divisions.

LESTER M. NICHOLS

WHITE PLAINS, NEW YORK
MARCH 1, 1954

CONTENTS

MAPS

CHARTS

I

THE BEGINNING OF THE END

As THE HUGE NAVY TRANSPORT, the "Breckinridge", slowly edged into its berth at Newport News, Virginia, on October 13, 1945, five thousand combat veterans of the Tenth Armored Division crowded to her starboard side to get their first look at America in more than a year. Excitement ran riot in the hearts of the battle-weary troops as they streamed down the gangplank to waiting busses which rushed them to Camp Patrick Henry for final processing. Two days later the men were enroute to army camps nearest their homes. Here final physical examinations were completed, papers put in order and final payments made to the happy Tigers. After months of blood, sweat and tears each of the homeward-bound men of the Division realized at long last his chief ambition.

Thirteen months earlier, the Division, after a false start, sailed from New York on the "Brazil", former Bermuda luxury liner, for an unknown destination. Originally, most of the Tigers including the Tenth's staff officer, Colonel Julian E. Raymond, had embarked on the "Alexander". Col. Raymond had sailed overseas on the same ship in the first World War. High tide did not come until midnight on September 13, so that by the time the huge troopship slipped away from her pier, most of the Tigers had retired in anticipation of arising in the morning far out at sea. Imagine one's astonishment then, at being awakened by the sound of automobile horns and seeing land less than 200 yards away through the porthole. Instead of riding the high seas, the Tigers were stranded in Brooklyn. During the night, the "Alexander" had been forced too far to the left in a heavy fog by an incoming British freighter and had run aground on a sand bar in the Narrows. The remainder of the day was spent being transferred

1

in a downpour via hastily-assembled ferryboats to the "Brazil", which had arrived from Europe only the day before and was quickly made ready for departure during the night of September 14. In the meantime, the remainder of the Division had sailed on other ships, leaving those on the "Brazil" to catch up, accompanied by a lone Navy destroyer escort for protection against marauding German submarines. On September 16, after eluding a dangerous fall hurricane, the convoy was sighted, to the great satisfaction of all on board the "Brazil". Two days later, the convoy was attacked by enemy U boats which were driven off by Navy destroyers—but not before they had succeeded in torpedoing one of the convoy's tankers. From that day on, appetites dwindled as the big troopship constantly shifted direction, zigzagging to elude unwelcome pursuers.

The "Breckinridge" arrives with its cargo of happy warriors

Embarkation scene at Marseilles, France

BREAKTHROUGH

Debarking at Cherbourg, France, the Tenth achieved distinction as being the first armored division to land on French soil directly from America. Then, after only a month of training, and having drawn new equipment, the Division was assigned to General Patton's United States Third Army, and was given its baptism of fire in the Mars La Tour area on November 2, 1944. Before the year's end, the Tenth Armored Division was to figure prominently in the capture of the 1,500 year-old fortress at Metz, France and to play a leading role in the epic defense of Bastogne in Belgium. And in 1945, too, its fighters were to contribute even more to its superb battle record. Though at times outnumbered and surrounded, these men fought back savagely to inflict crushing defeat upon the enemy in some the war's greatest tank and infantry battles. Moreover, Tiger task forces rocketed 600 miles through France, Luxembourg, Belgium, Germany and Austria, capturing 56,000 prisoners and 650 towns and cities along the

3

way. The Tenth's brilliant combat achievements were based on disciplined teamwork. While the spotlight is focused primarily on the tankers and doughs, and rightly so, these same men were the first to recognize the important role of supporting units. They placed supreme confidence in the Tiger engineers who cleared minefields and roadblocks to permit rapid penetration through enemy lines, in the artillery which so often broke up enemy attacks and dropped a protective blanket of fire in advance of the explosive Tiger forces, in the signalmen who kept lines of communication functioning under adverse conditions, in the ordnance which repaired or replaced their vehicles, in the medics who while under fire rescued the wounded from the battlefield to cheat death time after time, and in the anti-aircraft men who drove the marauding Luftwaffe from the skies.

Armored spearhead across Germany

RECORD BREAKERS

Throughout its battle history, the Division earned the respect and admiration of higher commanders including General George Marshall, General Eisenhower, Generals Bradley, Devers, Patton and Patch who bestowed more than thirty battle honors, awards and citations upon the fighting Tenth Armored Division.

On November 15, 1944, the Armoraiders participated in the capture of Metz. Its rampaging task forces encircled that ancient

4

fortress to seal the enemy's escape routes and at the same time, to prevent reinforcing of its strongly-held connected series of concrete and steel forts. For the first time in a century and a half, the Fortress was forced to capitulate to the infantry divisions which undertook the bloody frontal assault as armor supported the attack with steel and fire. Following this great battle, the Division lost no time as it smashed headlong into the heavily-defended Siegfried Line to fight its way across the German border near Eft on November 20, and become the first unit of General George S. Patton's United States Third Army to enter Germany. Less than a month later, it was the first American unit rushed north by General Eisenhower to help stop the German winter blitz at Bastogne and at the Belgian-Luxembourg borders. More than 56,000 Americans were killed as the Germans hurled 500,000 crack troops, 1,000 tanks and 800 planes into the Battle of the Bulge. In this, the scene of history's bloodiest combat, the Tenth Armored played a leading role in helping to push back the Nazi tide at Bastogne and in preventing the capture of the city of Luxembourg. On February 20, 1945, the Division, in an un-paralled achievement, punched through the world's most heavily fortified area to clear the Saar-Moselle Triangle and capture centuries-old Trier. After the war, one-time German chief of staff, Field Marshal Jodl, asserted that the capture of Trier was one of three main factors in the defeat of the German armies. The other two, he said, were the successful invasion landings and the swiftness with which the Allies crossed the Rhine. In capturing Trier, the Tenth Armored broke the hinges of the Siegfried Line and permitted large-scale operations to the north and south for the breakthrough to the Rhine.

ACCELERATED ATTACK

In mid-March, the Armoraiders raced across the Palatinate, the vast area between the Saar and Rhine Rivers, scooped up 10,000 prisoners from 26 German divisions and cut off the escape routes for an additional 30,000 hapless enemy. At the Rhine, the veteran Tigers were selected to lead General Alexander S. Patch's United States Seventh Army's assault into southern Bavaria and Austria. On the way, the Tenth became the first unit of the Seventh Army to cross the Austrian border on April 27, 1945 near Fuessen. At the same time, the unstoppable task forces of the Division smashed the myth of Adolph Hitler's vaunted Alpine National Redoubt. Throughout its combat history, the spearheading task forces of the Tenth Armored blazed a path of destruction to help force the once-powerful German war machine to its knees. The chaos left in the wake of the violent armored drive as it slammed through five European countries is almost indescribable.

Fortunately, most of the gallant fighting men of the Tenth were spared the loss of life, though the casualty rate skyrocketed in each succeeding battle campaign. Not enough credit can be given to the disciplined combat training undertaken in the pine woods of Georgia, and to the excellent battle leadership received from Tiger officers and non coms. Occasionally, Tigers were wounded under very unusual circumstances. One such incident was that of a young Tiger who was denied a Purple Heart medal, despite the fact that German shrapnel knocked out one of his front teeth. He was declared ineligible for the award when it was discovered that the tooth was false.

Dubbed "The Ghost Division" by the Germans, because it reappeared several times in different army sectors against the same enemy units, the Tenth Armored established itself as a great fighting machine of World War II. It fought under two American Army Groups, four operational armies and seven corps and provided a successful conclusion to every mission it was assigned. The battle story of the Tenth Armored Division is the story of teamwork and more, the story of a superlative string of victories in some of the greatest actions ever fought on the battlefields of Europe.

II

MARCH, MANEUVER AND SHOOT

ON MAY 16, 1942, virtually every general officer in the continental United States was present at Fort Benning, Georgia, to witness a series of combat demonstrations. Providing the troops for the battle problems were Major General Willis D. Crittenberger's Second Armored Division and Major General Terry Allen's First Infantry Division. On hand too, was Combat Command A's Brigadier General Paul W. Newgarden, of the "Hell on Wheels" Second Armored, and Captain John W. Sheffield, the Unit's S-3. During the pre-dawn hours of May 16, 1942, Captain Sheffield was busily engaged in supervising tank movements at one of CC A's control points on the Fort Benning Reservation. Suddenly, a command car cut through the tank column and abruptly stopped in front of Sheffield. "That you, Sheffield?" boomed a deep, clear voice from the car. The S-3 sprang to attention, saluted, and answered, "Yes sir!" as he recognized General Newgarden. "Hop in," he was told. Moments later the car sped away in the darkness. After they had travelled a short distance the General began: "John, I have some exciting news for you—in the next few months, there is going to be formed, a Tenth Armored Division. And I have been named its Commanding General." He continued, "I have decided to take you and Lieut. Rawley along with me." After a moment's pause, the General glanced at Sheffield expectantly and added, "You don't have to make up your mind right now, for I know only too well how highly you regard the Second Armored Division." Before the latter could speak further, Sheffield blurted, "Sir, I consider it an honor to be selected. I accept right now without reservations." Grinning, General Newgarden stuck out his hand and replied, "Good, I'll tell you more about the details later." As can be imagined it was a very elated young S-3 who carried out his responsibilities during the morning's final battle demonstration.

Seven weeks later, on July 6, both he and Lieut. Roger Rawley were relieved from assignment in the Second Armored and placed in the first cadre of the Tenth Armored Division at Fort Benning. On July 15, the Division was activated. 29 other key officers were assigned to the Tenth in the Division's first special order. Many of the newly-arrived officers came from the Third and Eleventh Cavalry Regiments. And equipment and areas for training were obtained from the Second Armored Division. From the outset, the Tenth was known as a "hot" outfit. Its nickname, "The Tiger Division" was selected through competition and was utilized throughout the Division's history. The rugged two-week training period was conducted in an area known as "Tiger Camp". "Tiger platoons" were chosen as a result of rigorous tests, "Tiger's Lair" was established at Lake Eibsee in southern Bavaria during the Occupation and the Tenth's own newspaper was called "The Tiger's Tale". The Division's tri-colored triangle shoulder patch was the same as that of all other armored units with the exception of the numeral 10. The yellow in the patch represents the cavalry which, in the early days of the war, was reorganized, mechanized and given armor. The blue represents infantry and the red color, artillery. The tank tracks indicate mobility, the cannon denotes firepower, and the lightning symbolizes speed of attack. Above all, the three colors stand for teamwork. Without artillery to soften the way ahead, engineers to span the rivers, tank destroyers to knock out enemy armor, anti-aircraft to down enemy planes, ordnance to

Crack "Tiger Platoon" in action

keep the vehicles in fighting trim and the medics to heal the wounded, it would be impossible for the tanks and infantry to operate effectively.

"Hurry up and wait"

FROM CIVILIAN TO SOLDIER

For the cynics, "esprit de corps" is likely to mean little. But to the men who spent three roaring, hellfire years as members of a superb fighting outfit, the word has a more significant meaning. For every Tiger knows what kind of spirit it took to help propel the Tenth Armored through Nazi lines of fire, stone and steel.

The initial discomfort of making the change from civilian ease to strenuous military life was soon overcome. Soft muscles were hardened. Technical training was quickly assimilated and every Tiger knew only too well the rugged assignment ahead. "Esprit de corps" meant bruised shoulders, tired feet, aching backs and frost-bitten ears. It did not come from speeches or flag waving. Instead, it stemmed from pride in oneself and pride in belonging to a crack outfit.

9

Major General Paul W. Newgarden was a superb leader. His troops sensed his genuine interest in their welfare and his leadership was clearly reflected in every Tiger. His many mottos provided an insight as to his personal beliefs. "Stand Up, Muscle Up, Clean Up, Carry Out Orders, March, Maneuver and Shoot", were his bywords. "If we are to be successful," he would say, "We must work like hell, play like hell and fight like hell." No man had more pride in his troops than did the Division's commander. On the streets of Augusta, Georgia, it was easy to spot a Tenth Armored Tiger. His cap was always set at a jaunty angle, his uniform clean and neat, and he walked along the street as though the world were his personal oyster. These were some of the important factors which explained later why the Division was so highly regarded by SHAEF, two army group, four army and seven corps commanders under whose command the Tenth functioned across the battlefields of Europe. The fierce pride of identity generated by General Newgarden in Georgia, blossomed into complete fulfillment later at the Saar, on the frozen fields at Bastogne and in the mountain passes of Southern Bavaria's Alpine Redoubt area.

CHIGGER INVASION

The first year of training was especially rugged. There was the Tiger Camp with its night problems, forced marches, endurance tests, "dry runs" and firing problems. Next came the Tennessee maneuvers, the scene of combat with chiggers, choking dust, sleepless nights, sore backs and aching feet. As always, the "enemy" was constantly pursued. The battle umpires, too, were on hand to declare tank, track and truck "knocked out" by a hidden "enemy" anti-tank gun crew.

The first week in September of 1943 found the Division on the move again, but this time it was a trek to its new home at Camp Gordon, Georgia. Here, the fine people of the neighboring city of Augusta welcomed the Division with open arms and made

Tankers come home to roost as Tenth Armored infantrymen find it tough scaling obstacle course at Tiger Camp

the ensuing year one of the best for the Armoraiders. Though
other divisions also trained at Camp Gordon, it has always been
felt that the Tigers were the Augustans' favorites.

On the morning of July 15, 1944, the residents of the city,
as well as the Tigers, were deeply shocked when they read a
screaming headline in the Chronicle: "General Newgarden Killed
in Plane Crash". With the General was Colonel Renn Lawrence
of Combat Command B. On that day, the two Tiger officers were
to have returned from a series of conferences at Fort Knox,
Kentucky, to participate in the Division's second anniversary
Review. Upon the death of the two commanders, it was at first
cancelled, but Mrs. Priscilla Newgarden insisted that it be held
as scheduled. During the Review, it was clearly evident that the
tragedy was shared by everyone. Their loss was so great a personal loss that it shook the Division from top to bottom.

SPECIAL SERVICES FOR THE ARMORAIDERS

From the very beginning, the welfare of the men of the
Division was given top priority by General Newgarden. In keeping with that policy, he made Major Russell C. Hinote, Tiger

11

Special Service Officer, custodian of the Division's Fund. Now, monies were available for an expanded program of athletics and entertainment. Captain Harry J. Steigelman and his two NCO's, Carroll M. Rines and Loren Wolfe, were responsible for the appearance of football, baseball and softball fields, volleyball courts and boxing facilities in the battalion areas. Lieut. Arthur Mathews and NCO's H. H. Smith and R. N. Smith organized soldier shows, dances, concerts and other entertainment. Coordinating the work of Bond and Red Cross drives, Mothers' Day observances and many other worthwhile projects were NCO's Stanley Morosko, Ray Moore, Ray Weinberg and Charley Mathis.

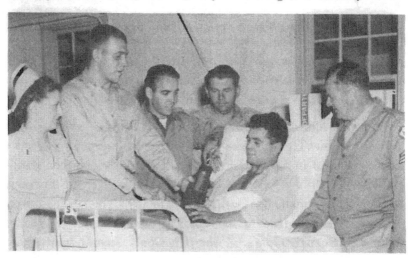

"Chuck" Taylor is presented Camp Gordon boxing trophy

During the first year, Colonel Thomas M. Brinkley's Third Armored Regiment dominated athletic competition, winning the Division championship in baseball, volleyball, track and handball. Another major title, the basketball championship, was won by the 55th Engineers. During the summer of 1943, the SSO operated a field post exchange for the benefit of the Tigers while on the Tennessee maneuvers, in addition to a program of sports, dances and other entertainment.

In the fall, the Tenth Armored was reorganized on a battalion basis. At the same time, Major Cortland A. Bassett replaced Major Hinote when the latter left the Tenth for a new assignment. Lieut. Henry Roberts was delegated the job of entertainment officer for the Division. Then too, each of 14 battalions named an SSO to further the extra-curricular activities of the Division. In October, NCO Joe Hirst joined the Tenth's SSO program and put to use his prior experience as traveling companion to golfer Walter Hagen. Later in the month, the Tenth participated with great success in the Post's boxing tournament, constructed an outdoor theater at Mirror Lake for troops in bivouac, and presented bi-weekly combined movies and stage shows to an average attendance of 2,000 men per show. At this time, Corporals Chuck Taylor and Martin Medvid were placed on special duty as boxing and weight lifting instructors.

Highlighting the heavy fall sports schedule was football, which drew over 100,000 military and civilian spectators. The Tiger Tankers overpowered the Infantry to the tune of 18-13 for the Tiger Championship. In January, the 419th Field Artillery, before an audience of 1,200, won the Inter-Battalion Talent Show contest. The citizens of Augusta were brought closer to the Division that month when Mathews, Moore, Gayeski and Weinberg presented a program over WRDW entitled, "Reveille In Rhythm". A one-hour variety show, it was presented six times weekly until the Division left for overseas in September, 1944.

Colonel Roberts speaks at Tiger Review in honor of the late Gen. Newgarden and Col. Renn Lawrence

The busy entertainment year ended when Pfc. Lemert Clark won a turkey shoot over 332 other Tigers. At the same time, the 11th Tank Battalion won the boxing crown, the 21st Tank Battalion took volleyball honors and the Provisional Battalion became Tiger basketball champions.

In early 1944, a new section of Information and Education headed by Lieut. James Lewis was added to the SSO program. He was assisted by big John Blank, former star collegiate football player. Heavyweight champion Joe Louis appeared at Camp Gordon, and shortly afterwards, "Tiger Tantrums" was presented in the Municipal Auditorium before 4,000 appreciative Augustans. It was so popular that it had to put on a repeat performance before another sell-out crowd in February. During the same month, a total of $88,000 was collected for the War Bond Drive, and the Division participated in a mammoth "Purple Heart Party" in the Municipal Auditorium. In the spring four

Lieut. Henry Roberts assists young Augusta belle for war bond drive

more diamonds were built for the baseballers and an additional 37 softball fields were constructed for 72 Company teams which took part in a giant softball program. The complete athletic participation of Tenth Armored men was a gratifying, if not an immense problem of organization and administration for the hard working SSO. In April, the 54th Armored Infantry Battalion was declared winner over the 132nd Ordnance Maintenance Battalion in the finals of a 14 Battalion glee club competition. Two brothers, Joe and Al Lynch, won the Division heavyweight and 150 pound wrestling titles, respectively. A month later, Mrs. J. G. Cameron of Cadiz, Kentucky, was selected "Division Mother" and was feted at her son's Company mess. Later, French, German and Spanish language books were issued, along with language records for courses of instruction. June of 1944 found the Tenth Armored collecting $141,500 in the War Bond Drive and the SSO making significant preparations for providing overseas services to the Armoraiders. "Music Memories", a program of popular music, was recorded by the superb Tenth Armored orchestra and distributed nationally.

INVASION BOOTH

When the Tigers awakened on the morning of June 6, 1944, they were surprised to hear loudspeakers near Division headquarters announce the Allied Invasion of France. Manning the speakers in a booth which was replete with large maps, was Lieut. James Lewis. His novel idea proved to be a huge success as virtually every Tiger visited the Booth at one time or another to view the progress of the Allies in the early stages of the invasion. In July, Chuck Taylor won the Post boxing title, indicating at that time his fistic ability. After the war he became a leading contender for the world's middleweight crown. The 419th Field Artillery won the baseball championship and Gil Dodds, the "Flying Preacher", demonstrated his track prowess in the latter part of the month. In August, the largest single social event ever staged by the Tenth was held at the Sports Arena. More than 1,000 girls, attending from the adjoining areas, graced the big affair. The Post golf tournament was won by Joe Rumsey of the 21st Tank Battalion, winding up all competitive sports until overseas occupation in May of 1945. During the Tenth's first two years of training, it was host to many distinguished visitors, including the late President Franklin D. Roosevelt; former governor of Georgia, Ellis Arnall; former Army Chief-of-Staff, General George C. Marshall; Anthony Eden of Great Britain; and General Jacob L. Devers, who later became commanding general of the Sixth Army Group overseas.

Invasion anxiety

Tenth Armored's Major General Paul Newgarden is host to the late President Roosevelt and Georgia's Governor Ellis Arnall

Now in its second year, the Tenth Armored quietly and earnestly prepared for its ultimate goal of battle under the guiding hand of Major General William H. H. Morris, Jr. He came to the Division with little fanfare and at a tremendous disadvantage as any commander would in taking the place of the Tenth's beloved Paul Newgarden. Immediately, General Morris expressed a desire for continued excellence in battle training. "The Tiger's Tale" reported that, "since the arrival of General Morris, the Division continues to devote itself to the task of training and further development of the characteristics of toughness, teamwork and tenacity, which have become so vital a part of the Division's tradition."

Very few Tigers knew of the circumstances behind the Army's selection of General Morris to lead the Tenth Armored. In July of 1944, General Morris commanded the XVIII Corps at Fort Dupont, Delaware. When he read of General Newgarden's death he immediately contacted General Marshall, then Chief of Staff, and asked that he be relieved of his Corps command and be assigned to the Tenth Armored Division which he knew was scheduled for early shipment overseas, although, in effect, it

Army Ground Forces Chief, Lieut. Gen. Leslie McNair
and Staff, visit Tenth Armored at Camp Gordon

meant a demotion for him. When asked why he decided on that
course of action, General Morris answered, "Hell, I've spent a
lifetime learning to lead troops into battle . . . and that's what
I want to do." During 1944 and 1945 General Morris skillfully
demonstrated his combat knowledge as he guided the Division
across five European countries. Commendations, battle awards
and citations were to come from Eisenhower, Bradley, Devers,
Patton, Patch and other top commanders as a result of the Tigers'
performance on the battlefield. More than thirty commendations
in all, were to be given to the Division.

When the Division sailed from New York on September 14, it was impossible to predict what the future would bring. But in any event, the Tigers were prepared for the worst. Their long period of training was behind them and ahead was the big test. On September 23, the Division entered the badly-wrecked harbor at Cherbourg, where its personnel were brought to shore in landing craft barges. Here, a large number of German PW's toiled to reconstruct the damaged piers and buildings. Waiting to whisk the Tigers to their training area were endless lines of trucks which, later in the day, rolled through the colorful Normandy port to Teurtheville. During the ensuing month of battle training, the Tigers were subjected to constant precipitation which soon transformed the area into a sea of mud. Mines were still hidden throughout the area and occasionally, Normandy cows provided an excellent detection service as they stepped on one enemy teller mine after another. Unfortunately, there was seldom enough left of the poor creatures to meet the needs of beef-hungry Tigers. In addition to receiving new equipment, forced

Second Anniversary Review for the late Major General Paul W. Newgarden and Colonel Renn Lawrence

19

Lieut. General Jacob L. Devers flanked by Lieut. Col. John W. Sheffield inspects Tiger Camp at Fort Benning, Georgia.

marches were the order of the day. Then too, battle problems were reviewed night and day. On September 5, the Division was assigned to the Third Corps of the U. S. Ninth Army and remained under that command for five days, after which the Armoraiders came under the control of the U. S. Third Army and its blood and fire commander, General George S. Patton. Then on September 23, the Tenth was assigned to Major General Walton Walker's XX Corps. From that date until April 1, 1945, the Tenth Armored was fortunate to be associated with that distinguished Corps through all but about five weeks of combat. On the first day of November of 1944, the Tigers supported XX Corps' containment of enemy troops in the Mars La Tour sector, close to menacing Fort Driant, key stronghold in the Metz fortress system. Here the men of the Tenth withstood their baptism of fire and readied themselves for the major battles that were to begin with the encirclement of the Metz fortress on November 15, and end in the capture of Mittenwald deep in the Bavarian alpine country, less than 30 miles from Innsbruck, Austria and the Brenner Pass.

Paris was not so gay when Armoraiders saw this familiar landmark.

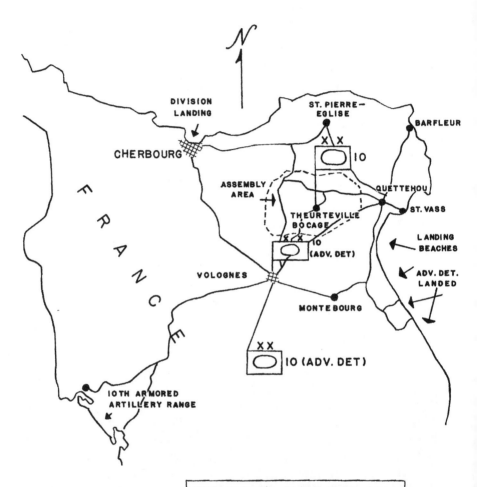

N

DIVISION
LANDING

ST. PIERRE-
EGLISE

BARFLEUR

CHERBOURG

XX
10

FRANCE

ASSEMBLY
AREA

QUETTEHOU

THEURTEVILLE
BOCAGE

ST. VASS

XX
10
(ADV. DET)

LANDING
BEACHES

VOLOGNES

ADV. DET.
LANDED

MONTEBOURG

XX
10 (ADV. DET)

10TH ARMORED
ARTILLERY RANGE

THE TIGER'S FIRST OVER-SEAS
ASSEMBLY AREA
SEPTEMBER 23, 1944

MAP I

III

THE CAPTURE OF METZ

THE METZ FORTRESS had stood for 1500 years on the Moselle River. Virtually impregnable against assaulting forces, it seemed to defy time itself. But in November, 1944, the United States Third Army, under General George S. Patton, shattered this precedent. Using three American divisions, "Old Blood and Guts" conquered the Fortress in a matter of days. Determination was the keynote as Patton ordered his troops to "go in shooting, no matter what, and goddamit, if you run out of gas, get out and fight on foot."

For the Tenth Armored Division, this was to be its first major battle. Everything it had learned in 28 months of preparation in the pine woods of Georgia was now to be put to the acid test. The battle plan was simple. Nowhere was George Patton's favorite expression, "grab 'em by the nose and kick 'em in the pants", used to greater advantage than at Metz. While the Fifth and Ninety-Fifth Infantry Divisions attacked Metz frontally, the Tenth Armored was to streak to the rear of the forts to cut off the retreating enemy.

H Hour for the Tigers was now a reality, and all that remained was to see whether the Tiger's claws were sharp enough for the kill.

On November 14, 1944, tank and infantry teams of Combat Commands A and B, led by Brig. Gen. Kenneth G. Althaus and Brig. Gen. Edwin W. Piburn, knifed their way southeast behind the forts from a point 23 miles north of Metz.

At the conclusion of the Tigers' first combat mission, this communique was issued by General Morris: "During the first three weeks of fighting, you have liberated one hundred square miles of France and occupied fifty square miles of German territory. You have seized 64 towns, captured over 2,000 German prisoners of war and you have repulsed 11 counter-attacks. You have destroyed personnel and material in substantial quantities. All this at a minimum cost in lives lost and vehicles destroyed."

Prior to the Tigers' first combat, an advance detachment, consisting of Major Roger Rawley, assistant G-2; Major John Sheffield, assistant G-3; Major William Taylor, assistant G-4; and bivouac details from all Division units set out from Teurteville Bogage to the city of Nancy. There, details for movement into the battle areas were to be worked out with General Patton's United States Third Army staff. And at that time Major Sheffield was ordered to report to the fiery General that the Tenth Armored Division was on its way. Upon his arrival at the Army Commander's Headquarters, located in an immense quadrangular barracks area at Nancy, he noted that a section of the roof was missing. This condition was brought about by American bombers which only a short time before had "skip-bombed" the quadrangle and killed a score of enemy troops who had been asleep on the top floor. They were still lodged in the wreckage above.

Later, when Sheffield asked to see the General, he was told that the latter was at the front lines and was referred to General Gay, the Army Chief of Staff. Somewhat indifferent to the news of the Tenth Armored's arrival, Gay told Sheffield, "I hope your Division will perform better than that other fouled-up outfit that calls itself a fighting division." Further conversation brought out the reason for Army's dissatisfaction. Sheffield was told how Patton, a short time before, had come upon the "fouled-up" division stalled on the road. Speeding ahead in his jeep to the head of the column, the General found that the lead vehicle was being held up by one enemy machine gun. At this juncture, a verbal explosion took place, and General Patton in his own inimitable fashion suggested that the division move on. Later, this same unit distinguished itself in combat at the Rhine and in campaigns across Germany.

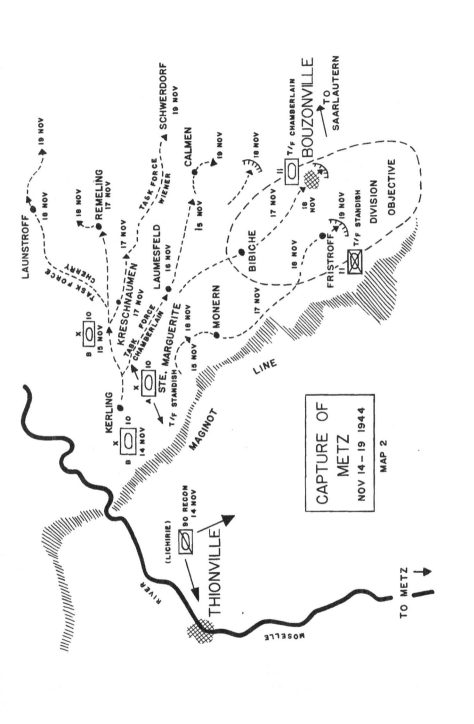

LAUNSTROFF

18 NOV

18 NOV

REMELING
17 NOV

SCHWERDORF
19 NOV

TASK FORCE
WIENER

CALMEN

18 NOV

18 NOV

T/F CHAMBERLAIN

BOUZONVILLE

TO
SAARLAUTERN

TASK FORCE
CHERRY

17 NOV

KRESCHNAUMEN
17 NOV

LAUMESFELD
16 NOV

15 NOV

17 NOV

BIBICHE

17 NOV

DIVISION

18
NOV

19 NOV

FRISTROFF

18 NOV

T/F STANDISH

OBJECTIVE

B

15 NOV

TASK FORCE
CHAMBERLAIN

STE. MARGUERITE

18 NOV

MONERN

17 NOV

x

10

KERLING

x

10

T/F STANDISH

15 NOV

LINE

B

10

14 NOV

MAGINOT

CAPTURE OF
METZ
NOV 14-19 1944

MAP 2

(LICHIRIE)

90 RECON
14 NOV

THIONVILLE

RIVER

MOSELLE

TO METZ

Before departing from Nancy, Major Sheffield was notified by Third Army that the Tenth Armored was to join the XX Corps and move up in the vicinity of Mars la Tour behind the 90th Infantry Division. Upon arrival there, General Morris was to swing Tiger Battalions into the line, one by one, in order to gain battle experience.

Thus it was that in early October of 1944, the Division moved into the worst bivouac area it was to occupy during its entire combat period. The area around Mars la Tour was much too small for movement. And it rained all the time, forcing the Tigers to bivouac in muddy fields. What the unit commanders had to say to the advance detachment about this situation is necessarily censored here. But despite these initial difficulties, Tiger Battalions rolled into action with the precision of a veteran division, in the Fort Driant area. Compared to other sectors, this was a relatively quiet place. Almost two weeks were to elapse before the Division was to become battle-hardened as the spearhead of the XX Corps drive to the Saar. Fortunately for the Tenth Armored, it had been superbly trained by the late General Paul Newgarden in Georgia. Now it was to be led into combat by a battle-wise commander. General Morris, prior to this time, had held successive commands with an armored regiment, an armored division and a training corps. A 1911 graduate of West Point, he had received the Distinguished Service Cross for gallantry in action in the St. Mihiel and Meuse-Argonne operations in World War I.

When the November battle for Metz began, the XX Corps under General Walton H. Walker was readied as a powerful attack force. Included in the command, in addition to smaller units, were the 5th, 90th, 95th Infantry Divisions, plus the newly-arrived Tenth Armored. All told, General Walker had 30 infantry battalions, 500 tanks and more than 700 guns for the big Metz offensive.

The Corps plan had two key phases. First, to destroy all German forces in the Metz area; second, to switch the axis of

The enemy makes sure that Thionville bridge cannot be
used by attacking Tenth Armored forces

advance to the northeast quickly to catch the enemy as they
pulled out of Metz.

In other words, the Tenth Armored, along with the 90th
Infantry, was to make a wide envelopment north of Metz. Corps
plans were to send the 95th Infantry Division to replace the Tenth
Armored. Yet, on November 8, the Tigers, to mislead the enemy,
moved so rapidly that their main columns were already on their
way north. Too late to call them off, Corps allowed the Tigers to
roll on to their objectives.

Details of the first commitment to battle of the Tenth Armored were finally worked out. On November 9th, the Tenth was
assembled around Malvange and Rumelange. These towns were
far enough west of the Moselle to provide safety from enemy observation. Here the Tigers waited for the call to battle. They
knew that they were to cross the Moselle in two columns, pass
through the 90th Division bridgehead north of Thionville and
strike with great force of impact to make a deep penetration in

27

the enemy's lines. Once they knifed through the Germans' defense, the Armoraiders' mission was to send their left column to roll eastward to seize a bridgehead over the Saar River near Merzig. The right column was to take the Division objective. This objective included Bouzonville, the center of arterial highway and railroad traffic running northeast out of Metz, plus a stretch of high ground about six miles north of Bouzonville on both sides of the Nied River valley. American domination of one of the main corridors, through which the Germans might send reinforcements to Metz or through which a retreat from that city might be made, was imperative to the success of the attack.

At the time, Tiger tankers questioned the use of the terrain for tank operations. The road net was limited. Only one good highway existed, the one which ran between Kerling to Bouzonville. The only other road suitable for the tankers was in a state of disrepair. Moreover, cross-country movements had to be ruled out because of the heavy autumn rains which made mire of the clay soil.

PATTON'S OBSERVATION

General Patton, on November 4, visited Tenth Armored units preparing for their first attack. After close scrutiny, he noted, "I ran into Combat Command B, commanded by Brig. Gen. Edwin W. Piburn, of the Tenth Armored Division, near Mars la Tour, the scene of the great cavalry battle of 1870, and they were looking fine and moving right into action with beautiful discipline."

General Morris had waited five days for word that was to send the Tigers into their first big battle. These days were marked by orders and counter-orders, new plans, and new estimates—all dependent on the swollen Moselle and the degree of the enemy's success in wiping out, by shellfire, the attackers' bridge sites.

As the Division began assembling near the bridge sites under cover of darkness on November 13, it rained buckets-full. Major

John W. Sheffield was drenched as he operated the Division Control Point four miles east of Ottange. A crossroads, it was here that Tiger units were feeding in from the south, west and north. And, to make certain that this movement was properly coordinated, a phone was placed at the Control Point. In this way, each unit was in direct touch with Division Headquarters. At midnight, as Sheffield deliberated his chances of being drowned or shot first, the field phone jangled. At the other end was Captain George Seignious, who said, "Hold on a minute, Major, Admiral Byrd wants to speak to you". A moment later a voice declared, "Major this is Admiral Byrd." Sheffield replied, "Uh-huh, and this is General Bradley . . . what can I do for you?" The Admiral countered, "This IS Admiral Byrd . . . I have a nephew in Colonel O'Hara's 54th Armored Infantry Battalion. I would like to see him. Do you suppose you can help me locate him?" Sheffield replied, "Yes, sir, I'll send a jeep down to Ottange for you." Hanging up the phone at this point, Sheffield wondered what kind of a joker was "loose on a night like this." A short time later, Lt. Col. William Eckles, Division G-2, rolled up to the Control Point. "Do me a favor, Bill," Sheffield pleaded, "Go pick up Admiral Byrd at Ottange." After much persuasion, Eckles agreed. But it was a very red-faced major who minutes later greeted Admiral Byrd at the Control Point in company of the Division G-2.

Rampaging Tiger tankers streak to enemy's rear to cut off reinforcement of Metz Fortress

The happy outcome of the night's zany doings found Sheffield producing one nephew for an admiral. At the time, the Navy hero was assisting in all river crossings as a liaison officer between Army Ground Forces and the Navy for SHAEF.

First Tenth Armored tanks to go into action against Germans in the Mars La Tour area in France

AT LAST — THE GREEN LIGHT!

At exactly 0930 on the morning of November 14, the largest Bailey Bridge in the European Theater of Operations was completed by the 1306th Engineer General Service Regiment. The way was now open for the Tigers to roll across the 190-foot span. During the afternoon, Brig. Gen. Edwin W. Piburn led Combat Command B across the river. His column wound its way along the east bank northward towards the 90th Division sector. The entire command had assembled near Kerling before daylight on November 15. Meanwhile, part of Combat Command A, under the direction of Brig. Gen. Kenneth G. Althaus, rumbled over the Malling Bridge, and before dark, two companies were shuttled across to take up their positions south of General Piburn's column.

CC B had the honor of leading the Tenth Armored's drive in the early morning of November 15. Snow and rain followed them as Task Forces Cherry and Wiener moved along the road east of Kerling. Tiger reconnaissance and a platoon of tankers were halted time after time to clear roadblocks, knock out anti-tank guns and pillboxes which blocked the highway. CC A pushed out of the congested bridgehead later in the afternoon and entered Lemestroff at the left of the line which was held by the 357th Infantry. General Althaus planned to keep a provisional recon squadron at the head of his command, in convenient fashion, but the big guns of the Germans were raising hell with the light Tiger armor, causing him to place them on the flanks in favor of our heavier armor.

TIGERS CLAW THE PANZERS

The Nazi 25th Panzer Grenadier Kampfgruppe and 416th Division blocked the way for a short time. But on November 16, Tiger armor was well inside German positions. Right off the bat, 250 prisoners were taken by the Tenth. Then CC A attacked in two task forces. Designated to make the main effort, Lieut. Col. Thomas C. Chamberlain blasted his way through Kerling and rolled southeast along the main highway to Laumesfeld, where our mortar, assault gun and artillery fire was plastered on the Germans there and on the high ground north of the railroad where the most resistance was expected. As expected, this preparation drew fire from an enemy artillery battery of four 88's hidden on the high ground bordering the town. After having disclosed their position, Tiger tank-infantry teams went after the big guns. Not to be overpowered, the enemy fought savagely and succeeded in knocking out three tanks and wounding twelve Tigers. By now, however, their positions were sufficiently pinpointed, allowing Chamberlain to mount a heavy infantry attack, supported by mortars, assault guns and P-47s utilizing napalm bombs. So violent was the attack on the 88's that their crews were almost completely wiped out. Those enemy fortunate enough to escape from the devastating attack quickly surrendered. The town was ours, and the

31

task force bivouacked here for the night. Before they called it a day at Laumsfeld, however, they had first to dislodge the Germans from Haute Sierck on the way. Here Task Force Chamberlain was hit hard by machine gun and rifle fire from the enemy hidden in the houses on the western fringe of the town. His recon platoon which led the column, was held up in the face of the Germans' withering fire. When the main body of the task force arrived, Chamberlain's doughs inched up to the occupied houses and directed the tank's 75 mm fire into the windows, literally blowing the enemy out of the houses. The place was soon cleared. Back at Laumsfeld, however, the Division lost one of its finest commanders in Captain "Red" Maddox. He was one of Chamberlain's crack task force leaders and one of the most popular men in the Division. On November 16, he was one of the first Tigers to enter Laumsfeld, and as customary, he rode the lead tank. When he got into the center of the town, he hopped off his tank and was promptly subjected to sniper fire from the top floors of the surrounding buildings. "Red" was an expert shot, having done a great deal of quail shooting back at Athens, Georgia, and in no time he racked up ten snipers and helped to clear out the remaining Germans. Shortly after the town was cleared, the former University of Georgia All-American football star was killed by a mortar as he crouched over a map to plan further movement of his Tiger Team.

COMBAT COMMAND B CONTINUES ATTACK

In the meantime, Combat Command B set out in a direct line to negotiate a distance of about eleven miles in an effort to seize a bridge intact over the Saar River at Merzig. To accomplish this mission, General Piburn sent Task Force Cherry and Task Force Wiener towards Kerling. Forced to stay on the roads because of the muddy terrain, these Tigers were slowed by many road-blocks and continuous enemy shelling. By nightfall, the two forces managed, however, to secure the wooded high ground three miles east of Kerling. Because the enemy had wrecked the bridges over the stream at the foot of the high ridge Combat Command B

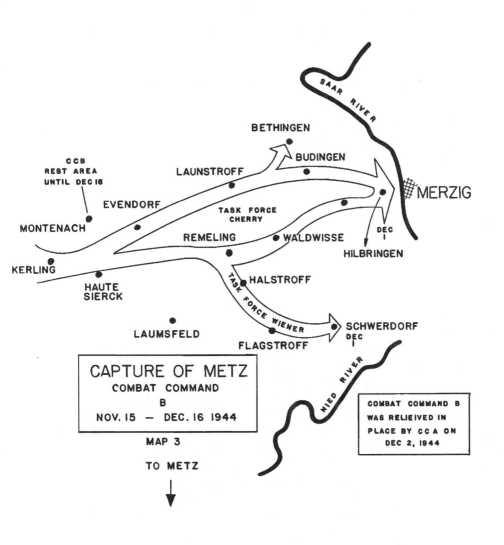

BETHINGEN

SAAR RIVER

BUDINGEN

CCB
REST AREA
UNTIL DEC 16

LAUNSTROFF

MERZIG

EVENDORF

TASK FORCE
CHERRY

MONTENACH

REMELING

WALDWISSE

DEC
1

KERLING

HAUTE
SIERCK

HALSTROFF

HILBRINGEN

TASK FORCE WIENER

SCHWERDORF
DEC

LAUMSFELD

FLAGSTROFF

CAPTURE OF METZ
COMBAT COMMAND
B
NOV. 15 — DEC. 16 1944

MAP 3

TO METZ

NIED RIVER

COMBAT COMMAND B
WAS RELIEVED IN
PLACE BY CCA ON
DEC 2, 1944

had taken the night before, further advance was impossible the next day. While waiting for the 55th Armored Engineers to put a treadway bridge across the stream, Piburn outlined a plan to split Task Force Cherry into two columns to launch an assault on Launstroff and Remeling and at the same time to push Task Force Wiener to Halstroff. At 0600 on November 17, Cherry scooted across the completed engineers' bridge and by sundown shoved his Tigers into Launstroff. At the same time, the right fork of his attack reached a position slightly south of Remeling. Meanwhile, Task Force Wiener inched along against strong enemy pressure to within throwing distance of Halstroff. Later in the day, this task force fought its way to Schwerdorf. Here Lieut. Col. Stanley Wiener was hit by enemy fire. After supervising his evacuation, Major Charles L. Hustead took command of the task force.

Division's artillery unit swings through muddy streets of Launstroff. Buildings are damaged by artillery fire

FIRST TO CROSS THE GERMAN BORDER

At exactly 1032 on the morning of November 19, Lieut. William Brown of Task Force Cherry halted his lead tank near Eft, Germany. For the United States Third Army, this was a moment of history. "Bill" Brown paused only long enough to glance at his map, then dismounted from his Sherman and walked across the German border. He was the first man in Patton's Army to set foot on German soil!

There, General Morris ordered Cherry to hold defensively and contain the Germans west of Merzig while the rest of the Division initiated the attack toward Saarburg. On November 20, the advance carried CC B forward about two miles and reached Hill 378, about three thousand yards from the Saar River and Merzig. Because of the closeness of the enemy, Tiger troops were subjected to continuous shellfire. Brig. Gen. Edwin W. Piburn, CC B's Commander, ordered his men on Hill 378 to fall back to positions on Hill 383 southeast of Wellingen. Actually, CC B had driven into a weakly defended portion of the Saar Heights Stellung, the line which constituted the last German battle position west of the Saar River. Thinking this was the main American advance intended to roll up the Saar Heights position, the enemy 25th Panzer Division under Balck was thrown into battle as shock troops. In late afternoon on November 21, this counter-attack drove in on the left wing of CC B. A small Tiger outpost force that had been screening east of the Heidwald woods was driven back along the road toward Launstroff and lost a platoon of tanks. At daylight, the enemy continued the attack but was blotted out by the gunners of the 420th Field Artillery, who shelled the woods until the Germans broke.

By November 20, all three columns had crossed the German border. Cherry's north column was hit by a strong German counter-attack as it probed west of Budingen. The enemy assault was thrown back with heavy losses, however, and the ensuing days were spent in locating enemy positions in patrolling actions. On

November 26, the woods east of Waldwisse were cleared, and the town of Bethingen was captured but was relinquished quickly as a result of a heavy enemy artillery concentration.

PHASE ENDED

More important, though, was the fact that Combat Command B had all of its Tigers within four miles of the bridge at Merzig. By afternoon of November 29, CC B reached Hilbringen, located only a mile from the command's objective. At Hilbringen, the Germans had all the odds stacked in their favor. It is difficult to imagine the enemy's advantage here over CC B, for both Hilbringen and Merzig were at the bottom of a "V"-shaped valley and faced each other across the Saar River. Behind them, the mountains rose abruptly and were honeycombed with pill boxes. In each of them was a dreaded 88. Then, too, there was only one road running down Hill 378, and every foot of the way had been plotted by the enemy. This avenue of death immediately became known to the Tigers as the "shooting gallery".

On November 30, as the 55th Engineers reached the bridge, they were rocked backwards in the face of a tremendous explosion. The Germans had blown up the objective. On December 1, Combat Command B took Hilbringen. This ended the phase for the command, with the exception of reorganizing its lines. General Morris on December 2 brought in Combat Command A to relieve Piburn's weary Armoraiders, who trudged back to the vicinity of Montenach for a brief rest. A rest that was vitally necessary for the greater battle that CC B was to fight at Bastogne later in the month.

COMBAT COMMAND A DRIVES SOUTH

While Combat Command B was charging eastward towards Merzig, Althaus and his raiders of Combat Command A continued their drive to the south towards Bouzonville. Task Force Standish barrelled its way along the road east of Lemestroff and went on

The enemy's dragon teeth are pulled from the vaunted
Siegfried Line

to grab Ste. Marguerite. Tiger losses in tanks and men in both
combat commands were relatively light. Because of the poor roads,
General Morris sent out splinter task forces on November 17 and
18. The Germans, no longer organized, tried to stop our tanks,
utilizing small groups. They banged away at the Tigers with
bazookas and anti-tank guns with but little success. The tanks
and armored doughs bagged 600 hard-pressed Germans during
the two days.

Suddenly on November 18, the skies cleared, giving our
supporting P-47s a chance to blast away at the retreating enemy.
Task Force Chamberlain, after two days of heavy fighting, reached
the Nied River, across from Bouzonville, where it found the
bridges blown. But his Tigers discovered another bridge near
Filstroff. Though damaged, it was still usable, providing them with
an opportunity to scramble across.

Another Task Force commanded by Major William R.
Desobry, knifed its way to Schwerdorf the same day. Then on

November 19, Desobry's Tigers were attached to CC A's Task Force Chamberlain for operations east of the Nied River. On the same day, the Filstroff bridgehead had become a reality. Troops A and B of the 90th Recon were reinforced and, led by Major Leyton, scurried through the lightly-held bridgehead and struck south toward Bouzonville. At this point, they were hit by the German 73rd Regiment and lost 36 men. Following them were tanks and doughs of Chamberlain's Task Force, who took advantage of the cavalry's exploitation. In the midst of this operation,

NCO Thomas J. Roberson examines captured enemy anti-tank weapon at Rustroff, France

Chamberlain was ordered: "Cease all operations east of the Nied River. Destroy the Filstroff Bridge and assemble in the vicinity of Laumsfeld." A sudden change of tactics became necessary, as the 6th Armored Division, driving up from the southwest, was nearer to the target at Bouzonville than we were. But more important, XX Corps designated a far more significant mission as General Walker decided to use the Tenth Armored to clean out the Saar-Moselle Triangle—one of the most heavily fortified areas in the world. And, as usual, Division Headquarters became the subject of criticism for "applying the brakes," just as the Tigers were rolling in high gear east of the Nied River. Nevertheless, the operation was a complete success. Combat Command A, with brilliant leadership from General Althaus, performed magnificently in penetrating the Koenigsmacher bridgehead—an area bristling with enemy defenses—then swinging around to the enemy's rear to Bouzonville, disrupting installations and wrecking communications everywhere in the area.

Now, the 90th and 95th Infantry Divisions had put a strangle-hold around the inner rim of the circle while the Tenth had made certain that German reserves could not break in from the east to help their beleaguered comrades within Metz. Thus, the first phase in the battle for Metz was over. As directed, Chamberlain's Tigers destroyed the Nied bridge, after having scampered back to the west bank. Then in black-out they rolled through the 90th Infantry Division to jump into the Division attack on the enemy at the Saar River in the north.

With the help of the 90th Infantry, CC A was to slam into the German 416th Infantry Division with such impact that the Germans were sent reeling north behind the Orscholz

Tank trap is backed up by hidden enemy pillboxes as part of Maginot Line near Monneren, France

Switch Line. The big attack launched by XX Corps now got under way northeast to the Saar. At General Walker's urging, General Morris ordered Combat Command A into the Saar- Moselle Triangle on November 20. The new mission for the command was to seize a bridgehead over the Saar, some twenty miles to the north, near Saarburg. Originally, the Third Cavalry was assigned to this task, but because of the absence of heavy armor, the cavalrymen were unable to accomplish their mission. At 1000 hours on November 19, Combat Command A was in receipt of the new orders, and on the next day, after having reversed its direction, it swung into the positions held by the Third Cavalry. Known as "Task Force Polk," the Third Cavalry was one of the most efficient and highly-trained units ever to operate with the Tenth Armored. Commanded by West Pointer Colonel Polk, this unit was a "jack-of-all-trades" for XX Corps. They were likely to be sent on any kind of mission, and they never failed to give a first class performance. The fact that later, on November 27, Task Force Polk relieved an entire Tiger combat command indicates the man-sized job this unit was called upon to perform. In deploying his Command along a six-mile front, Althaus made use of the Cavalry's assault guns, which put heavy fire on the Germans, as Task Force Standish jostled its way on the left flank and Task Force Chamberlain rumbled into the right flank.

HOOK AND JAB

Althaus' intention was to send the right task force against the sector of the German line north of Borg while the left task force jabbed at Tettingen and hooked around the German flank near Besch. In the early hours of November 21, the CC A Armoraiders moved into the attack in four columns. Behind were four battalions of field artillery to give additional fire support when they hit the Orscholz line. The attack on the right gained some initial success, although here, as elsewhere, the enemy fought with desperation. Task Force Chamberlain's eastern column, Team Eisberg, jumped off from the cover of the Saarburg forest in

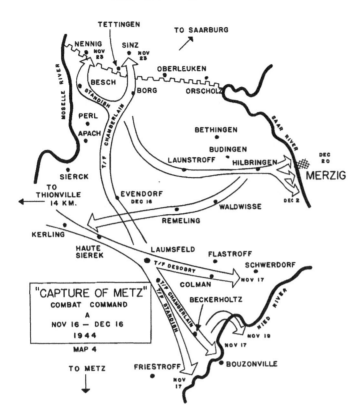

"CAPTURE OF METZ"
COMBAT COMMAND
A
NOV 16 — DEC 16
1944
MAP 4

an oblique attack toward the village of Orscholz and drove to the outworks of the Orscholz line. About 1400 yards from the village, the Tigers were stopped by severe artillery and mortar fire. So little was known then of the enemy's works that the fight became exploratory in nature. Our artillery ranged in on each pillbox and bunker as their locations were spotted by the armored doughs. In the meantime, Colonel Chamberlain's western column attacked Borg along the main road leading toward Kirf and into the gap discovered earlier by the Cavalry. Still, dragon's teeth barred the way. The enemy had also blown a large crater in the highway to block our tanks. But our dismounted infantry was able to penetrate beyond the crater and the dragon's teeth only to be checked by small arms and shellfire from field fortifications backing up the anti-tank barrier.

41

German homes at Perl provide hiding place for 609th
Tank Destroyers waiting to move up front

Task Force Standish on the left flank was stopped almost as
soon as its advance began, by a long anti-tank ditch reinforced
by pillboxes and dragon's teeth. During the day, engineers and
armored infantry attempted to throw bridges over the anti-tank
ditch under intense German fire, but with slight success. At the
end of the day, CC A was still held in check by the German line,
except at the one point where one small Tiger group worked its
way past the crater. Colonel Chamberlain decided that further
preparations were necessary before continuing the attack on the
right. He withdrew his task force to Borg, leaving CC A in about
the same positions it had occupied at the beginning of the day's
operations.

CC A continued a systematic penetration of the Orscholz line.
It attacked with dismounted doughs as Lieut. Col. W. P. Clapp's
engineers slowly and painfully yanked the dragon's teeth. Together, they systematically reduced the troublesome enemy pillboxes, bridged the anti-tank ditches and crater. Task Force Standish, at dawn on November 22, dispatched a force of tanks and

42

infantry to execute a flank attack against the German right wing as outlined in CC A's original plan. These Tigers managed to fight their way into Nenning, only to find that here the Orscholz line ran in a north-to-south line behind the village — thus covering the enemy flank. The Germans fought with terrific intensity to eject the Tigers from Nenning, and in the early afternoon were successful in forcing back our forces, who withdrew under a barrage of protective artillery fire. This unsuccessful venture cost the Tigers nearly sixty casualties and six tanks. Team Eardly, of the right wing of Task Force Standish, was more successful. Dismounted, this team attacked along the main road between Wochern and Tettingen. A platoon of Tiger doughs kicked in a section of dragon's teeth just outside of Tettingen and forced their way into that village—only to be driven back. On CC A's right wing, Task Force Chamberlain progressed satisfactorily along the large hogback ridge whose eastern side was marked by the Borg-Kirf road. Chamberlain's armored doughs jabbed north along the road and broke through the dragon's teeth east of the Campholz Woods and went on to establish a small "bridgehead"' some eight hundred yards in depth.

Thus it was that on the night of November 22, CC A held only one opening through the dragon's teeth. The field fortifications beyond this anti-tank barrier were intact all along the line, making the task of the Tenth Armored extremely dangerous. As it was, the Tigers of CC A were deployed over a very extended front. The experiences of the past 48 hours clearly showed that more infantry was needed if the Orscholz line was to be breached.

General Morris ordered the 328th Regimental Combat Team of the 90th Infantry Division, which previously had been attached to the Tenth Armored, to pass through CC A's lines and capture the villages of Sinz and Munzingen about three miles behind the center of the Orscholz line. To help them, CC A put a platoon of tanks across the anti-tank ditch south of Tettingen, but this assistance was not enough. In fact, some of our tanks in error fired on the hapless men of the 328th, causing a number of casualties.

And after three days, the combat strength of the 328th, already drained from continuous action north of Metz, was further reduced by the Germans. Another enemy, trenchfoot, was also taking its toll in the cold, mud and rain. By the evening of November 25, General Morris concluded that the 328th was no longer able to absorb the punishing resistance put up by the Germans. General Walker agreed with the Tiger General, and, on the following day, units of the Tenth Armored relieved the 328th—which was accorded high praise from General Morris for its superlative fighting abilities. Colonel Clark, the Regimental Commander, from Atlanta, Georgia, was suffering from pneumonia, yet would not tell anyone. When General Morris ordered him to the rear, he had a temperature of 103°.

Though the Tenth Armored was blasting away at full strength, in the Orscholz line, the Germans were not ready to give up. They made one last but unsuccessful attempt to drive the Tigers out of Tettingen. At 0130 they infiltrated into Tettingen and barged into Borg. With flamethrowers and automatic weapons, they blasted away at the Tigers, but our armored doughs hunted them down from house to house and rocked them into submission. American operations, however, were halted against the Orscholz line. Oberleuken and Nennig remained in enemy hands, and the big attack for a bridgehead at Saarburg was abandoned by the Twentieth Corps.

During this time the Corps offensive along the main axis toward the Saar was carried very rapidly northeast by the 90th and 95th Infantry Divisions. They moved with such speed that flanking protection on the north by the Tenth Armored was lost. Therefore, General Walker advised Morris to swing all of the Tenth Armored in a new atack to the east. The 27th of November found Task Force Polk in relief of CC A—whose mission was to screen on the far north flank of the XX Corps. Subsequently, all of the Tenth Armored was regrouped to clear the remaining Germans from the west bank of the Saar in the Division zone.

On November 30, all armor was assembled and began to attack toward the river. Through a low-hanging mist, the armored doughs led CC A's tanks in the attack, while CC B on the right drove as far as Merzig. There the enemy blew up the last two Saar bridges in this sector. Very few troops remained on the west bank to oppose the Tiger Division, and by December 2, the last resistance in the Merzig sector west of the Saar was ended with the capture of Drisbach, on the north boundary of the Division zone.

Tenth Armored tanks employed as artillery prior to the battle for Metz

At this time, General Walker ordered General Morris to set up an outpost line on the west bank of the Saar between the 3rd Cavalry and the 90th Infantry Division. This position required only one combat command of the Tenth, so CC B was turned back to the Montenach rest area as previously described.

Meanwhile, CC A stepped up its activities. It shuffled its armor and put on a round-the-clock firing binge to center attention on itself while the 90th Infantry prepared for the real attack to the south. CC A's shelling continued until midnight on December 5. This barrage brought about intense counter-battery fire from the Germans. At the time it was thought to be answering fire—but apparently the Germans were using their shelling to hide

45

troop movements in preparation for the Bulge battle later on.

At the end of this operation, the Division lost a truly great general officer in the person of Kenneth G. Althaus, who had to be replaced because of his physical condition. He was an experienced battle commander, having fought in many World War I campaigns, and he had the respect and admiration of every Tiger, who knew him. One cannot be surprised to learn that even as he led the Division's advance detachment to Europe, he hid the fact that he was suffering from an acute case of arthritis in his right shoulder. Had the Division Surgeon known that at the time, the General would never have been permitted to leave the States. All through September, October and November of 1944, Althaus was handicapped with excruciating pain, and finally, the combination of that and the heavy responsibility of sending men into battle day after day overpowered him. The superlative service rendered to the Division by General Althaus under extremely trying conditions is further testimony to the skill and courage that he possessed. Because of his ability and that of all the Tiger Troops, no other unit of the Third Army was to push deeper into enemy lines during 1944.

Target practice for machine gunners across swollen Moselle near Apach, France

HARVEY'S CHARGE

One of the most outstanding examples of bravery during this period of combat was "Harvey's Charge," led by Lieut. Allen P. Harvey, Jr. A combined task force of the 61st Armored Infantry Battalion and the 21st Tank Battalion had been stopped in an area bristling with anti-tank gun emplacements, pillboxes and an estimated battalion of enemy infantry with artillery support. In order to coordinate its advance with task forces on its flank, it was necessary to initiate a swift thrust forward. Lieut. Harvey stepped forward to lead a volunteer skeleton force in a dangerous charge.

The column moved out with Harvey mounted in the lead tank. As it gathered speed, the Germans raked it with everything they had. But the speeding tanks and halftracks raced on for five miles. On the way, they captured three important towns in less than thirty minutes. This depressed the Germans to such a degree that they decided to withdraw—despite their superiority in· numbers and firepower.

FIRE ON MY POSITION

In another action during the early days of battle, a young, cool-headed Tiger officer made quite a reputation for himself and his tank crew. Trapped in a Sherman, after an 88 shell had jammed the hatch cover, Lieut. Mater E. Hawkins and his crew would have been a sitting duck for the enemy, especially since the tank's 75 gun jammed. Hawkins immediately prepared artillery data and radioed for fire directly on his position. Instantly, a shower of projectiles screamed overhead, as time-fire was brought down on the enemy doughs. They fell back in helpless confusion before the deadly barrage, leaving behind their dead and wounded as the entire Tiger crew scrambled to safety.

ERRANT DRIVER

Technician Fifth Grade Joseph A. Walsh normally performed the duty of driving for B Company of the 54th Armored Infantry Battalion. One day, however, he left the rear echelon to bring supplies up to the front. He reached B Company just as it was going into action around Borg, Germany. He decided to tag along "to see what it was all about." And for the next five days he found out, and at the same time, earned the right to call himself a combat Tiger. During this period, Walsh constantly drove his vehicle into fire, picking up wounded men and rushing them back to the aid station. In the course of his exhausting mission, he wore out two jeeps and two halftracks—all lost to artillery and mortar fire.

TO KINGDOM COME

The Third Platoon of D Company, 11th Tank Battalion, rolled into the little town of Kalemburg on a cold November night. No opposition appeared, so Lieut. John J. Maher set up an outpost just outside the town. During the rest of the night, the Germans rained a steady hail of mortar fire on the tiny command post. Next morning, Maher and his platoon went into the town. There they found fifteen wounded Germans and 83 others who were anxious to surrender. But there was more to come. The Tiger tankers found mortars set up everywhere. Mines were strewn all over the place, and a German staff car was loaded down with ammo. Much radio equipment was in evidence, and bazookas lined the road; but the big surprise was the town church. From the door right up to the altar, mortar ammunition was piled high. In the words of one of the tankers, "they had enough stuff to blow us to kingdom come."

KNOCK OFF

When Combat Command A occupied Eft on the German border, they were subjected to their first intense shelling from the big enemy guns located on the Siegfried Line. Brig. Gen. Kenneth A. Althaus resorted to a new kind of psychological warfare. He summoned the town burgomeister and informed that portly gentleman that if the shelling did not cease immediately, he would pull his troops out of town in the morning and "level it to the ground." The result? All quiet on the western front!

Tenth Armored tank is completely destroyed by an
enemy "88". Note gun barrel and hole on right side

KALTENBORN WAS THERE

On the next to the last day of November, H. V. Kaltenborn,
distinguished news commentator for the National Broadcasting
Company, visited Combat Command B's headquarters near Bethingen, Germany. He was impressed with the Division to the extent
that he devoted his entire broadcast to America from Verdun that
night to the Tigers. What he had to say about the Tenth Armored
is as follows:

"In a dilapidated German village at the front, I found a brigadier general (Edwin W. Piburn, Combat Command B) preparing an attack by one of the combat teams of the Tenth Armored
Division. It was his task to take some high ground overlooking
the Saar River. The front of the attack covered less than two miles.
He had only a few hours to line up his infantry, his armor, and his
artillery, and to get everything ready. The lives of thousands of

49

Men of Third Tank Battalion rest briefly amid ruins
of Launsdorf, Germany

his men were involved on that little two-mile front. He took a few
minutes to outline to me his plan of action. He had done his best
to safeguard his men in the course of its development, but he knew
that some, perhaps a few score, would lose their lives. Yet, it was
his duty to order them into action. But it was also his duty to see
that they fought under the best possible conditions which his re·
sources or his ingenuity could provide. I could see that he felt his
responsibility for the lives that were in his hands.

"After spending some hours with this commander and his
men, shortly before they went into action, it was only natural
that I looked over the next day's communique with special interest.
I wanted to know just how this particular attack had come out and
whether or not there had been losses. Finally, I found the seven
words mentioning the action: "We occupied high ground west of
Merzig." I always come home from a trip to the front in a chas-
tened mood. I know so much better what our men are suffering. I
have learned how hard the way is along every mile of advance on

every front. I know, too, that even though our daily communiques say nothing about cost in blood, we pay in precious American lives for every mile we gain. Our people at home should be reminded more often, when they are told of minor gains, what those minor gains have cost.

"The Tenth Armored Division of the Third Army saw action in France exactly two months after it left an Atlantic port. Yet, only a few weeks later, it was a veteran battle division with nearly a thousand Purple Hearts earned in that short period of fighting. During those weeks it won every important objective assigned to it despite the fact that it was fighting against some of the best German divisions on the Western Front. It was the first division of the Third Army to enter Germany. I mention it particularly because it was my host. I know that there are any number of divisions in our army with the same fighting spirit and the same record of outstanding success.

A SUCCESSFUL ACTION

"Just before I arrived at the front, the German village of Bethingen had been captured. This was a small action. Its purpose was to give an an infantry company its first taste of offensive warfare under conditions that would make a tactical success almost certain. When a unit has never experienced active warfare, it is highly important that it should taste success the first time it goes into battle. So, whenever possible, the wise commander plans that first action so carefully and so completely that it is almost sure to succeed. The officer (Colonel William L. Roberts, Combat Command B) who prepared the capture of Bethingen took the trouble to explain it to me in full detail. He worked it out as a highly coordinated operation. There was minute planning of the use of artillery and mortars and smoke to blind the enemy. From the beginning we had superior observation. All our men had been well trained for their specific tasks. They had excellent leaders. The entire action (executed by B Company, 20th Armored Infantry Battalion, commanded by Captain "Bud" Billett) went off exactly on schedule as if it had been a carefully prepared maneuver. We captured the town, we eliminated an enemy's observation post, we took thirty-eight prisoners. We inflicted considerable losses in killed and wounded on the enemy and the entire operation cost us only one man killed and two wounded. But from the commanding officer's point of view, the most important result was the heightened fighting morale of an infantry unit which had earned its spurs."

ACK ACK ADVENTURE

No one particularly searches for trouble, especially when it might easily result in annihilation, but the men of the 796th AAA Battalion on December 16, figured in an escapade that had all the earmarks of suicide. The trouble began at Nohn, a small German town some 20 miles from Division Headquarters located in the

55th Armored Engineers bridge German tank trap near Tenth's CP at Apach, France

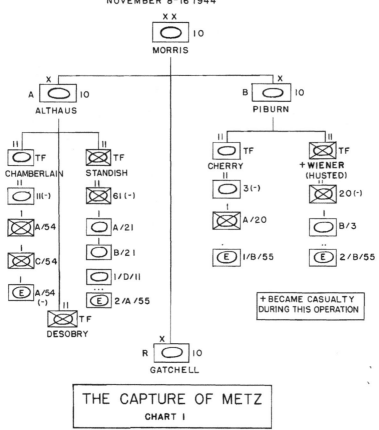

TENTH ARMORED DIVISION
COMBAT ORGANIZATION
NOVEMBER 8-16 1944

THE CAPTURE OF METZ
CHART I

area of Sierck-les-Bains. After sustaining a heavy all-day enemy artillery shelling, the 796th anti-aircraft men decided to find out "where the hell all that stuff was coming from." At 1500, with but four B Battery halftracks at hand, Major W. F. "Jack" Madison formed his "task force" consisting of Captain William R. Hughes, Lieut. Ward and Lieut. Palmaccio. Together with their ack ack crews, they set out to locate the enemy artillery and troop concentrations. When they reached a point approximately three miles east of Nohn they spotted a cluster of buildings behind which was located the long familiar line of dragon's teeth. Proceeding according to plan, Captain Hughes dashed down the hill

Tigers' 50 caliber machine gun rakes building

and through the woods which bordered the enemy strongpoint. To protect his movement on foot, the four halftracks, partly hidden at the edge of the woods, opened fire on the buildings. In a matter of minutes, all the buildings were on fire and about 50 enemy were killed by the intense fire from the halftracks. Then as Hughes' allotted time for observation of enemy artillery emplacements was rapidly expiring, the tracks directed their fire at the dragon's teeth. The Germans immediately retaliated as Major Madison hoped they would. Within three minutes 88's and mortar fire answered them—in quantity. Captain Hughes noted their positions and hurried back to the halftracks with the knowledge that the Tenth's own artillery would soon be able to give the jerries "some of their own medicine." However, one of the tracks became stuck in the mud and had to be winched out by another and by this time the enemy began to find the range. In the meantime, the other two tracks took off in a big hurry, followed by the third track which had succeeded in extricating the fourth vehicle. The latter tarried in the area only long enough to hook its dangling cable and it too scurried for cover. However, all four tracks, in their hurry to evade mortar and 88 fire, forgot one important detail. None of them waited for Captain Hughes, who by this time had reached the pre-arranged meeting point. Each track thought the other had picked up the Battalion S-3. And while the latter wondered, "what the hell has happened?" Major Madison reappeared over the horizon in search of his lost comrade. Acting like "old mother hen", the major stood up on his halftrack and watched Hughes duck into an apple orchard. He hesitated briefly, then, probably saying a prayer for the captain, took off again for Nohn. In all probability he would have lost his entire crew had he tried to rescue Hughes, for by this time the Germans zeroed in on the position. Hours later the Captain returned after having successfully dodged both enemy mortar fire and infantry in the woods. This particular expedition was but one of many actions by the crack ack ack men. On many occasions 796th batteries and platoons served as spearheads for Tiger armor and infantry as well as providing anti-aircraft protection and security. The best testimony to their value was in the large number of enemy planes their deadeye gunners bagged during their partnership with the Tenth Armored Division.

Lieut. Gen. George S. Patton and Major General Walton H. Walker leave Tenth's Headquarters at Apach

SIEGFRIED LINE

14 May 1945

To: Officers and men of the 10th Armored Division and attached units:

1. On Friday, 11 May 1945, General Jacob L. Devers, commanding the Sixth Army Group, presented to me the Distinguished Service Medal. The citation reads as follows:

"CITATION FOR DISTINGUISHED SERVICE MEDAL
Major General William H. H. Morris, Jr.,
United States Army

As Commanding General of the 10th Armored Division in France and Germany during the period 2 November 1944 to 10 January 1945, General Morris brilliantly supported the XX Corps in its operations against Metz. Elements of his Division advanced along the left flank of the XX Corps and overran the city's outermost defenses and eliminated the last hope of the Germans to reinforce the Metz garrison. With the fall of the city, General Morris directed his forces east and northeast, battering against a wall of ingeniously constructed concrete abutments, anti-tank ditches and pillboxes. In spite of thick mud, and murky weather which prevented air support, his armor continued to roll back the enemy through the heavily fortified Siegfried line, and to gain approaches to the Saar river. Occupying the strategically important west bank of the Saar, General Morris directed a series of brilliant crossing feints which diverted the attention of the enemy, permitting elements of an infantry division to negotiate a crossing. When a strong hostile counterattack threatened to penetrate the Allied battle line on 17 December, General Morris swiftly placed elements of his command in defensive positions which repulsed the enemy. His shrewd tactical judgment and the gallant conduct of his men contributed greatly to the annihilation of the German spearheads seeking to push the Allied Armies back from the border."

2. This award is indeed a great personal honor but I feel that actually it is a glowing tribute to each and every one of you who served so valiantly with the 10th Armored Division. I am deeply grateful for your support.

W. H. H. MORRIS, JR.,
Major General, U.S. Army
Commanding, 10th A.D.

GERMANY

3 December, 1944

To: Officers and Enlisted Men, 10th Armored Division:

Tigers of the Tenth, your accomplishments against the enemy have earned high praise from our Corps and Army Commanders. During the first three weeks of fighting you have liberated one hundred square miles of France and occupied fifty square miles of German territory. Many of your home town papers have already announced the Tigers as the first of General Patton's divisions to enter Germany. You have seized sixty-four towns, captured over two thousand prisoners of war, and repulsed eleven counterattacks. Enemy personnel and materials you destroyed in substantial quantities. All of this has been at a minimum cost to yourselves in lives and vehicles destroyed.

I take this opportunity to commend each officer and enlisted man of this great fighting Division for an outstanding performance in our first test before the enemy.

W. H. H. MORRIS, JR.,
Major General, United States Army
Commanding, 10th Armored Division

METZ

24 November, 1944

To: Commanding General, XX Army Corps.

Radiogram received from General Marshall which is in substance herewith quoted:

"Congratulations on the capture of Metz and the splendid advance your Corps are making in spite of floods and mud and bitter enemy resistance. My very personal congratulations to Eddy and Walker on the grand show their troops are putting on toward bringing this war to a triumphant conclusion."

I personally wish to add my commendation and congratulations for the splendid advance which you and your Corps have made. With such troops, the triumphant conclusion of the war is inevitably near.

G. S. PATTON, JR.,
Lieut. General, United States Army
Commanding, 3rd Army

28 November 1944

To: Commanding General, 10th Armored Division.

It is with supreme pride and gratification that I publish to the command the following letter of commendation:
To: Commanding General, XX Corps.

1. The workmanlike manner in which your Corps accomplished the capture of the heretofore impregnable city of Metz is an outstanding military achievement.

2. Please accept for yourself and pass on to the officers and men of the XX Corps my high commendation for the superior manner in which you accomplished your difficult mission.

G. S. PATTON, JR.,
Lieut. General, United States Army
Commanding, 3rd Army

I thank each officer and man of the XX Corps for the part he played in this operation. Such aggressive action and battlefield cooperation and the will to carry on in spite of adverse conditions will have full significance in the victory of tomorrow.

WALTON H. WALKER
Major General, United States Army
Commanding, XX Corps

IV

THE BATTLE OF THE BULGE

ROLLING NORTH ALONG THE Thionville-Luxembourg highway in the late afternoon, combat vehicles of the Tenth Armored Division came to a sudden, grinding stop. The date was December 17, 1944. The night before, General Morris had been alerted to move the Division to the north. Unknown to most of us, the Tiger General had already dispatched Colonel Basil G. Thayer, Lieut. Col. John W. Sheffield and Major Roger Rawley at 2030 on December 16 to Bastogne to confer with Troy Middleton, commanding general of the VIII Corps. In the early hours of December 17, Thayer returned in time to join the Division which was already on the move. In the meantime, General Morris had hurried, in advance of the Tenth Armored, to Bastogne for further orders from General Middleton. With him was Major "Mutt" Jordan, who was later killed in action.

While Tiger troops waited for word from General Morris, as they huddled around their vehicles on the highway, they seemed to sense that "something big" was in the wind. Tension increased to fever pitch by the time Colonel Thayer returned to relay orders to the commanders. Now, everyone learned the truth. As they sped northward, they knew that instead of becoming the "palace guard" in Luxembourg, as many had predicted, the Division was to be hurled in the face of a new German winter blitz. Von Runstedt's top field commanders were already sweeping in from the east with a mighty panzer force made up of the Fifth, Sixth and Seventh German Armies—backed up by ten tank and fourteen infantry divisions.

This was the pulverizing enemy attack that created the Bulge. Its purpose was to break through unsuspecting American divisions in the Ardennes and then to proceed westward to capture the important supply points of Liege and Antwerp. Thus, while the Tenth Armored was getting its combat operation orders on that fateful day of December 17, Von Runstedt had already launched his devastating panzer-led offensive across a 75-mile front—which at that time was protected only by five United States divisions.

We couldn't know at the time that it was Hitler himself, who, while lying in a hospital bed in August of 1944, after an unsuccessful attempt on his life, had hatched the master plan for the Ardennes Offensive. Though top German generals were opposed to the plan, Hitler ordered that it be carried through. Now the plan was set, and along with it, the fate of the armored Tigers.

The night before, on December 16, while the Tenth Armored was licking its wounds and reorganizing after a holding action on the Siegfried Line, the enemy Juggernaut was penetrating the Belgian-Luxembourg borders. It was this grim threat that resulted in the sudden shift of the Division to Luxembourg and Bastogne the next day—a day that none of us will ever forget.

Fortunately for the Nazis, the great Blitz was given birth under an all-engulfing fog. As a result, it partially escaped detection by our intelligence and enabled them to crash a mighty mailed fist into the unsuspecting forces defending the 75-mile arc—until now, a stable and relatively quiet front.

On orders from General Middleton, the Tenth Armored was to be sent to a quartering area in the vicinity of Luxembourg upon their arrival. However, this instruction was discarded because of the developing enemy situation. As the Division approached that city, General Morris was being briefed by Middleton on the grave situation faced by the Fourth Infantry Division and the Ninth Armored Division on their front east and northeast of Luxembourg city. At the same time, Middleton requested that General Morris go into immediate conference with General Barton and General Leonard of the Fourth and the Ninth. Furthermore, he was asked to assist them with the problems they faced as the

White-washed halftrack provides setting for two Tenth
Armored doughs as they try on new waterproof boots
in northern Luxembourg during the Bulge

Germans threatened to break through their defenses. It was while
the Tiger commander was en route to Barton's Headquarters with
Lieut. Col. Sheffield that he sent orders to Thayer on the Luxembourg highway to lead the Tenth Armored to the area between
the Fourth Infantry and the Ninth Armored Divisions. When they
reached their destination, the leading Tigers rolled headlong into
the enemy. Combat Command A, under the brilliant generalship of
Edwin W. Piburn, attacked the same day and thus accomplished
the magnificent feat of racing 75 miles in a single day and ending
it locked in combat. Without stopping, they rammed into a very
surprised German attacking force; and while the Tenth Armored
blasted away at the underbelly of the Bulge, the Seventh Armored
Division was holding at the top near St. Vith. Here was the first
stopping action being performed by two armored divisions. Each
one was miles away when the breakthrough was effected, but because of armor's great mobility, they were able to move directly
to the hinges of the Bulge and check the enemy's enlargement
of the mouth, and at the same time, to canalize his movement to
a relatively narrow front.

When General Morris arrived at the Command Post of the Fourth Infantry Division at Luxembourg he was grabbed by Major General Barton who, after hugging him said, "Dammit Bill, am I glad to see you." Afterwards, the two generals and Sheffield studied the Fourth Infantry's situation map. The latter described it as "a map that looked like it had a bad case of measles." Virtually every infantry unit was marked by a red circle, indicating the havoc inflicted upon it by the marauding German attack.

FARMED OUT

Because the First Army sector was hit hardest by the onrushing Germans, the Tenth Armored was "farmed out" at once to that headquarters. For three days, from December 17 to 19, the Tenth Armored was placed under the command of Major General Troy Middleton's VIII Corps of the First Army. But on the third day the Third Army left flank was extended to include Luxembourg and part of Belgium. This brought about the quick return of the Tenth to General Patton's command. The fiery Patton quickly made General Morris provisional corps commander with the responsibility of protecting the Third Army's right flank. The details of high command conferences to determine the Allied preparations to meet the enemy blitz are revealed by General Morris who described them to the author later. The Division Commander told of a big meeting at Verdun, called by General Eisenhower. In attendance were the Supreme Commander, General Bradley, General Devers, General Patton and other high-ranking American officers. There, it was decided that the Seventh Army would relieve the Third to permit the latter Army to move to the Bulge. After leaving that conference, General Patton called General Morris at Luxembourg and told the Tiger Commander to meet him at XX Corps Headquarters at Thionville at 1700 on December 19. When General Morris arrived there, he found General Patton and General Walker discussing the situation. "Patton was mad as hell," he recalled, " and he was pacing the floor, his hands on his two pistol butts. He turned to me and said, Morris, I'm making you a provisional corps commander. You are in charge of the right flank around Luxembourg until the Headquarters of the XII Corps arrive." Then Patton named the Fourth, Fifth and Eightieth units included in the provisional corps. In the talk that followed, Patton told how he planned to move Third Army to the Bulge and directed General Morris to hold there until additional troops arrived and to be prepared to counterattack with the Corps when directed. At this juncture, Morris inquired, "How long am I expected to hold"? Patton answered, "Four or five days and dammit, you had better hold!" After the Conference, General Morris returned to Luxembourg to assemble the division commanders now under his jurisdiction. Plans for a counterattack were outlined to them by the Tiger leader and the machinery for coordination was set by the time General Eddy of the XII Corps arrived at noon on December 21. On the next day, another meeting was held by Patton at his Luxembourg Headquarters. Present, in addition to Morris, were Generals Walker, Gay, Eddy, Millikin and several division commanders. This time, Third Army's plan for an immediate counterattack was plotted by the assembled commanders against the face of the German salient. Highlight of the rapid-fire proceedings came when General Patton hurriedly sketched the responsibilities of each of the corps and division commanders and then turned to the entire group and announced grimly, "Now we've got those bastards just where we want them". On December 22, General Morris relinquished his provisional corps command to General Eddy's XII Corps and returned to lead the Tenth Armored. On December 23, he was informed by Third Army that the big counterattack plan had been junked and that he was to help strengthen the shoulder of the southern underbelly of the Bulge and hold. A few days later, before departing with the Tenth for Metz, General Morris met with General Patton and asked the latter why the counterattack had been cancelled. The reason, he was informed, was because of the dangerous situation which had developed at Bastogne. To the very end, Patton insisted that a mistake had been made, holding that the counterattack should have been initiated to "drive those S.O.B.'s back to the Rhine".

CRITICAL OPERATION

Earlier in the blitz when the Tenth first reached Luxembourg, General Morris lost no time in organizing the Division's fighting power effectively. As has been described, he directed CC A under General Piburn, to attack immediately in northern Luxembourg. Meanwhile, Combat Command B was held in reserve by him. But not for long. Later in the day CC B was ordered on to Merl, a western suburb of the City of Luxembourg, where they bivouacked for the night of December 17. Then in the morning, Colonel William L. Roberts moved his CC B Armoraiders on Bastogne. For the first time since our arrival in Europe, Combat Command B was virtually on its own as circumstances dictated the splitting up of the Tenth Armored. Combat Command B was headed for the fiery inferno at Bastogne while Combat Command A and the Reserve Command geared themselves for the flaming battles at the southern hinge of the Bulge. For, as a direct result of the smashing enemy attack over a wide portion of the front, the Tiger Division was soon to play a leading role in one of the most crucial military struggles of all time. And for the first time in its combat operations, the Division fought under two distinguished Corps at the same time, as Roberts' Combat Command B functioned under VIII Corps at Bastogne while the remainder of the Tenth pushed forward under the XII Corps at the city of Luxembourg.

SLUGFEST

As described, after racing 75 miles, Combat Command A without pausing, rammed into Von Runstedt's elite troops in the vicinity of Berdorf and Echternach, some 20 miles north of Luxembourg. Here, the enemy spearhead was already choking off isolated pockets of Fourth Infantry doughs and was fanning out over a 30-mile front to menace the city of Luxembourg. To throttle the dangerous enemy threat on the Fourth Infantry's front and to claw Von Runstedt's flank, General Morris directed Combat Command A to counterattack the enemy drive. Brig. Gen. Edwin W. Piburn, one of the most decorated general officers in the Army, hurled three crack task forces against the enemy blitz in accordance with the Division Commander's order. One of them, Task Force Chamberlain, slammed into the Germans before 1700 on the day of arrival and along with Task Forces Riley and Standish, fought a blistering battle for three crucial days. In the meantime, General Morris received a report that two Nazi divisions were heading for a three-mile gap that separated the Ninth Armored and Twenty-Eighth Infantry Divisions. In desperation, he plugged the gap by sending Lieut. Col. Cornelius A. Lichirie's 90th Cavalry Recon Squadron there. Fortunately, the Recon Tigers were not required to hold off the two enemy divisions as German commanders directed them to attack elsewhere. The fighting at Berdorf and Echternach was a slugfest all the way. Always outnumbered but never outfought, the men of the Tenth Armored managed to hold the enemy at bay long enough to permit the Third Corps to assemble a powerful attacking force with which to drive the Germans back across the Sauer River line and to rescue marooned elements of the Fourth Infantry Division.

On December 19, Task Force Chamberlain halted the greatest enemy penetration at Mullerthal's "bowling alley", a deep draw which echoed the discordant noise of battle. At the same time, Task Force Riley ran a three-mile gauntlet of fire on three separate occasions to rescue Tiger doughs cut off in Echternach. Task Force Standish, meanwhile, smashed its way to Berdorf, the scene of some of the war's most bitter fighting. The enemy fought with fury at both places, inflicting heavy casualties on the Tigers, but soon had to divert part of its men and machines to the north as a result of the VIII Corps' attack east of Bastogne. A description of the furious battle waged at Berdorf was provided by a United Press war correspondent who related how, "A handful of men from the Tenth Armored and Fourth Infantry Divisions halted the Nazi drive toward Luxembourg City for three days during the early stages of Von Runstedt's great counter-attack. 250 men, commanded by Captain Steve Lang of the 11th Tank Battalion, Tenth Armored Division, beat off attack after attack launched by two German panzer battalions, holding the town of Berdorf during 72 hours of furious fighting in which 350 Germans were killed, and 7 enemy tanks knocked out. The greatly outnumbered Americans also destroyed 3 German halftracks. The tankers and doughs defending the tiny town lost only 4 dead, 20 wounded, 1 tank and 4 halftracks.

HOLD AT ALL COSTS

"The motley unit withdrew from the town in perfect order after they had booby-trapped it. Not a man was hit during the withdrawal which was carried out according to Captain Lang's plans. The stand enabled relief forces of Americans to move up and prevent further German advances. Had there been a breakthrough at Berdorf, the Nazis would have had a clear road to Luxembourg City.

Belgian church escapes destruction but rectory is leveled by the Germans' artillery

"The armored units under Lang joined what was left of two companies of the 12th Regiment, Fourth Infantry Division, on December 18 and entered Berdorf. Their orders were to hold the town at all costs.

"During the first night they not only held but actually advanced 350 yards against vastly superior numbers of the enemy. They used explosives to blast their way from building to building.

"One lieutenant among the defenders of Berdorf appeared to have a charmed life. His tank was hit by a bazooka which set his 50 caliber machine gun afire. He rigged up two 30's from a knocked-out tank and kept shooting.

AMMUNITION LOW

"A rifle grenade bounced off a turret and just missed him. Then another bazooka rocket hit his tank, injuring him slightly.

"On the 19th, the Germans attempted to drive into the town from the north and were beaten off by heavy weapons fire. Lang directed artillery fire to beat off three thrusts by German tank columns.

"The Germans mounted an attack in force from the northeast and west on the 21st after laying down a murderous artillery barrage. The fight lasted an hour and a half, but Lang's tankers and infantrymen held firm, and the Nazis again retired. By now the ammunition of the little garrison was low, and there were wounded in urgent need of evacuation. Lang was informed that he was virtually cut off. So the men went back to battling off two more attacks with what ammunition they had. When the supply was just about exhausted a relief train of two M-4's and three halftracks got through to them. The train that brought in supplies took back the wounded. At 1600 the afternoon of the 21st, Lang received orders to withdraw. He loaded his tanks with 15 infantrymen each—four inside and 11 clinging to the outside. Artillery fire masked the noise of the engines starting. The withdrawal was made without the knowledge of the Germans. The engineers were the last to leave. They set off explosive charges in all vehicles that had to be abandoned."

MEN OF DISTINCTION

Every combat veteran knows that absolute coordination and disciplined teamwork are necessary to emerge victorious from battle. News accounts of Tiger battles almost always included the tankers and the doughs at the scene of action and rightfully so, but rarely were the exploits and the less-sensational efforts of the remainder of the Tiger team highlighted in the press. For example, in the United Press story there was no mention made of Private First Class Elmer L. McCann of the 419th Armored Field Artillery in the hard fighting at Berdorf. Yet, the value of his work there can not be overestimated. On December 20, McCann, despite heavy enemy artillery and rocket fire, crawled from his forward observer position, laying wire to the artillery so that effective fire could be placed on the enemy who had encircled Berdorf. This hazardous effort had to be made to offset radio relay failure from the forward observer position. To make matters worse, the intense enemy fire shattered the wire at three different locations forcing McCann to expose himself to a shrapnel shower again. On December 21, Staff Sergeant Thalen Bowen of the 420th Armored Field Artillery, though beset by enemy sniper fire, risked his life repeatedly as he called for Tiger artillery fire to thwart an enemy counter-attack despite the fact that the artillery fire had to be directed practically on top of his position. The end result was translated into extremely valuable time gained by our forces at the expense of a stalled enemy. These are but two descriptions of personal valor by supporting Tigers. They represent the kind of initiative and devotion to a cause that was typical of most of the unheralded Tigers who daily backed up tanker and dough with supplies, medical attention, counter-intelligence, air support, vehicle maintenance, signal needs, special services, chemical warfare, engineer support and countless other vital services.

CORPS CONSOLIDATION

By December 21, XII Corps had moved to the city of Luxembourg. There, it assumed control of the Fourth, Fifth and Thirty-Fifth Infantry Divisions plus the Tenth Armored Division—less Combat Command B. Also included were the Second Cavalry Group and Combat Command A of the Ninth Armored Division. On the next day our intelligence reported the enemy's probable capabilities. His advance to the west could be continued. He could also attack north and south to expand the shoulders of the salient. Finally, he could commit his reserve armor to the Echternach area to endanger the east flank of First Army's counterdrive. His decision was known almost immediately as pressure on the Tigers mounted in the Echternach area.

On December 22, XII Corps prepared an intensive attack in a zone from Ettelbruck to Echternach, then south to Wormeldange which was east of Luxembourg. At this time, Combat Command A was at Imbringen about 5 miles northeast of Luxembourg. In the meantime, the Reserve Command was enroute to Nommern. The foul weather which favored the movement of the German blitz continued its pattern of heavy fog. But on the next day, General Patton's prayer for good weather was answered. Through the Third Army Chaplain, his prayer was issued to the troops. In it he begged, "Almighty and most merciful father, we humbly beseech thee, of thy great goodness, to restrain these immodest rains with which we have to contend. Grant us fair weather for Battle. Graciously harken to us as soldiers who call upon thee that armed with thy power, we may advance from victory to victory, and crush the oppression and wickedness of our enemies and establish Thy justice among men and nations. Amen."

Along with cold and clear weather on December 23, reconnaissance elements of the Division advanced to within a mile of Diekirch as Combat Command A and the Reserve Command prepared to attack in force. On this day, for security reasons, 1,200 fragmentation hand grenades were issued to military police in the rear areas to combat enemy troops believed to have been parachuted behind our lines—including those who had infiltrated our positions in civilian garb. It appeared later that more damage had been done to the morale of front line Tigers—as a result of the wild rumors of spies and saboteurs who were supposedly running loose behind our lines—than the minor success achieved by a few enemy who managed to operate for a short time in our rear areas. The total estimated strength of the enemy opposing the United States Third Army north of the Moselle River was 11 Divisions—about 88,500 German troops. On the day before Christmas, 143 enemy planes bombed and strafed Third Army positions 94 times. But in retaliation, Army's anti-aircraft units shot down 17 of the marauders with an additional 6 probably destroyed. The same day, December 24, Piburn's Armoraiders captured Mostroff and continued to drive north. Then on Christmas, 202 days after the Allied landings on D Day, the Tiger commands along with the Fifth Infantry Division pushed their way west of Echternach. Haller and Waldbillig were cleaned out and Belfort was encircled. Further south at Metz, the Sixth Armored Division, having completed its job of refitting, prepared to move up to the XII Corps zone to relieve the Tenth Armored. At 2000, the next day, XX Corps relinquished its control of the Sixth Armored and its attached troops to the XII Corps and in the big switch got back the Tenth Armored along with the Division's attached troops. Then, on December 26, after having been relieved by the Sixth Armored, the Tenth swung around south to the XX Corp's sector where it continued to press the enemy along that Corp's front.

On December 28, General Walker's "Ghost Corps" issued the following order to the 90th, 95th, attached troops and Tenth Armored:

"Hold present sector to include the Saarlautern bridgehead. On Army's order, advance north to clear enemy from area between Moselle and Saar Rivers. Be prepared to follow XX Corps to the northeast". During the day on December 28, the Tenth Armored also managed to improve its defensive positions. Then, on December 31, the Division, minus Combat Command B, moved south to Metz for rehabilitation and training, ending the most hotly-contested battle in the Division's brief but rugged operational history since its November baptism of fire at the swollen Moselle.

The southern anchor of the great defensive battle waged by Combat Command A and the Reserve Command was secured at last. The period of jabbing and sparring to keep the Germans off balance was over. Now the Division readied itself to deliver a solid punch as part of General Patton's great offensive against the Bulge got underway. And, as an act of crowning glory, the Tenth Armored Division received the everlasting gratitude of Prince Felix who visited General Morris in Luxembourg. Before the Division departed for Metz, the Crown Prince brought to the

Scene after battle

Division the heartfelt thanks of his people and declared that the Tenth had saved Luxembourg from certain capture by the Germans as a result of the courage and superior combat shown by the Armoraiders.

While in the process of rest and reorganization at Metz, both Combat Command A and the Reserve Command nevertheless were on call by XX Corps in the event of operational need by General Walker. The Tigers were rewarded with nearly six weeks of rest at Metz partly as a result of the crushing defeat inflicted upon the retreating Germans after the Bulge was deflated by the Allies. During the period from December 26 until February 8, the Tigers had been attached to no less than three different army corps and two armies. Though the Tenth moved short distances several times in carrying out assigned missions no major combat was undertaken. Most of the time was devoted to rest, rehabilitation and re-equipping. In the latter part of January of 1945, small unit training was the order of the day.

DEMOLITION DEMONS

During the first three days of the Division's counter-offensive against the charging enemy, the Ninth Armored Division prepared for the worst and consequently had at hand an extensive plan for prepared demolitions. Combat Command A, now operating in the Ninth's zone, took over part of the demolition responsibility. As a result, Captain Morris Wientraub's Company of the 55th Armored Engineers found themselves engaged in hurried demolition activities. On one occasion, when one of Wientraub's engineer platoons arrived to fix dynamite to a small bridge spanning a stream west of Lorentzweiler, they found that the bridge had been previously destroyed by the retreating enemy. However, in the meantime, a band of hardy Luxembourgers had managed to repair most of the span by the time the engineers appeared on the scene. Wientraub's Tigers immediately set to work with their sticks of dynamite. Finally the civilian repair-

Three Tiger tankers enjoy brief Christmas respite from
Battle of the Bulge and open packages from home

men's curiosity got the better of them and they gathered around
the engineers to learn what they were doing there. When they
saw demolitions being attached to the structure, they dropped
their tools and without a word of explanation left the site.

BOMBS AWAY

During the wild battle in Berdorf one of Captain Lang's
Tigers found a cache of Schnapps. The stuff tasted so good that
he proceeded to liquidate the entire supply. About the time that
he had lost touch with the situation, the Germans attacked his
three-story building. While his platoon fought the infiltrators from
room to room, the young Tiger buzzed around in a make-believe
world. Soon the Germans worked their way up to the floor be-
neath him. The shooting finally penetrated his happy mind and he
proceeded to lend a hand. Leaning precariously out of a top
floor window, he raised his arm back and with mighty heaves,

73

threw grenade after grenade into the room below. With each toss he yelled with great glee, "bombs away". He was untouched throughout the entire melee.

LITTLE GROUPS OF YANKS BROKE UP BIG NAZI PUSH
by Hugh Schuck

War Correspondent, The New York Daily News

"With the U. S. Third Army, Jan. 4 - As details of fighting in the early stages of Field Marshal Karl von Runstedt's break-through emerge from a shroud of secrecy imposed by disrupted communications and censorship, it becomes more and more apparent that the initial impetus of the German drive was broken by isolated American units which chose to fight to the last cartridge against overwhelming odds.

"It was such a last-ditch fight by Major General Raymond O. Barton's 4th Infantry Division and part of Major General William H. H. Morris' 10th Armored Division which kept the Germans from capturing the City of Luxembourg and its road network over which Lieutenant General George S. Patton later moved his divisions to launch a counter-attack. And it was that kind of American resistance that centered around Berdorf, 17 miles northeast of the City of Luxembourg.

ARMOR SPLIT UP

"The 10th Armored Division was the first Third Army unit rushed north to help stem the German tide. By forced march the 10th Armored Division reached Luxembourg on December 17, the day after the attack opened. There it was split, one part being scattered to the northeast to bolster various units, while the rest rushed toward Bastogne.

"Incidentally, it was the 10th Armored Division which met the German drive head-on outside Bastogne, threw it back on its heels and saved the city. The 10th Armored repulsed attack after attack in eight hours of continuous battle before the first elements of the 101st Airborne entered the city and joined in its defense. Ironically, the 101st got credit for the defense of Bastogne because censorship permitted it to be mentioned before the 10th Armored Division.

"Berdorf was nearly encircled the morning of December 18 when two platoons of tanks and two of armored infantry from the 10th drove through heavy artillery fire to reinforce two companies of the 12th Infantry Regiment of the 4th Division, which had been holding out there.

"Then for three days this force of about 250 men commanded by Captain Steve Lang of Chicago threw back the best the Germans had to offer, killing 350 of the enemy and destroying large numbers of German tanks and armored vehicles, while losing only four dead and one medium tank.

"All during the day of the 18th, Lang attempted to attack, but the German pressure and artillery fire was too heavy. That night he set fire to a house at the edge of town, and the light prevented the Germans from infiltrating in the dark hours. The next morning the Germans attacked with artillery and rockets, but in the face of this Lang managed to advance about 350 yards.

TANK CHIEF BATTERED

"That day Lieutenant John F. Gaynor of Ocean Avenue, Freeport, L. I., platoon commander of the 11th Tank Battalion, wore most of the fur off his rabbit's foot. His tank was hit by bazooka fire, setting his machine gun ammunition ablaze, and artillery knocked out his last machine gun.

"But under cover of tanks commanded by Sergeant John Shea of 29 Sullivan Place, Bronx, and Sergeant Francis J. Cleary of Roxbury, Mass., Gaynor pulled back and removed machine guns from a knocked-out tank to replace his own.

"No sooner were the guns in place when another bazooka shell struck his turret.

"All that day the Germans attacked and were beaten off. At 4:30 the next morning the Germans massed for a surprise attack. Three times they tried. Three times they were pushed back.

"Later that morning the Germans struck northeast and west under heavy artillery fire. For an hour and a half the defenders beat back the Germans, and then just as American ammunition was running low the enemy pulled back to reform.

HALFTRACKS COME THROUGH

"When Lang called back for supplies and ambulances to evacuate his wounded he was told he had been cut off from the rear, but later in the day Sergeant James C. Halligan of Rutherford, N. Y., broke through with two medium tanks and three half-tracks loaded with supplies. With the halftracks he evacuated the wounded.

"And at four that afternoon Lang ordered a withdrawal if possible. He divided his tanks, guns and halftracks into four units which left at eight-minute intervals under cover of artillery fire, which also covered the noise of his retreat.

"He got his entire force out of town without the Germans knowing it, leaving demolitions and mines to delay the enemy further.

HEAVY GUNS GO TO WORK

"The Germans didn't discover Berdorf had been evacuated until the next morning, for as soon as Lang had pulled out, the artillery kept pounding it for hours.

"By the next morning, however, other American units had dug in on high areas back of the town, further blocking the Germans.

"The defense of Berdorf and Echternach, three miles to the southeast, by the 12th Regiment of the 4th Infantry Division, stopped the left flank of von Runstedt's drive, preventing him from swinging south and grabbing the rich prize of the city of Luxembourg before stronger units could be thrown into line."

Sergeant Walter W. Streetman guards against Luftwaffe attack. Sheets help prevent air detection

LUXEMBOURG

31 December 1944

TO: Officers and Enlisted Men, 10th Armored Division

"The Division Commander commends the officers and enlisted men of the Division on the fine work they did during their recent operations in Luxembourg. The missions accomplished by the Division will have far reaching results.

"During the past year, the Division has been successful in every operation in which it has participated. May next year bring us similar success.

Happy New Year."

W. H. H. MORRIS, JR.
Major General, United States Army
Commanding, 10th Armored Division

28 December 1944

TO: Commanding General, 10th Armored Division
THRU: Commanding General, XII Corps

"1. On 16 December 1944, a general German offensive was launched along the greater portion of the Western Front. This division was in position and holding a front of approximately thirty-three miles east and north of the city of Luxembourg.

"2. Substantial penetrations were made by the Germans in sectors north of this division, and he sought desperately to expand the shoulders of his penetration to the south. At stake were the City of Luxembourg, Radio Luxembourg and military installations of vital importance.

"3. On 17 December your command was ordered to the support of this general sector. Working closely in conjunction with the 12th Infantry Regiment, holding the northern flank of the 4th Division sector, three task forces of your CCA were committed.

"a. Task Force Riley passed through our lines, contained an enemy force in Scheidgen, and succeeded in supplying one company of the 12th Infantry Regiment isolated in Echternach;

"b. Task Force Standish aided in the defense of Berdorf;

"c. Task Force Chamberlain supported our attack and aided in securing high ground overlooking Mullerthal.

"4. Your immediate and accurate appraisal of the developing enemy intentions, and the complete cooperation tendered by you, together with the vigor with which your troops undertook these missions, contributed ultimately in denying to the enemy any expansion southward of his penetration. Regroupment later of the Allied forces to the north was based upon an extension of the line we had fought for and held.

"5. Maj Gen R. O. Barton, commanding this division during the period cited, desired that expression be made of his appreciation for the complete cooperation extended, and the outstanding performance given by you and your command. In transmitting this commendation, I desire to add that I am in full accord with General Barton's opinion and take this opportunity to concur with his expression of high regard."

H. W. BLAKELEY,
Brigadier General,
U. S. Army, Commanding,
4th Infantry Division.

V

BLOODY BASTOGNE

ON DECEMBER 19, 1944, most of the Western Front was afire. Supplying the torch was Hitler himself who, in a final desperate gamble, flung virtually all his remaining military strength against the ever-pressing Allies in the hope of regaining the initiative in the west. A delayed Associated Press communique on December 26 spelled out in detail the magnitude of the enemy's great winter blitz which hit Combat Command B with all its crushing force as it reported that, "Powerful and aggressive enemy forces composed of elements of eight German Divisions smashed headlong into Combat Command B of the Tenth Armored Division and its attached units in the early hours of December 19, 1944. The bloody Bastogne epic rocked the entire world with its ominous outcome, for it was here that the enemy spearhead struck violently in an effort to capture the important Bastogne road junction, vital to the success later, of capturing Antwerp, largest supply point for allied troops on the western front."

Just before noon on December 18, the Tigers of Colonel William L. Roberts' Combat Command B were ordered to assemble at Bastogne. At that time, while no one could foresee the bloody road ahead, there was ample evidence that the small Belgian town of Bastogne was to be a key point in the days to come. And supporting the Tigers' apprehension was the directive issued to Colonel Roberts by Major General Troy Middleton, commander of the VIII Corps, which stated, "When your troops arrive in Bastogne, place one third of your forces each in Noville, Longvilly and Bras." Each of these towns was situated about seven kilometers distant on key roads, leading from the north, east, and southeast into Bastogne. The roads were extremely important to the enemy as avenues of attack for their panzer forces. To block and hold these roads and to cover the concentration of the 101st

Airborne Division in Bastogne was the man-sized job assumed by Combat Command B.

As yet unopposed by the enemy, the able Roberts brought his Tigers into Bastogne at nightfall. By midnight of December 18, the Command had taken positions as ordered. Along the way, they passed many friendly units headed for points west. At the same time, Eighth Corps Headquarters was busily evacuating the city. In their hurry, they were forced to abandon considerable equipment. Left behind, too, was the huge American Red Cross supply dump of donut flour which was later issued to appreciative units at Bastogne in lieu of other rations which were to become almost non-existent. During this frenzied activity, CC B, soon to be dubbed "The Stone of Bastogne", quietly established its Headquarters in the Hotel Le Brun, right in the center of Bastogne—a city as yet untouched by battle and heretofore virtually unmentioned in news reports on the war in Europe.

TWO DAYS OF WHITE HELL

The first Tigers to be attacked were Major William R. Desobry's Noville defenders. This small but determined force had arrived and assembled at 2300 on December 18. On hand were 30 light and medium tanks of the 3rd Tank Battalion, half of the 20th Armored Infantry Battalion, a platoon from the 55th Armored Engineers and part of the 90th Recon Squadron. Despite the fact that it was dominated by two ridges a half mile away, Noville was on high ground. Upon arrival, Desobry instructed Captain Gordon Geiger of Headquarters Company, 20th Armored Infantry Battalion to set up a perimeter defense of Noville. Anchoring this line were three forward strongpoints 800 yards from the main force, on the roads to Bourcey, Houffalize and Vaux. These were manned by three weakened infantry platoons and tank sections. Though they began to mine the area to support the roadblocks, the engineers had to stop for fear of blowing up stragglers streaming into Noville. A message from Roberts to Desobry instructed the

BASTOGNE

COMBAT ORGANIZATION OF CC B
18 DEC 44 — 16 JAN 45

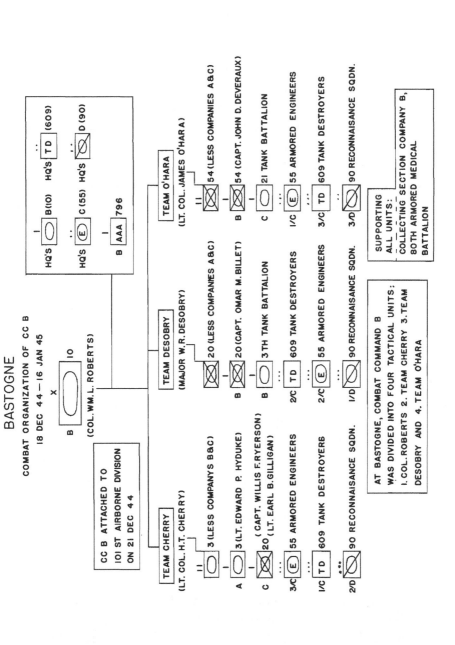

CC B ATTACHED TO
101 ST AIRBORNE DIVISION
ON 21 DEC 44

(COL. WM. L. ROBERTS)

HQ'S   B(10)   HQ'S   TD   (609)
HQ'S   E   C (55)   HQ'S   D (90)
B   AAA   796

TEAM CHERRY
(LT. COL. H.T. CHERRY)
3 (LESS COMPANYS B&C)
3 (LT. EDWARD P. HYDUKE)
(CAPT. WILLIS F. RYERSON)
20 (LT. EARL B. GILLIGAN)
A
C
3/C   E   55 ARMORED ENGINEERS
1/C   TD   609 TANK DESTROYERS
2/D   90 RECONNAISANCE SQDN.

TEAM DESOBRY
(MAJOR W.R. DESOBRY)
20 (LESS COMPANIES A&C)
20 (CAPT. OMAR M. BILLET)
B   3TH TANK BATTALION
2/C   TD   609 TANK DESTROYERS
2/C   E   55 ARMORED ENGINEERS
1/D   90 RECONNAISANCE SQDN.

TEAM O'HARA
(LT. COL. JAMES O'HARA)
54 (LESS COMPANIES A&C)
54 (CAPT. JOHN D. DEVERAUX)
B   21 TANK BATTALION
C
1/C   E   55 ARMORED ENGINEERS
3/C   TD   609 TANK DESTROYERS
3/D   90 RECONNAISANCE SQDN.

AT BASTOGNE, COMBAT COMMAND B
WAS DIVIDED INTO FOUR TACTICAL UNITS:
I. COL. ROBERTS 2. TEAM CHERRY 3.TEAM
DESOBRY AND 4.TEAM O'HARA

SUPPORTING
ALL UNITS:
COLLECTING SECTION COMPANY B,
80TH ARMORED MEDICAL
BATTALION

B   10
X

latter to "fill your unit with any stragglers you can lay your hands on". But most of these men were either exhausted or demoralized and could not be utilized by the defending Tigers except for a superbly led infantry platoon of the 9th Armored Division which plugged a hole in the perimeter with excellent results. To prepare for the enemy avalanche, Desobry emptied the streets by moving his vehicles to side roads. Then he told his men to hit the sack for a few hours of sorely needed rest. This command was disregarded as the Tigers watched the lessening flow of stragglers entering the town. At 0430, traffic ceased altogether. Everyone apprehensively waited for the enemy attack that was sure to follow. At 0545, the sound of approaching vehicles alerted the defenders to a "wait and see" preparedness.

HALT!

Then as the vehicles ground to a noisy stop a few feet from the Bourcey roadblock, a Tiger sentry yelled, "Halt!" At this juncture, someone in the lead half track barked commands in German. In the next instant, dozens of hand grenades were hurled into the vehicle by Desobry's men. As they exploded, the screaming of the wounded coincided with their efforts to scramble out of the wrecked track. The remainder of the column hit the ditches to slug it out with the Tigers. The battle was now joined as the leading elements of the German Second Panzer Division crashed into Desobry's outnumbered defenders. In the rear area, Von Luttwitz, Commander of the crack 47th Panzer Corps, bent intently over his battle maps, secure in the knowledge that his panzers were rolling with ease towards Bastogne. Several hours later both he and his panzer commanders were forced to revise their operational timetable as Desobry's fighters grimly threw back the surprised and confused enemy.

As the battle continued in pitch blackness, Sergeant Leon D. Gantt of the 20th Armored Infantry decided to pull his men back about 100 yards when enemy grenades began to find their mark.

In the ensuing minutes, the battered Germans swung their remaining halftracks around and bolted for safety in order to report the unexpected American strongpoint. Then at about 0630, three tanks rumbled up to the Houffalize roadblock guarded by Sergeant Major I. Jones and his Tigers. At a distance of 75 yards, the Sergeant triggered a burst of fire over the tank's turret, and he too yelled, "Halt!" He was answered by a shower of 50 caliber machine gun lead which barely missed him. The small arms fire ended abruptly as the enemy tanks opened up with their big guns on the two American tanks which had been supporting the roadblock. Though hit and knocked out by several rounds from the German tanks, the crews of both the Mediums miraculously escaped death. At this point Private John J. Garry of the 20th Armored Infantry crawled into a ditch to aid the wounded tankers and was hit by shrapnel. Meanwhile, the two wrecked Mediums blocked the road, preventing enemy armor from moving forward. But the battle continued as the Tigers fought the enemy in hand-to-hand combat. Finally, the fog, which had been drifting in increased density, forced both sides to withdraw. At 0730 the Houffalize outpost pulled back into Noville. Shortly afterwards, three enemy Mark IV's slipped into the town under cover of the swirling fog. A Tiger Sherman, its armor-piercing shells exhausted, stuck its snout around the corner of a building and opened fire with high explosives. These hits only stymied the enemy for awhile. Finally, two German tanks backed out and disappeared while the third impaled itself on a burning halftrack. A sharp-shooting armored dough calmly stood in the shadows of a protective doorway and picked off each of the enemy as they bolted out of the stalled tank.

The Tiger outpost at Vaux was not attacked by the Germans, but in accordance with instructions from Major Desobry, it, too, moved back into Noville. During the night of December 18, Captain Geiger had seen to it that all roads leading to Noville were blocked. In addition, he then arranged an infantry screen in an arc just beyond the buildings, and placed three Tiger Mediums to guard the southern and western approaches to Noville. Finally, Geiger utilized a 57 mm and a 75 mm assault gun to cover the outposts at Bourcey, Houffalize and Vaux roads. When the two outposts moved into the defensive arc, the Germans took advantage of the enveloping fog and moved their tanks up on the road to fire round after round directly into the town. Fortunately, no one was hurt, though the enemy tanks got three halftracks and a jeep.

At 0830 on December 19, two enemy Tiger tanks smashed their way to within 60 feet of the Noville Force's machine gun positions, the 57 mm gun and a medium tank. Grabbing their bazookas, the machine gunners timed their shots with the two larger weapons, and together they destroyed the charging German tanks. An hour later, the enemy deployed in small groups and tried unsuccessfully to penetrate the perimeter. Among the many Tigers who helped stop the enemy from breaking through the perimeter were Lieut. Benador and Sergeant John P. Griffin. They manned the Tigers' 57 mm anti-tank guns and, along with their crews, blasted away at the small German groups from the high ground at Noville with telling effect.

FOG LIFTS

Suddenly the fog lifted. At that moment the Noville garrison saw before it a terrifying spectacle. On every flank except the rear, German tanks were pushing towards Noville. Before them was an entire German armored division! Too busy to give up in the face of these fantastic odds, Major Desobry, Captain "Bud" Billet, Captain Geiger and other Tiger commanders plotted to stop the relentless enemy. As the panzer division pressed forward on December 19, it shelled Noville constantly. Instead of quitting the town, now a mass of flames, the Tiger defenders countered the German drive by firing every available weapon. During the ensuing hour, the wild noise of battle was ear-shattering, as Tenth Armored guns dueled with enemy tanks which rolled to within 200 yards of Noville. The 420th Field Artillery Battalion in the

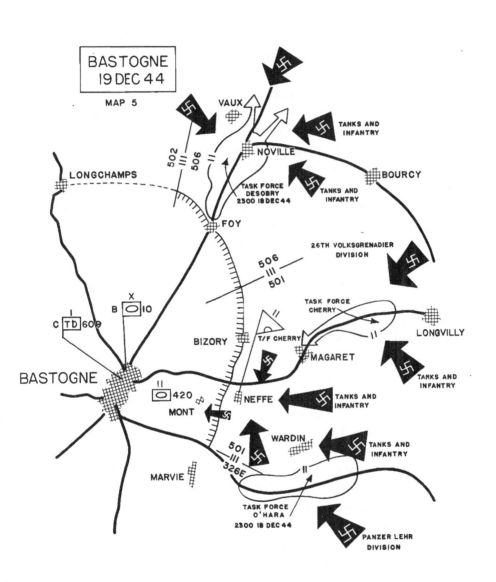

BASTOGNE
19 DEC 44

MAP 5

VAUX

502 | 506

LONGCHAMPS

NOVILLE

BOURCY

TASK FORCE
DESOBRY
2300 18 DEC 44

TANKS AND
INFANTRY

TANKS AND
INFANTRY

FOY

506 | 501

26TH VOLKSGRENADIER
DIVISION

B | X | 10

C | TD | 609

BIZORY

TASK FORCE
CHERRY

T/F CHERRY

MAGARET

LONGVILLY

TANKS AND
INFANTRY

BASTOGNE

420

MONT

NEFFE

TANKS AND
INFANTRY

WARDIN

TANKS AND
INFANTRY

501 | 326E

MARVIE

TASK FORCE
O'HARA
2300 18 DEC 44

PANZER LEHR
DIVISION

meantime slammed away at enemy infantry and armor, loosing its big projectiles as fast as it could load and fire.

During this melee, a sharpshooting platoon of 609th Tank Destroyers arrived to add its much-needed fire power to Desobry's command. As the fog continued to rise like a great curtain, enemy Mark IV's and V's were observed scooting across the distant ridge line. Like ducks in a shooting gallery, they were knocked off one by one by the TD's. Altogether, nine were hit. Three of them exploded, and one charged to within a quarter of a mile of the town before it was destroyed. But the most amazing shot of all that morning was by a gunner on a 90th Recon armored car. With only a 37 mm gun, he knocked out a big enemy Panther tank. Later, two more German tanks tried to crash through the perimeter. One was eliminated by a direct hit from the 105 mm assault gun and the other was destroyed 75 yards away from one of our Mediums. Hidden in a draw were four other enemy tanks. As one of them made the mistake of lumbering up on the road, it was hit by a tank destroyer. The three others beat a hasty retreat. To the east, the Second Panzer Division lost three more tanks to Tiger accuracy. Behind these tanks were sizeable groups of German infantry who were caught in the open as the fog lifted. As they turned and ran, our machine gun fire cut them down. Though completely outnumbered, our losses were relatively light in comparison with the heavy enemy casualties. The defending 20th Armored Infantry company lost 13 killed, 4 vehicles destroyed and 1 tank destroyer wrecked.

By noon the flaming Noville battle had burned itself out and, except for occasional shelling, all was quiet on the defenders' front and flanks. Ordinarily, Desobry would have had great cause to rejoice at the iron-clad defense put up by his men. But despite his severe losses, the enemy now was strongly entrenched behind the three ridges and, with the exception of one approach, could dominate Noville. Worse, his great fire power could level the town from behind the ridges. For this reason, Desobry asked Colonel Roberts for permission to withdraw to Bastogne. The latter, mindful of original instructions from VIII Corps, told the worried Desobry to continue to hold, that replacements were on the way. Earlier, General McAuliffe had heeded Roberts' plea for reinforcements and had dispatched two battalions of the 506th Parachute Regiment. Under the command of Lieut. Col. Joseph La Prade, one battalion hurried to Noville while the other raced to Foy. Arriving at noon on December 19 with his Troopers, La Prade huddled with Desobry at Noville and together, they prepared an attack to seize the high ground. As both Tiger and Trooper stalked out in the attack in the late afternoon, they were subjected to intense enemy shelling and in addition, their attack was met head on and stopped in its tracks by an enemy drive which had been planned for the same hour. Before the unsuccessful counter-attack was launched, Lieut. George C. Rice, Battalion S-4 of the 20th Armored Infantry, raced back to Foy for desperately needed ammo for the paratroopers. Loading his jeep with hand grenades and M-1 ammunition, he hurried back to the 506th Battalion and distributed the load to the moving paratroopers. Then he scrambled back to Foy again, and this time he brought back a truckload of ammo which was placed in 5 separate piles along the road to enable the Troopers to grab what they needed as they marched along.

At nightfall, enemy tanks came out from behind the ridges and pushed to within 1500 yards of Noville but were driven back by the deadeye 609th tank destroyers. Failing again to crash through the perimeter, the Germans instead rained a steady hail of shells on the weary Desobry-La Prade forces. As the two commanders worked over their maps in planning a defense for the night for the town, an 88 hit the front of the command post, killing Colonel La Prade and wounding Major Desobry. Major Charles L. Hustead then took command of Tenth Armored forces there and prepared for a night enemy attack he felt was sure to come. Fortunately for all, the anticipated attack never materialized, but fighting continued to rage on the outskirts of the infantry-defended perimeter. Bazooka and small arms fire kept the enemy at bay during the remainder of the night. Again, permission to get out

Supply Drop at Bastogne

of Noville was denied to the exhausted defenders. This time, General Middleton, VIII Corps commander, insisted that Noville be held, explaining, "If we are to hold Bastogne, you cannot keep falling back." For Major Desobry, the problem of defense was no longer important. When he was removed by the 80th Medical Battalion corpsmen from his command post, he was unconscious. And a few hours later, the field hospital caring for him was overrun, looted and destroyed, and he was taken prisoner by the Germans.

In the two days at Noville, the Tenth Armored defenders knocked out a record 31 enemy tanks, repulsed two major German attacks and held at bay an entire panzer division which thought it was opposing a much stronger force. Outnumbered at times by ten to one, the Noville defenders fought with raw courage in the face of almost certain annihilation. Only these men will ever know the punishment those precious hours cost.

The next day, General McAuliffe and Colonel Roberts decided to withdraw the Noville force to the vicinity of Foy, which was another vital point on the new perimeter. Pressure was such, that by mid-morning, the force was almost completely surrounded.

It was necessary now 'for the force to fight its way out. Valuable assistance was given by concentrated artillery fire along the east side of the retreat road, while an attack was generated by the 506th Airborne Battalion along the west side to relieve pressure. The column was organized, wounded were carefully loaded into the vehicles, supply dumps were blown and in an erratic fog, the movement by the harrassed Noville defenders got under way. However, the unit was stopped by the enemy, by breakdowns, shortages of drivers, burning tanks and one snafu after another. At this juncture, two groups were organized. One was commanded by Major Hustead and the other by Captain Billet. These forces, in enveloping movements, propelled themselves into Foy and methodically eradicated the enemy there to permit the remainder of the column to move. Assisting the Noville units at Foy was Battery B of the 796th AAA. This was the only anti-aircraft unit to operate at Bastogne and it was 'instrumental in helping to free Foy from enemy domination. Commanded by Lieut. John R. Walker, Jr., the Battery had been ordered to proceed to Noville on December 20 to support Tiger units there. On the way, the Battery was blocked by the Germans at Foy. Here, a Tiger lieutenant delivered a message to Walker which directed the latter to keep going on to Noville. When Walker was apprised of the enemy roadblocks and anti-tank guns confronting him at Foy he objected to the order. The lieutenant at this point, shrugged and said, "Okay, I was told that if you didn't want to, or couldn't proceed, that I am to turn you over to the airborne battalion in the area." By that time, however, the Billet-Hustead forces pushed to Foy and utilized the crack anti-aircraft battery to good advantage in kicking the Germans out of that place so that the remainder of Team Hustead was able to break out of Noville. During the same night, Major Hustead outposted Foy with doughs and the ack ack men. All night long, these Tigers could hear enemy tanks on the move around them but there was no further action there until morning. At that time Lieut. Walker attempted to return alone to Luxembourg to confer with Lieut. Col. Ormand K. Williams, his battalion commander, but found that Bastogne had been surrounded and had to return to Foy.

TEAM CHERRY AT LONGVILLY

While the delaying action was taking place at Noville, Lieut. Col. Henry J. Cherry, Commander of the Third Tank Battalion, had proceeded to Longvilly. There he found Combat Command R of the Ninth Armored Division already in position. At 0200, the Task Force Commander proceeded to Bastogne to request permission from Combat Command B to remain in the Longvilly-Magaret area to back up the Ninth Armored unit. In the meantime, Cherry's Tigers, on the road between Longvilly and Magaret on December 19, received word that the Germans had raided Magaret and had sliced in between the main force of the Battalion and its command post. When Cherry attempted to rejoin his command he found that he could not get to them through Magaret and was forced to proceed to Neffe, where he established his Command Post. At 0600 his Recon platoon was attacked by the Germans at an outpost position at the crossroads at Neffe. After a fierce fight, during which the platoon knocked out an enemy tank with a bazooka, three members of the unit made their way to the CP. There, they reported enemy strength in the village to be two tanks and two infantry platoons. Meanwhile, the remainder of the Recon platoon, unable to cope with the strong German attack on the roadblock, was forced to withdraw towards Bastogne. By 1000, four additional enemy tanks, including a Tiger Royal, an armored car and about 100 more infantry entered Neffe from Magaret. It was this enemy force which bore in on Cherry's Headquarters Company Tigers all during the day of December 19. It knocked out a Medium and encircled the Chateau in which the CP was located. The western approach to the building was covered by machine gun and tank fire and enemy infantry worked their way to within five yards of the heavy stone structure only to be cut down by the Armoraiders. Earlier in the morning, a depleted platoon of engineers arrived at the Chateau from Mont and were sent to guard the Chateau from the high ground to the south later in the afternoon. They were never seen again by Cherry's men. At 1430, a platoon of paratroopers from the 101st Airborne arrived to reinforce Cherry's small force but by this time the Chateau was a mass of flames—the result of enemy grenades and high explosive shells. No longer able to hold the old Chateau, Cherry ordered the CP to be moved to Mont, a small town two miles distant. Before he quit the inferno, Cherry radioed CC B: "We're not driven out, we're burned out; we're not withdrawing, we're moving." Dusk was settling as the tiny group of fighters left the Chateau, firing in every direction. Cherry himself emptied two tommy guns enroute to the parked vehicles. He was the last to leave and his vehicle was hit a dozen times by enemy fire, wounding two of his men. Later Cherry was awarded the Distinguished Service Cross for his actions at the Neffe Chateau.

THE RED BADGE OF COURAGE

While Cherry's Headquarters Company Tigers defended the Chateau, other units of the Team were engaged in blistering combat. Lieut. Hyduke, who was killed at Bastogne later, arrived in Longvilly at 1920 on December 18. His mission was to locate desirable gun positions before daylight and to hold them at all costs. From midnight on, stragglers from the Ninth Armored and 28th Infantry Divisions passed through Lieut. Hyduke's position. When questioned as to the situation to the east, the reply was always the same: "Jerries coming . . . tanks, lots of tanks." Despite constant movement to the rear by broken units of other outfits, Hyduke's Tigers held fast. Soon enemy artillery fire increased in intensity and endangered the column, which could not move off the road due to a steep bank on the left and marshy terrain on the right. Jammed-up vehicles from other units further complicated the situation. To eliminate the congestion, VIII Corps had given permission earlier to CC B to commandeer any withdrawing units. Colonel Cherry was notified of this decision but his Force found it virtually impossible to grab up the hurrying stragglers, so great was the panic and utter disorganization of the hard-hit units coming in ever-increasing numbers from the east. The next morning at about 0100 one Medium was destroyed by artillery fire which dropped in at regular intervals. Then at 1300, the Germans bore in on the front and left flanks and disabled a light tank and two halftracks. Five minutes later, enemy fire got two Mediums which were located about 150 yards in front of the now-burning halftracks. This attack forced additional friendly units to pull out which only added to the chaos as their vehicles double-banked the column on the road, making movement extremely difficult. Then too, the 40 stragglers picked up by Lieut. Hyduke, and assigned to guard the left flank, took off—leaving only 23 Tigers of Company C of the 20th Armored Infantry to guard that important flank. Though Hyduke's Armoraiders were subjected to intense enemy artillery, mortar and tank fire, they held their ground until 1330, when Cherry ordered the Column on to Magaret. The withdrawal was costly as the unit lost 5 of its 7 light tanks, a recovery vehicle and a tank dozer. In addition, the halftracks in front of the Column had to be abandoned—all because of the lack of room to turn and the enemy's strong attack on the flanks. As the unit continued in its efforts to extricate itself, two more Mediums were destroyed by direct anti-tank weapons and our doughs were subjected to heavy machine gun fire. At the edge of town another Medium was cut off from the Column and when last seen was fighting off a dismounted enemy attack. The seventh and last Medium received a hit on its tracks and was put out of action. Finally, the remaining two light tanks and the forward observer tank were destroyed by their own crews to keep them from falling into enemy hands. By 1500, the remainder of the Column fought its way to the western outskirts of Magaret to join Captain Ryerson's Team there.

PANZERS POUNDED

When Lieut. Hyduke became locked in battle with the streaming enemy panzers, Captain Ryerson's Team had been located about two miles east of Magaret and not far behind the former's Column. Ryerson got word that the enemy had jammed in behind him and sent a patrol back to Magaret to clean out that place and, at the same time, hold the road open. At 0300 on December 19, this patrol found three enemy tanks and 120 infantry in Magaret, a discovery which helped them decide to get back to Ryerson in a hurry. Then Ryerson notified Cherry who directed him to use his entire Team to push the enemy off the road to Magaret. Turning his Team around, Ryerson headed for the town and immediately was hit hard by enemy artillery. Just east of Magaret, he was stopped by anti-tank, small arms and mortar fire. The lead tank commanded by Lieut. Bolden was destroyed and its commander killed. Ryerson sent dismounted infantry in an attempt to knock out the anti-tank gun, but the armored doughs were pushed back by heavy artillery fire coming from Magaret and could not carry out their mission. Then Ryerson deployed his tanks to support the infantry but even they were unable to generate enough power to bull their way into the town. At this juncture, Lieut. Hyduke and his depleted force joined Ryerson and together with a group of stragglers, the new Team was organized into squads. But Ryerson became enraged when he learned that his force had dwindled to only 40 men, as a result of the quick disappearance of the recently-acquired stragglers. Nevertheless, he formed four squads of infantry and, with tank support, tried to crash into Magaret but again was unsuccessful. After persistent attempts, by nightfall, three buildings in the northeast end of the town were brought under our control and were held for the rest of the night despite pounding from direct enemy tank fire and heavy artillery fire. During that night Ryerson lost three vehicles to the enemy, who used flares to help sight on the tanks and tracks. The remainder of the Team's vehicles were moved out to the edge of the town to avoid further losses. And additional enemy attacks were repelled there with the aid of the 420th Armored Field Artillery Battalion. Just before daybreak, Ryerson brought his vehicles back to Magaret and loaded them with the wounded. Then, in accordance with task force orders, the column moved out at 0730 on December 20. With tanks in the lead and dismounted doughs around them, the shot-up force pushed north along the trail to Bizory. The enemy did not emerge lightly from the Teams' determined stand as it lost 15 tanks, 1 armored car, 2 halftracks, 3 anti-tank guns, 184 Germans killed and an undetermined number wounded. Our Teams lost 11 Mediums, 7 light tanks, 17 halftracks, 1 tank dozer and 2 recovery vehicles. In addition 1 Tiger officer was killed, 1 officer and twenty enlisted men wounded and 2 officers and 44 men were missing. Cherry's Tigers were a tower of strength and fortitude as they held off numerically superior

Tank tracks in snow show movement of Combat Command B's units near Bastogne. Woods provided effective shelter

enemy forces to help prevent Bastogne from being captured on December 19. The enemy never penetrated in strength any closer to Bastogne than at Neffe. All during the flaming battles in the enemy's struggle for continued movement west, the Team organization remained intact and communications functioned efficiently despite terrifically heavy pressure.

ENEMY SOFTENED

It was not fully known until studies were made after the war, just how enormous was the German strength in front of Cherry's divided forces in front of Magaret. Later, German commanders testified as to the power they had generated there. Cherry, at the Neffe Chateau, was in touch with Ryerson by radio only. Though the Team Commander had no force with which to aid Ryerson, his advice and instructions via radio were vitally important to the latter. Actually, the enemy force that struck Ryerson consisted of parts of three enemy divisions. They were the Second Panzer, 26th Volks Grenadier and the Panzer Lehr Divisions. The Second Panzers had to move through Tiger units east of Longvilly, and turn north and then west, towards Noville. At the same time, some of their tanks were detached to strike Ryerson's Mediums which had been seen in the haze. Meanwhile, the 26th Volks Grenadiers bore in on Cherry's Tigers who were directly to their front. And, as the Panzer Lehr commander, operating against Wardin, heard the sound of battle he dispatched post haste, part of his panzers to strike Cherry from the southwest. It is difficult to imagine the utter hopelessness of Team Cherry's situation in view of the tremendous forces arrayed against it, plus the factors that the Team was confined to just one road, and to maneuver was out of the question. Yet despite these critical problems, most of Cherry's men were saved along with a few trucks and other vehicles. Later, Colonel Roberts noted that the destruction of Cherry's Team was a minor victory for the Germans in a tactical sense but CC B's Commander reminded the author that, "strategically, Cherry's Armoraiders softened the enemy," and, "more importantly, their stand gained precious time for General McAulliffe's airborne battalions to deploy east of Bastogne." "In fact," he said, "the 501st Infantry was stopping an enemy attack from Magaret on Bastogne at the same time and later that day, it turned back another attack north of Magaret's at Bizory."

BACK TO BASTOGNE

Shortly after noon on December 20, Team Ryerson reached Bizory and contacted the 101st Airborne Division units there who were responsible for the defense of that sector. Here the Team's tanks were placed in support of the paratroopers and subsequently knocked out four German tanks which attempted to pierce the perimeter. And hour after hour, they helped to repel numerous enemy attacks. On December 20, in the afternoon, Cherry's Headquarters were ordered to move into Bastogne from Mont. Then, on December 21, Team Ryerson was directed to move into Bastogne. This force was joined by Team Hustead, which had so gallantly defended Noville earlier. To consolidate the battle-decimated units, Colonel Cherry reorganized the Ryerson-Hustead Teams and prepared to lead them as a mobile reserve for the 101st Airborne. His primary mission now was that of counter-attacking enemy thrusts directed at Bastogne from any direction. Supporting Task Force Cherry was his Third Tank Battalion minus Company C; the Second Platoon, Troop D, 90th Armored Reconnaissance Battalion; the Third Platoon, Company C, 55th Armored Engineers and Company C, 20th Armored Infantry Battalion. An idea of the fluid battle situation at Bastogne is illustrated by the activities of Captain Ryerson's Tigers there. On December 26 Ryerson, who was killed at Bastogne shortly afterwards, was sent out to plug a gap in the northwest corner of the perimeter. Seizing the initiative, his Team flushed the woods to its immediate front and killed 70 Germans, took 7 prisoners, knocked out an enemy tank, four mortars and numerous small arms. Because of men of this calibre, the enemy was unable to make a single penetration of the perimeter. For the Team, the entire period was indescribably

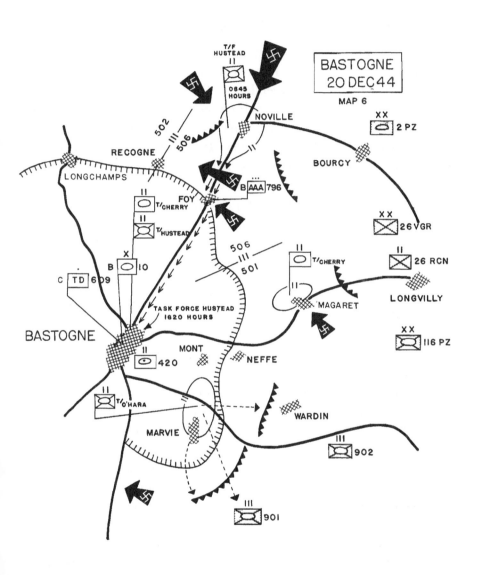

BASTOGNE
20 DEC 44
MAP 6

difficult. Everyone including the Airborne Troopers was continuously subjected to intense artillery fire and the Luftwaffe pounded the encircled forces with nightly strafing and bombardment.

TEAM O'HARA AT BRAS, WARDIN AND MARVIE

During the two-day nightmare, a third Tiger Team, commanded by Lieut. Col. James O'Hara, located itself at Bras, just south of Wardin. On December 19 this Force was set to receive an attack. It spent the day repelling small enemy groups and participated in aggressive patrolling against a force which became diverted towards Cherry's men. In addition, O'Hara's fighters occupied Wardin. The strong patrols sent out by O'Hara were successful in keeping the enemy off balance—delaying any major German effort that day. By nightfall, O'Hara was forced back to Marvie to escape a flanking operation by the Germans. At 0645 on December 20, Team O'Hara's roadblock, located about three-quarters of a mile east of Marvie on the Wiltz-Bastogne highway, was heavily shelled by the enemy. The enemy's movements could be heard but not seen due to the thick fog. Later in the morning, O'Hara's men detected enemy activities near the roadblock and became more apprehensive as the sound of German armor in the rear grew louder. Shortly after 0900 the fog lifted for a brief moment revealing about a dozen Germans in the act of trying to remove the roadblock. Quick thinking on the part of O'Hara's Tigers resulted in catastophe for this group as the 420th Armored Field Artillery Battalion was called upon to deliverer a hail of high explosive in their midst. After the Germans were driven off the block they put smoke around it to conceal any further movements on their part. To block any possibility of an enemy infantry attack, Team O'Hara put its assault guns and mortars to work at the roadblock and prevented enemy penetration there. It is very likely that because of the Team's action here, the enemy was forced to direct their attack towards Marvie where a platoon of O'Hara's tanks had taken up defensive positions the previous night. At 1125 on December 20, Team O'Hara's units in Marvie were hit hard by enemy artillery fire. This was followed by an attack of four tanks and six halftracks. As the ten enemy vehicles sped towards Marvie they fired round after round into that town and knocked out two of the five light tanks which were no match for the heavy enemy tanks. Request was made by the platoon leader to quit Marvie and it was granted by O'Hara. When the enemy tanks and tracks reached a position about half a mile away from Marvie, O'Hara's Mediums perched on the high ground above the town opened up and knocked out four of the charging enemy vehicles. The German panzers did not see the Mediums firing at them from the high ground, so intent were they on crashing into Marvie. At about the time the enemy tanks were destroyed, a second wave of halftracks had closed in to within a few yards of the outlying houses of the town. This time O'Hara's Tigers were powerless to stop them and they smashed into Marvie. Here they were met head on by part of the Second Battalion of the 327th Glider Infantry who routed the Germans after a wild house to house fight which ended at about 1300. Later in the day, on December 20, the first snow flurries fell and as the ridges became white and the drifts deeper, the most pressing problem became that of getting the defenders indoors in order to escape the icy blasts of the Ardennes winter. On December 21, three of O'Hara's tanks along with airborne infantry support thwarted another enemy attempt to capture Marvie in the early afternoon. However, this attack was followed by more powerful enemy thrusts during the ensuing three days and the tanker-trooper teams at Marvie were hard put to maintain their hold there. Now O'Hara's losses mounted with each passing day of bitter combat.

ENEMY AT BAY

At the end of the crucial twenty-four hour period, the 101st Airborne Division was able to place several battalions on the front. Three were abreast and astride the road west of Neffe. They repulsed two heavy attacks while the other two battalions inched towards Noville.

Thus the Tiger armor, which had stopped the Second Panzer Division at Noville and slowed up parts of three Nazi divisions at Longvilly, had bought, at a high cost, the time needed for the 101st Airborne Division to organize and deploy around Bastogne. It is likely that without the determined stand taken by the CC B Tigers east of Bastogne, the defense of that city would not have been possible. Subsequent newspaper accounts, movies and magazine articles about the Battle at Bastogne have given little attention to the significance of the Tigers' role, but the men who fell and those who survived are themselves the most eloquent testimony that the first twenty-four hours were the most punishing and the most crucial of the German winter blitz. Fortunately, too, for the Americans, a local Belgian so exaggerated the strength of Cherry's Team that General Bayerlein, Commander of the Panzer Lehr Division, needlessly slowed down his attack several hours. This slowdown helped to provide the time urgently needed by the Airborne Troopers to get into position for the continued defense of the key Bastogne road net. During those first twenty-four hours, not only were the Tigers in an extremely critical position, but all the American armies as well. Radio intercept provided the Germans with information that airborne troops were moving to Bastogne. Knowing of no armor movement, they expected to breeze into the city with little resistance. However, the delay at Noville, where the Second Panzer was held up for thirty-six precious hours, coupled with the effective roadblock at Longvilly, the two repulses at Neffe and the setback at Bizory all contributed to an abrupt halt of the Forty-Seventh German Panzer Corps. This resulted in a major upset of enemy plans, giving General McAuliffe time enough to bring in his troops and drape them around the Bastogne perimeter.

ONE MAN SHOW

The writer has described in general the story of Bastogne on December 19 and 20 for Combat Command B. The details of individual heroism could make many volumes if they were available. Fortunately, one such account is at hand. It is the story of a

Company B, Third Tank Battalion, gunner. While his account of of the two-day action at Noville is undoubtedly extraordinary, it certainly gives adequate insight as to what the situation was like and, most of all, the terrific ordeal that CC B's Tigers underwent during those forty-eight hours.

ASN 13011643

Private First Class Delmer D. Hildoer, 13011643, was a gunner in a medium tank of B Company, Third Tank Battalion. Along with his company, B Company of the Twentieth Armored Infantry, a platoon from Troop D of the Ninetieth Recon, a squad from Company C of the Fifty-fifth Armored Engineers, and a platoon from Company C, 609th Tank Destroyer Battalion, all found themselves under Major William Desobry's command at Noville at midnight on December 18. The description of the events that followed explain why the German attacks at Noville failed—and why the Germans thought they were opposing a large and powerful force. This is the account of Tiger Hildoer in his own words. He says: "CC B came into Bastogne on December 18 at 2200 hours without any contact being made with the enemy. Our task force moved out and entered Noville at 2400 without making contact. The town was small and deserted. Our objective was to take the town and set up a road block. This was done. Our lines of defense were approximately 800 yards outside of town on three roads—each road having two tanks and an infantry outpost. The central building in town was the command post. My tank was a command tank with a 538 radio. It was placed against the wall of the CP. Captain Schultz, my C.O. reported to the CP and was retained there. Upon orders I was to receive a report from each outpost every hour on the hour—which I relayed to the CP. This was done by radio. The time was now 0200, December 19.

ALL QUIET

"Everything was very quiet. Soon received report that a lone Second Armored tank had come through our outpost. At about 0500 received message that tank column was approaching. Relay message. Answer is to stop column and investigate. Receive message that they are firing on us—then silence. Our defense is alerted, and the enemy deploys for attack. Estimated enemy forces are 40 tanks and 3 infantry companies. Attack us furiously, and wounded become a common sight. Litter bearers are everywhere, and the town is under direct artillery fire. Our halftracks, jeeps and trucks in town become flaming masses. Several buildings are on fire. Due to my unfavorable position to fight, I got an O.K. from the CP to move to left side of town and away from the direction of attack.

HELL BREAKS LOOSE

"Now the town is between me and the attack. I realize that an attack will come on my side of town so I took up a position between two hay stacks. I have a range of 3,000 yards to the front, rear and left of unobstructed fire. Also have 3,000 yards of the main road under my fire. Things are quiet, so to occupy my time, I map the terrain in my view and fire my 30 caliber at prominent points in the terrain so I have accurate range of all terrain markers on my map. Suddenly, I saw two turrets come up over ridge at about 3,000 yards under glasses. They are M 4's of our own but also a Mark VI comes into view—so I know they are our tanks being used by the enemy. When they get to about 2500 yards I begin firing. Without a tank commander, I pick my own targets. Luckily, I had the range. Knocked out one of the first two tanks with three shots. While it burned, I fired at the Mark VI. Right off, seven more tanks come into view. I can see ricochets from the 37 on a nearby armored car bounce off the tanks—so I know I'm on my own. Still shooting, I think I hit four more but more Tiger tanks keep coming. Hit them numerous times but with no effect. My CP sees that I'm in trouble and sends a 105 over. He fires, but has no effect. Luckily, four Tigers stop in ravine at bottom of our little hill. They turn sideways to us, and the 105 gets them."

ENEMY DOUGHS HIT

Hildoer continues. "During this attack, my bow gunner gets the enemy infantry accompanying the tanks. At 11:15 I observe about 100 enemy infantry break from the woods at my left. Range is 3,000 so I waited until they got to 2,500. Open up on my 50 caliber and stop them cold. The ones that were left run back to the woods—but come out again, only this time there are about 250 of them. While I waited for them to get closer, I fired four rounds of HE into those woods. At 2,000 yards I open up on them but they keep coming. Burned out my barrel so hurriedly changed barrels. A few reach a small ravine 800 yards from me and stop. During the afternoon, four more similar attacks come. I'm short of 50 caliber ammo, so when halftrack nearby gets hit, run over and unload all 50 cal. ammo and spare barrels.

TROOPERS ARRIVE

"Meanwhile at 1430 a Battalion from 101st Airborne pulls into town. I asked officer who was leading the column what the score is. He says they are going to attack at 1500. At 1445 a heavy barrage comes in and the 101st digs in. They didn't attack while I am with the outfit . . . Now it gets dark so I moved closer to town. I'm very short on ammo. Captain Schultz comes over from the CP to ask about our ammo. He pats us all on the back. Said he saw everything from the CP and was going to recommend us all for some ribbons. He sends the Company jeep over for ammo for us. Since everything is quiet, we stow our ammo and eat and I arrange guards for the night. Hoped to get some sleep. Skrofichie, my driver, had first watch. Then came Goolkasion, my loader, and my assistant driver, Lester, came up next. He was a new man and I didn't know him. During his watch, he woke me. Said tanks were coming. Sounded like a thousand. They seemed to be about 1,000 yards from us when they stopped. I didn't think we would get an attack before morning. but kept my crew alert anyway.

MORE LEAD

"At about 0500 on December 20, the enemy opened up with a concentrated barrage. They were firing directly into the town. Their machine guns filled the air with lead. I moved back to my position of the preceding day. During breaks from the smoke from the burning buildings, I think I got three more tanks and burned out a barrel on my 50 cal., stopping two infantry attacks. At 1000 during another infantry attack, I burned out my last barrel. I ran to a halftrack and got another one. While changing it, an artillery shell exploded on the back deck of my tank. Dazed me and filled my hands with shrapnel. Goolkasion's arm was almost cut off and he was bleeding bad. The 101st had an aid station set up in a building 300 yards away. I asked him if he could make it back alone. I didn't want to leave the tank shorthanded. He said he could, so I watched him walk into the aid station. I wrapped a handkerchief around my hands and pulled to the rear of town until I could get a loader. Radioed the CP for permission, then moved across the road from the aid station. Saw some men to our rear in the glasses. They were the enemy. Got my assistant driver in the turret just in time. Three tanks attacked from our rear and we routed them in nine shots. I was pretty shaky and couldn't judge the range so good. Just about then I got word that an artillery shell hit the CP and killed a colonel and a major from the 101st.

WANT TO BE A TANKER?

"An enlisted man came by and. I asked him if he wanted to be a tanker. I put him in the bow to fire the 30 cal. CP sends me a gunner from a knocked-out tank. I radio the CP that we are surrounded and gave my position. The enemy finds my position and starts shelling us. During the barrage, I saw an infantry attack coming so opened my hatch to fire at them. A shell explodes on our tank and knocks me down. A piece of shrapnel takes my right ear off. I'm bleeding bad, so talk it over with my crew. Decide to go to the aid station. Told them I wanted it bandaged up and some sulfa powder on it, then I would come back. Ran to the aid station and got treated. They gave me a shot of morphine and I got a little sick. They wouldn't let me leave the aid station and made me get up on a jeep to be evacuated. The jeep went ten yards and came under machine gun fire. I grabbed a rifle and hit the ditch. The morphine made me feel like I was drunk. I couldn't see anything so I jumped up and ran back to my tank. Got back in time to receive a message to retire to Bastogne. It was just 1700. There were two tanks on the road in front of me. Captain Schultz waved me down and got in. I sat on the floor of the turret behind the driver. The Captain was now firing the 50 cal. We had to break through small groups of enemy infantry. We came on our other two tanks which had come under fire and were stopped on the road. We went around them. We were then hit twice on the gun shield after going 300 or 400 yards. Luckily, the shells didn't penetrate. The next shot came through the driver's side and killed Skrofichie and the new man from the 101st. I never knew what his name was. Another shot came through and put 15 pieces of shrapnel in my right leg. My gunner and loader, Lester, both got hit in the legs. Captain Schultz wasn't hurt but the tank was burning and as Lester went to get out they shot him in the face. He fell back in. I boosted him out and went out after him. As I got out on the right hand side of the tank, I saw the German tank that hit us. It was about 100 yards away. There were three Germans near the tank and I knew I was going to get it. I grabbed a tommy gun from the side of the tank and shot them before they got me. I jumped up and joined Captain Shultz and the other two on the other side of the tank and we crawled halfway to Bastogne. A jeep came out and picked us up. The Captain went to the aid station with us and I never saw him after that. I heard that he was killed a month or two later. At 1800 on December 20, I was evacuated to Luxembourg. I was one of the last out before the town was surrounded. Later I was evacuated to the States."

So ends the story of Private First Class Delmer D. Hildoer, ASN 13011643. In his case, death took a holiday. Hildoer was in the hospital for eighteen long months recovering from his wounds. He was given a new ear and, luckily, his hearing was not impaired. With the exception of shell fragment wounds on his hands and leg, he is good as new again and has reenlisted in the Army.

ARMORED-AIRBORNE PARTNERSHIP

Combat Command B became attached officially to the 101st Airborne Division on December 20. Up to that date, the two forces, though independent, worked together harmoniously. Both General McAuliffe and Colonel Roberts had anticipated a knock-down fight on a linear front. However, without the protection of support on their flanks, the armor and airborne units had to drop back. The new combined mission was to hold, at all costs, the spider-like network of roads leading into Bastogne. On December 21, McAuliffe returned from Corps Headquarters at Neufchateau armed with fresh intelligence about the enemy blitz. The General conferred with Colonel Roberts and they decided that the Tigers and Troopers would stand fast—there would be no further withdrawal to the west, at least for the time being. As senior commander, McAuliffe had the choice of getting out of the mess— there was still time—or sticking it out. He and his commanders chose to fight to the bitter end, knowing that the Germans would stop at nothing to control the roads for their big push. Thus was the die cast. Only God and courage could help them now.

THE DIE IS CAST

The battle had developed into a circular action. No longer was this combat with the usual front and rear. Almost at the beginning, the 101st Division's hospital was captured and some of their trains were lost. CC B's trains were sent out on the 21st and with great luck, these trains managed to evade the giant trap. (They returned to Bastogne on January 27, loaded down with new supplies and Christmas-New Year's turkeys for the beleaguered Tigers.)

106

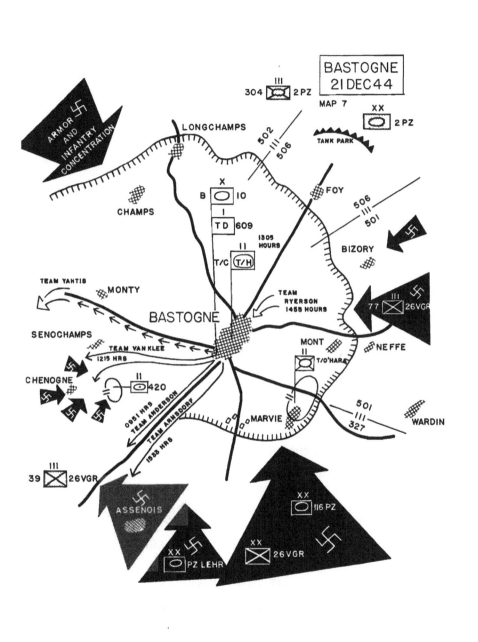

BASTOGNE
21 DEC 44

MAP 7

304 | 2 PZ

2 PZ

TANK PARK

LONGCHAMPS

502
506

FOY

506
501

BIZORY

CHAMPS

B 10

TD 609

1305 HOURS

T/C T/H

TEAM YANTIS

MONTY

TEAM RYERSON 1455 HOURS

BASTOGNE

SENOCHAMPS

TEAM VAN KLEE
1215 HRS

MONT

T/O'HARE

NEFFE

77 26VGR

CHENOGNE

420

0951 HRS
TEAM ANDERSON

TEAM ARNSDORF
1533 HRS

MARVIE

501
327

WARDIN

39 26VGR

ASSENOIS

116 PZ

PZ LEHR

26VGR

ARMOR AND INFANTRY CONCENTRATION

The fluid battle situation proved to be a tough defense' problem even for the battle-experienced Roberts. He told the writer, "I had expected to fight as I had been taught—front, flanks and rear—in other words, a linear battle. But I found that we had to do a circular job. The books never said anything about this type of operation. So we improvised. What a helluva way to fight a war."

Because Von Runstedt's blitz failed east and northeast, his commanders tried a new push from the south, southwest and west. But still they were unable to drive the Americans out. However, in spite of superior forces, their attack washed, like a great wave, around the defenders. And on December 21, Tigers and Troopers were completely encircled. This situation, though anything but funny, caused one airborne staff officer to observe: "Good—, now we can attack in any direction."

STRAGGLERS TURN DEFENDERS

On December 18, Colonel Roberts was given Corps permission to commandeer any troops and units withdrawing west. One such unit was Team Pyle of the Ninth Armored. This team, which had fourteen tanks, became the backbone of the Bastogne rear. Almost immediately, it was called upon to repulse a heavy panzer attack which wheeled in from the west where the 420th Armored Field Artillery Battalion found itself in the dangerous position of holding 4,000 yards of front, in addition to providing artillery support for the encircled defenders. The use of Team Pyle and other stray units was of enormous help to Combat Command B. More than 600 infantrymen, seven 155's of the 771st Field Artillery Battalion, Company C of the Ninth Armored Engineers, and the 969th Field Artillery were absorbed. They operated with great effectiveness throughout the duration of the encirclement.

THE BIG FREEZE

December 21 was cold and freezing. The first snowfall forced an immediate change in tank tactics. Until now, the tanks had to stay on the roads to avoid being mired down in the soft ground.

Now, they were no longer bound to the roads. Both the enemy and the Americans had to cope with the snowy weather. Tanks and other vehicles had to be parked under sheets or be whitewashed. The unfortunate Belgians, in addition to other woes, were sheet-blitzed before they knew what had happened.

Inside the fourteen-mile perimeter, the fighting increased in intensity. Elements of ten German divisions hammered at the city from every direction. The food supply dwindled to a dangerous low. Only a few gallons of gas remained, and the artillery battalions were down to eleven rounds per gun. On the brighter side of the picture, there was valuable help from a number of units besides the 101st. One of these was the 705th Tank Destroyer Battalion. Its gunners were deadly throughout the terrible days at Bastogne. Commanded by Lieut. Col. Templeton, later killed, the twenty-four tank destroyers established an enviable record of marksmanship. These weapons and CC B's tanks and tracks were to be found everywhere in the battle-filled perimeter. The thin line of steel and men made up for lack of strength with experience and guts. All types of armor were in great demand in every unit. It was found that a few tanks stationed with the doughs on the line contributed greatly to morale and helped to anchor small groups in their positions, though this is contrary to the teaching that all tanks should be kept in reserve.

PROBE, THRUST AND READJUST

From December 21 through 23, our troops were subjected to probes and sudden thrusts. Constant readjustments had to be made to counteract the pressing German offense. But on the evening of December 23, a determined enemy attack, launched from the southeast, smashed into Team O'Hara and the 327th Glider Infantry near Marvie. Three main thrusts pushed our lines back and three Nazi tanks clattered right up to the city. These were eventually disposed of, and our forces were able to re-stabilize their positions by morning. How this was done was something of a miracle, considering the overwhelming odds. December 23 was the day our Air Corps was waiting for. It made excellent use of the clear, crisp weather to plaster the Germans in full force. With new squadrons appearing every thirty minutes, the besieged Tiger-Troopers got the kind of support they had prayed for throughout the battle. The panzers took a crushing beating that gave our forces badly needed hours to reorganize.

ULTIMATUM

Only the day before, ironically, the Germans had delivered an ultimatum to surrender. The ultimatum declared:

December 22, 1944

To the U. S. A. Commander of the encircled town of Bastogne.

The fortune of war is changing. This time the U. S. A. forces in and near Bastogne have been encircled by strong German armored units. More German armored units have crossed the river Ourthe near Ortheville, have taken Marche and reached St. Hubert by passing through Hompre-Sibret-Tillet. Libramont is in German hands.

There is only one possibility to save the encircled U. S. A. troops from total annihilation: that is the honorable surrender of the encircled town. In order to think it over, a term of two hours will be granted beginning with the presentation of this note.

If this proposal should be rejected, one German artillery Corps and six heavy A.A. Battalions are ready to annihilate the U. S. A. Troops in and near Bastogne. The order for firing will be given immediately after this two hours' term.

All the serious civilian losses caused by this artillery fire would not correspond with the well known American humanity.

The German Commander

Lt Gen Heinrich von Luttwitz

CG of XXXXVII Panzer Corps

Von Luttwitz, Commander of the 47th Panzer Corps, thought he had our troops in the bag. Instead he got "Nuts" for an answer.

110

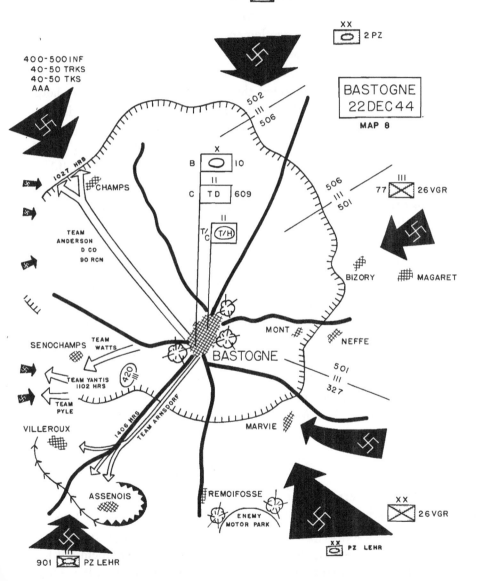

304 2PZ III

2PZ XX

400-500 INF
40-50 TRKS
40-50 TKS
AAA

BASTOGNE
22 DEC 44

MAP 8

502 III 506

B 10 X

C TD 609 II

506 III 501

77 26 VGR III

T/C T/H II

1027 HRS

CHAMPS

TEAM
ANDERSON
D CO
90 RCN

BIZORY

MAGARET

SENOCHAMPS

TEAM
WATTS

MONT

NEFFE

BASTOGNE

TEAM YANTIS
1102 HRS

420 III

TEAM
PYLE

501 III 327

1406 HRS

TEAM ARNSDORF

MARVIE

VILLEROUX

ASSENOIS

REMOIFOSSE

ENEMY
MOTOR PARK

26 VGR XX

901 PZ LEHR

PZ LEHR XX

The German errand boys who received the message didn't understand what "nuts" meant. So the word was deciphered for them. "Go to hell" was the translation.

During the operation of our much-needed air support, one of the most popular gentlemen to be found was Captain "Ace" Parker. An Air Corps air-ground whiz, he went to work with two VHF radios, supplied by Headquarters Company of CC B. During the three days he operated the sets, he was inundated by helpful hints of "kibitzers". But the value of air support for the defenders was considered by some observers to be equal to that of two divisions. In all, the Air Corps performed a devastating job that has been overlooked by historians. The results were visible immediately. As the P-47s approached, Parker would require half to orbit while the other attacked targets "Ace" knew about. When their ammo was expended, the second flight of '47s had its fun. As the squadrons left for home, they were required to make a reconnaissance circuit to find targets for the next squadrons which came over in 30-minute intervals throughout the day.

An interesting sidelight occurred around "Ace" and his radio tank which had to be roped off eventually to give him operating room and protect him from goggle-eyed kibitzers. On one occasion, Martha Gelhorn, correspondent and ex-wife of Ernest Hemingway, was kibitzing, and "Ace" noticed that the fly boys did not use drawing room language. He tried to shut them up because a lady was present. But Martha stopped him, declaring, "I like that language in times like these."

DEAD GIVE AWAY

The Germans were caught with their armor down. The clear weather had left their vehicles exposed. Snow tracks of tanks hidden in the woods gave them away. And when ground troops flushed out additional targets, artillery smoke would point them out to the pilots. Yet, in spite of the urgently-needed help from the Air, our ground defense was growing weaker by the hour. Our commanders knew only too well that holding out much longer was almost impossible without ammo, gas, food, and medical supplies. Most dangerous was the fact that artillery ammunition was nearly exhausted—a tell-tale sign to the Germans of our plight. The shortage became worse as some battalions ran completely out of ammo; others were down to their last few rounds per gun. Small arms ammo was at a premium, too. The airborne troopers were limited to two meals per day and there was grave danger that the food supply would give out completely. While it could, the 420th Field Artillery Battalion provided effective support. Its range of 12,400 yards was far superior to the 4,500 yards of the airborne artillery. The 420th fired in all directions because of its greater range and its ability to quickly lay in any direction. When their high explosive ammunition was exhausted, the cannoneers discovered that it was effective to fire one round of colored smoke to deceive the enemy into believing that an air attack was ordered to follow the smoke marking round. The Germans often took cover, and consequently their attack was stalled as a result of the artillerymen's ruse. The airborne artillery had to be close-up to the line in most cases, which made for a narrow fire sector. However, soon both Tiger and Trooper cannoneers were to be nearly silenced for lack of shells.

THE BIG DROP

Fortunately, the problem was solved later the same day. The drone of hundreds of approaching C-47s was the answer. For beleaguered Tigers, it was the day of days, as they viewed the beautiful sight of falling colored parachutes, bringing from heaven, supplies to help them hold out. Added drops were made the day before and after Christmas and again on December 27. The 420th got its ammo on the last drop, and it wasn't until CC B's trains rolled in that supply needs were fully met. But the Air had turned the trick. Without it, the situation would have been hopeless. Among other things, even the parachutes were utilized by the improvised hospital for bedding.

IN RETROSPECT

The value of artillery at Bastogne cannot be emphasized too much. For the first several days of the encirclement, the 420th Liaison pilots were the eyes for the entire area. They flew in and out from the outside at high altitudes to escape enemy flak. One of the pilots, Lt. Harold Cole of Kansas City, Missouri, was shot down, wounded and captured by a German AAA unit upon whom he was adjusting our fire. Later, the 101st was able to establish an airstrip within the perimeter for use by all planes.

THE WOODCHOPPERS

Lovingly referred to as the "Woodchoppers" was B Battery, 796 AAA Battalion Self-Propelled, commanded by Lt. John Walker. They did a great deal to augment the fire of the ground weapons during the siege. So powerful were their multiple machine guns, used many times with telling effects, that they stopped one German ground attack after another. As mentioned earlier, this battery earned the respect and confidence of Hustead's men at Foy and at Senochamps on December 20. It was at the latter place that Walker's ack ack men were dubbed "The Woodchoppers" for the spray job they directed at any enemy infantry concentration in the woods there. This was but the first of many such devastating direct fire operations the Battery was called upon to deliver in support of the Tenth Armored Teams. At Bastogne, Walker's unit provided excellent AA defense each night against marauding enemy bombers and each morning returned to the center of that place to make themselves available for more of their now-famous "spray jobs." On December 29, during a Luftwaffe attack on Bastogne, Walker's advance command post was subjected to a direct hit which killed five men, destroyed his command track and three ammunition trailers. Not to be forgotten too, were the booming big guns of our 420th Artillery which stopped the enemy cold at crucial stages of the battle. The first big assault on Neffe is a case in point. That attack, as well as the heavy assault on December

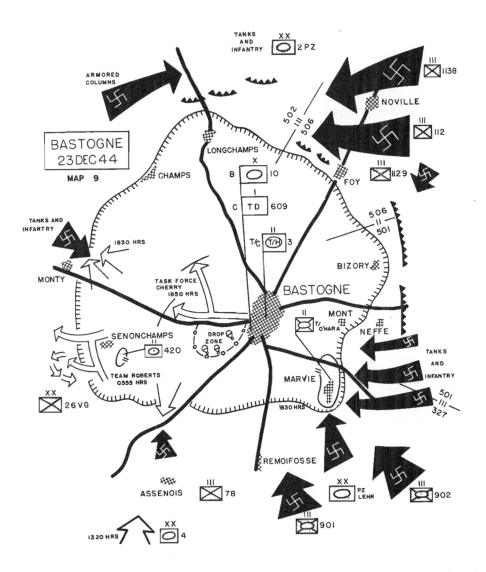

TANKS
AND
INFANTRY   XX □○□ 2PZ

ARMORED
COLUMNS

BASTOGNE
23DEC44

MAP 9

CHAMPS

LONGCHAMPS

502
III
506

NOVILLE

FOY

III 1138

III 112

III 1129

X
B □○□ 10

I
C □TD□ 609

II
T/C □T/H□ 3

506
501

BIZORY

TANKS AND
INFANTRY

1830 HRS

MONTY

TASK FORCE
CHERRY
1850 HRS

BASTOGNE

II
T/O'HARA

MONT

NEFFE

SENONCHAMPS

□○□ 420

DROP
ZONE

TEAM ROBERTS
0555 HRS

MARVIE

TANKS
AND
INFANTRY

501
III
327

XX □×□ 26VG

1830 HRS

REMOIFOSSE

ASSENOIS

III 78

XX □○□ PZ
LEHR

III □○□ 902

1320 HRS   XX □○□ 4

III □○□ 901

23 by the Germans, was smothered. This is ample testimony to the real value of the armored artillerymen. The eighteen guns of the 420th Armored Field Artillery Battalion, commanded by Lieut. Col. Barry D. Brown, blasted away day and night against the enemy. With these men and their cannon, American fortunes were considerably enhanced. Colonel Brown was killed in action at Bastogne. He was replaced by Lieut. Col. Willis D. Crittenberger, Jr. Of Colonel Brown, General Morris said, "The artillery commander performed a superlative job in effectively directing his artillery against the enemy. He was very important in the successful defense of Bastogne."

Because of circumstances, CC B did not operate as a unit after its first deployment east of Bastogne on December 19. During the siege, its operations were defensive in nature until the first week of January of 1945. After the first 24 hours Team O'Hara was the largest component of the Command. After the first day, it successfully held a sector of the perimeter at Marvie. O'Hara's losses were considerably less than those of the other two Teams.

Combat Command B's Colonel Roberts is congratulated by General Maxwell Taylor after receiving Silver Star. Germans' artillery fire disrupted ceremony at Bastogne

It steadfastly resisted multiple pressures by the Germans while astride the main road during that period. In January, Team O'-Hara went on the offensive with substantial results against the now-stalled Nazi blitz.

The next largest force was commanded by "Hank" Cherry. This was a force made up of the remnants of the Noville and Longvilly Teams. Organized at the beginning with eight tank crews and with some patchwork, it grew to ten. When pressure was applied to any part of the front, Cherry's reserves were thrown against the invaders. During the Bastogne epic, these Tigers counterattacked no less than seven times. Getting this force back to the center after a successful push was difficult. When the infantry saw the tanks arrive, they welcomed them with open arms—and moved over—expecting Cherry's men to remain. The first time Cherry's Armoraiders came in to help, it took three days to get them back again. Such were the problems of command during those hectic days of defense by the rugged Tigers.

TEAM SNAFU

Team Snafu was the name given to a gritty bunch. This was the heterogeneous collection of 600 stragglers commandeered and used for practically every purpose. The 28th Infantry Division evacuated 250 of them before the Command was cut off and encircled. The remainder proved to be a valuable asset in the defense of Bastogne. Two hundred of this group were operating as part of Team Pyle and its 14 tanks. Others were organized to combat any penetration at the many entrances to the city. Some of these men had been cooks, truck drivers, ordnance and repairmen. But their prior calling made little difference. They put up a gallant and forceful fight that contributed so much to the job that had to be done by Combat Command B. Some were already so exhausted at the beginning that they had to be given 48 hours' sleep. Once recharged, they could be used effectively. Team Snafu was also known as the "Fire Brigade." One of the Tiger tank crews who figured prominently in the patched-up band of fighters was commanded by Staff Sergeant Palmero Domenicona. He, along with Corporal Donald Nichols, loader Sergeant Frank Bullano and driver Sergeant Dean Wagner all contributed greatly to the cause, as did all the other valiant men both within and without the Tenth Armored Division. And, some of the Bastogne defenders were lucky, while others were less fortunate. One Lieutenant and 30 men from the 101st reporting from hospitalization—arrived just in time to get themselves surrounded in Bastogne. They attached themselves to the 420th Field Artillery. Within three days, every one was a battle casualty.

DIRECT HIT

Casualties and vehicle losses continued to skyrocket. At night the Luftwaffe plastered Bastogne from the air. At 0715, on December 30, Colonel Cherry's Headquarters was hit by two aerial bombs which killed five Tiger officers and buried the entire headquarters personnel. At another time, all the men of another Headquarters Company were killed from a direct hit on their building. An improvised CC B hospital was hit and burned: casualties numbered 22, including a heroic Belgian nurse. The havoc continued until after January 1. At that time, a radar-controlled antiaircraft battalion was set up in position around Bastogne. With their accurate shooting, the triple A gunners knocked down ten marauding aircraft the first night. After that, no more sky Nazis were in evidence.

CHRISTMAS EVE IN BASTOGNE

On the night before Christmas at CC B's Headquarters, it was reported that the Fourth Armored Division was making excellent progress in its drive to break through the panzer ring of steel around Bastogne. As the Fourth Armored advanced north of Arlon, it looked as though long-awaited relief was at hand. In their great joy, McAuliffe and Roberts shook hands, thinking the worst was over—that the German blitz was a thing of the past. But

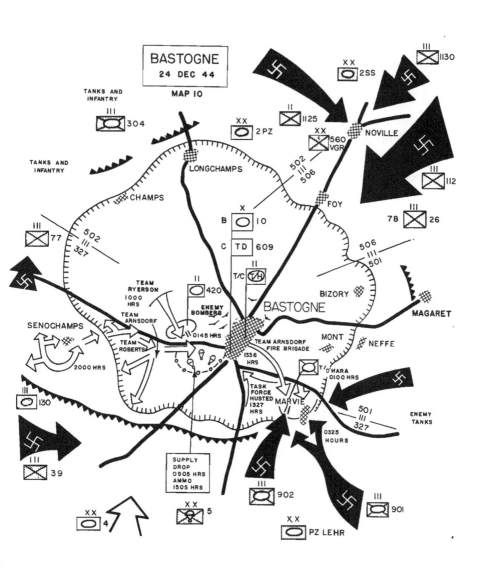

BASTOGNE
24 DEC 44
MAP 10

even at the moment an enemy attack in division strength with tanks was preparing to strike the city from the northwest. So even in their last hour of hope, the Tigers wondered if the Fourth Armored would make it in time. The 15th Panzer Grenadier Division, supported by 18 tanks, made a last do-or-die attempt to capture the city. They attacked about 0300 to avoid air detection and got as far as Hemroulle, a half mile from Division Headquarters in the city. There they were stopped by tanks, TD's and infantry. Cherry's fighters were once again alerted to hop into the flaming battle, but by the time they arrived, there was little to do except mop up the remnants of the German forces. In this battle, a Nazi tank was captured intact and taken south by CC B for training purposes, when it was relieved in January.

HELP ARRIVES AT LAST

For the Germans, it was the beginning of the end. At exactly 1630 on December 26, the Fourth Armored's CC R, led by Lieut. Col. C. R. Abrams, blasted its way into Bastogne. To do this, they had to smash enemy resistance at Assennois, slightly southwest of the city. The Tigers' Christmas present, though a day late, was delivered. The iron ring of German panzers was pierced and the rescue was begun. Aiding the encircled forces were 35 American field artillery battalions which fired 94,230 rounds at the stubborn enemy. Despite the arrival of the Fourth Armored Division though, hard fighting was still required of all units. This was necessary in order to widen the corridor during the ensuing days. The next day, wounded were evacuated and supply trains wheeled in. Along with the supplies came swarms of war correspondents and official observers. The sickening sight of gutted buildings, smashed tanks and vehicles, was mute testimony of the hell that Bastogne had been for eight long days.

Later in the day, General George S. Patton arrived. He was accompanied by Major General Maxwell Taylor, Commander of the 101st. General Taylor was in Washington for conferences

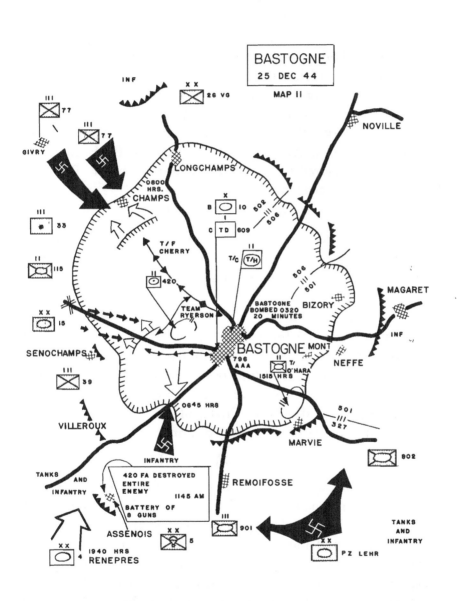

when the Bulge attack had begun. For this reason, Brig. Gen Anthony McAuliffe became the acting 101st Airborne Division Commander. Still attached to the 101st, CC B was not finished with Bastogne. In the early days of January, Team O'Hara, in cooperation with airborne doughs, made several attacks against the stubborn Germans. O'Hara's Team suffered very heavy losses. Ironically, Combat Command B lost as many Tiger officers and men after January 1 as they had during the "holidays" at Bastogne. "Hank" Cherry's final effort was a push west through Senonchamps, to help widen the perimeter. Then CC B's Headquarters were finally moved to Petit Rosiers, just southwest. This move was made to make way for fresh troops.

WELCOME RELIEF

Twenty-nine days from the begining of the German blitz, the Tigers left Bastogne. And most of them would never see Bastogne again. On January 16, CC B, in a raging blizzard, quit Bastogne. Pausing at Metz for only thirty minutes, the Command continued on to the area of Fifteenth Corps in the Seventh Army, where replacements filled the badly decimated battalions and where much-needed rest was at last granted to Bastogne's defenders, even though they were in XV Corps reserve on a front which expected an enemy drive. In a period of 30 days, Combat Command B had been assigned to the Third, First and Seventh Armies—further testimony to the extreme mobility of armor!

BASTOGNE BATTLE ENDED

The most spectacular battle of the war was over. More than 56,000 Americans were killed in the enemy's winter blitz. The Germans had thrown 500,000 crack troops and 1,000 tanks into the greatest, and final, blitzkrieg of the war. This German land power, coupled with 800 Luftwaffe planes, struck with lightning speed against thinly-held American lines in the Ardennes. The 101st and the Tenth Armored Division took the full force of the Germans' furious assault at Bastogne and at the underbelly of the

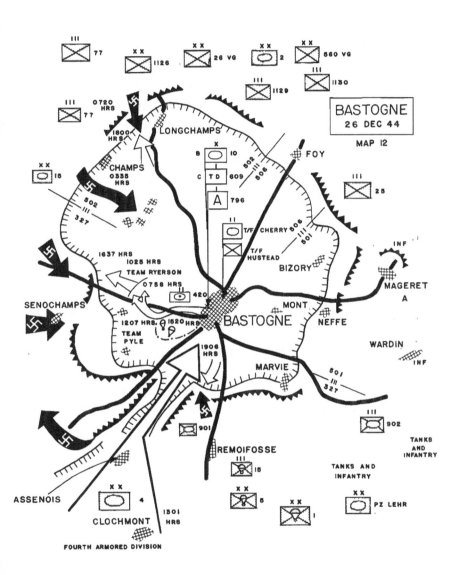

BASTOGNE
26 DEC 44

MAP 12

Map showing the Bastogne area, 26 December 1944, with unit positions including Longchamps, Champs, Senochamps, Foy, Bizory, Mageret, Marvie, Mont, Neffe, Wardin, Remoifosse, Clochmont, Assenois, and Bastogne. Units include the 77, 1126, 26 VG, 2, 560 VG, 1129, 1130, 25, 15, 502, 327, 506, 501, 420, 901, 902, 5, 4, Pz Lehr, Fourth Armored Division, Team Ryerson, Team Pyle, T/F Cherry, T/F Hustead, with times marked (0720 HRS, 1800 HRS, 0335 HRS, 1637 HRS, 1025 HRS, 0758 HRS, 1207 HRS, 1520 HRS, 1906 HRS, 1301 HRS). Labels include "TANKS AND INFANTRY".

Bulge, in northern Luxembourg. It is no wonder that our Tiger lines were cut to shreds. The odds were incredibly stacked against the Armoraiders.

Every unit in the area covered itself with glory, and no one division was the whole show. Combat Command B did not win the battle of Bastogne alone. But many military students believe that without our armor, Bastogne would have fallen to the Germans immediately. They would have been free to control the vital highways leading into Bastogne, free to smash their way west to create, perhaps, another "Bastogne" elsewhere in Belgium. The importance of Combat Command B's effort is already a matter of record in military history.

For Combat Command B, the credit due the three task forces of Desobry-Hustead, Cherry and O'Hara cannot fully be measured. When the chips were down, those forces reacted magnificently. Not to be overlooked is the first-rate support received from the sharpshooters of the 705th Tank Destroyer Battalion, the superb 420th Field Artillery, tough Ninth Armored fighters, the dead-eye 609th Tank Destroyers, the tiny group of stragglers from many other units, and most of all, the help obtained from those rugged paratroopers of the 101st Airborne Division. Of the Troopers, Colonel Roberts had this to say, "Those 101st men were absolutely tops—they were taught to fight surrounded—and few divisions could have accomplished the same success. Their officers and particularly the staff of the division were superior in every respect. They didn't scare easily."

SERVICE UNITY

The heat of battle fused Tiger and Trooper into one great fighting machine. Friendships were made during Bastogne that were not forgotten after the war was over. In Nice, France, after VE Day, a group of Tigers, celebrating peace, managed to get embroiled in a street fight. It was a rip-roaring brawl in which the Tigers were once again outnumbered. Taking a licking from a

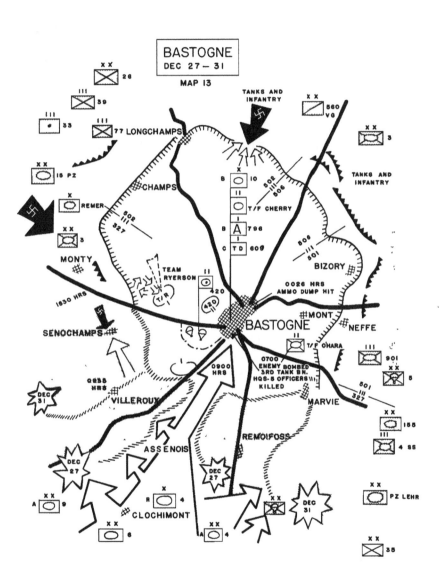

BASTOGNE
DEC 27 – 31

MAP 13

rival group of soldiers, the wearers of the Tenth Armored patch were in trouble. In the meantime, a few Troopers of the 101st happened along. Seeing the Tiger patches, they joined the fray and helped to rout the opposition—out of sentimental attachment for their former comrades-in-arms. Perhaps this is what the Department of Defense later had in mind when it called for unity in the services.

RECOGNITION

General George C. Marshall, then Chief of Staff, signed the following Distinguished Unit Citation which was presented to these Combat Command B units: Headquarters and Headquarters Company, Combat Command B; Third Tank Battalion (less C Company); Twentieth Armored Infantry Battalion (less A Company); Fifty-Fourth Armored Infantry Battalion (less A and C Companies); 420th Armored Field Artillery Battalion; Troop D Ninetieth Cavalry Squadron; Company C, Fifty-Fifth Armored Engineer Battalion; Company C, Twenty-First Tank Battalion; Collecting Section, Company B, Eightieth Armored Medical Battalion; Company C, 609th Tank Destroyer Battalion (less 1st Platoon, with 2nd Platoon, Reconnaissance Company attached); and Battery B, 796th Anti-aircraft Automatic Weapons Battalion.

The Citation read: "Essential to a large-scale breakthrough into Belgium and northern Luxembourg, the enemy attempted to seize the key communications center of Bastogne, Belgium, by attacking constantly and savagely with the best of his armor and infantry. Without benefit of prepared defense, facing overwhelming odds and with limited and fast-dwindling supplies, Combat Command B of the Tenth Armored Division maintained a high combat morale and an impenetrable defense despite heavy bombing, intense artillery fire, and constant attacks from infantry and armor on all sides of their completely cut-off and encircled positions. This masterful and grimly determined defense denied the enemy even momentary success in an operation for which he paid dearly in men, material, and eventually, in morale. The outstanding courage, resourcefulness and undaunted determination of this gallant force are in keeping with the highest traditions of the service."

17 January 1945

To: Commanding General, 10th Armored Division, U.S. Army

1. The undersigned desires to take this means to commend the officers and enlisted men of Combat Command B, 10th Armored Division, for their most excellent work in the defense of Bastogne, Belgium, during the period 19 December 1944 to 17 January 1945.

2. During the period in question this organization was attached to the 101st Airborne Division and took an active part in the historic defense of Bastogne. During a part of the time, the entire garrison was surrounded by the enemy and isolated from contact with friendly troops.

3. This unit, under the command of Col W. L. Roberts, U. S. Army, performed an outstanding service. I doubt that service has been rendered by an armored unit in the U. S. Army which can parallel the accomplishment of this splendid group of officers and men.

4. While all the officers and men of this command performed a notable service and it would be difficult to single out individual cases, yet I feel that this communication would not be complete without special mention of the unit commanding officer, Colonel William L. Roberts, 13597. The action of an organization typifies the caliber of its commander. The high type of leadership on the part of Colonel Roberts deserves special mention."

TROY H. MIDDLETON
Major General, U. S. Army
Commanding, VIII Corps

20 January 1945

To Commanding General, Officers and Men of the VIII Corps

1. The magnificent tactical skill and hardihood which you and your Command displayed in slowing up the German offen-

sive, and the determined valor and tactical prescience which caused you to retain possession of BASTOGNE, together with your subsequent resumption of a victorious offensive, constitute a truly superb feat of arms.

2. You and the officers and men of your Command are hereby highly commended for a superior performance.

3. You will apprize all units concerned of the contents of this letter.

G. S. PATTON, JR.
Lieut. General, United States Army
Commanding, 3rd Army

BASTOGNE

24 December 1944

To: The officers and men of CCB, 10 AD

You have been doing a spendid job regardless of conditions. During the freezing weather, whether night or day, with your superb team mates of the 101st Airborne Division, you have stopped numerous strong attacks of seven divisions. You are making history and we are all proud of your exertions. Troops of two armies are battling their way forward in order to defeat the enemy's attack and to relieve BASTOGNE. They are nearby at this moment, and advancing.

The CG 10 AD informed me today that he was proud of his splendid group known as CCB of the 10th Armored Division and that he desired that I extend his Holiday Greetings to you along with mine.

Col. WILLIAM L. ROBERTS
Commanding Officer, CCB

SNAFU BECOMES SYNONYM
OF VALOR IN 10TH ARMORED
By James Cannon

WITH TENTH ARMORED DIV., Belgium, Jan. 6.—The fortunes of war bilked this armored division out of the full credit it

Bastogne heroes homeward bound. Lucky Tigers were
Standing, left to right: Gerald Stevens, Vester Smith,
Ignatius Vaznonis, Ray Yantis, Angelo Yequierdo, Oscar
Thomas. Kneeling: Robert Mays, Hugh Doyebi and
Odeno Scanzillo.

deserves for its valorous part in stemming the Nazi breakthrough.

Junior officers and non-coms who were compelled to a-
bandon the accepted tactics of mechanized warfare in the crazy
tides of one of the most important actions of the war threw the
book away and "fought guerilla fashion with tanks."

Not only did they figure prominently in the defense of Bastogne but they also blocked the surprise German counter lunge
which started to roll Dec. 16, northeast of the city of Luxembourg.

THIN LINE HOLES FAST

After travelling 75 miles on the 17th, they flamed into action on the afternoon of the same day to reinforce the Fourth Inf.
Div., whose thinly-strung line was the only barrier between the
enemy and the city of Luxembourg.

By the afternoon of the 18th a task force of the Tenth was
rolling into Bastogne. It is largely responsible for holding the city

until the first element of the 101st Airborne Div. arrived on Dec. 19 to make one of the bravest stands in the history of men at war. From the time it went into action until the Fourth Armored Div. broke through the ring around the city the Tenth fought continually, driving into any section of the area where a fresh break through threatened.

In support of a battalion of the 101st and elements of the Ninth Armored Div., units of the Tenth figured in the destruction of a German counter-attack southwest of Bastogne. This action has been described by participants as the fiercest battle of the Bastogne defense.

ATTACKED FROM THREE SIDES

Col. William L. Roberts of the Tenth, who directed the defense of Bastogne until the 101st arrived, dispatched units of his outfit north and east of the town to defend the approaches at Noville, Longvilly and Bras. With the 101st they held until Dec. 21, although attacked from three sides. Then they fell back to high ground. At Longvilly the tankers were cut off and surrounded, but shot their way out.

During the fighting around Bertonge the Tenth is credited with destroying at least 60 tanks. This does not include armor ruined around Berdorf, Echternach and other places. The Tenth retook Waldbilling on Dec. 20 in conjunction with the Ninth. It plugged a big gap with less than a battalion of cavalary reconnaissance troops during the early critical stages, when a breakthrough might have changed the course of the battle.

But what pleased the Tenth most was the fact that it took the GI word of despair, snafu, and made it a synonym for gallantry. That was the name the Tenth Armored officer gave his task force of clerks, cooks, radio operators and other non-combatants of this uivision, plus stragglers trom other outtits, who inflicted such heavy casualties. It is probably the first time that snafu ever showed up on official papers.

130

VI

THE SAAR-MOSELLE TRIANGLE

F OLLOWING THE BATTLE OF THE BULGE, the Tenth Armored Division, except for Combat Command B, was given a brief respite in the comparatively luxurious surroundings at Metz, where it had assembled on December 27. For a time, the weary Tiger was able to lick his wounds and rest for the long battle journey across Germany yet to come. On January 17, the Division moved southward to Faulquemont, France, where it was rejoined by Colonel Roberts' Combat Command B. Upon its arrival there, the Tenth was placed in XV Corps reserve of the United States Seventh Army—with the exception of Division Artillery—which supported new American divisions rushed to Europe without their own artillery. For nineteen days the Tigers were engaged in a three-fold program of unit training, providing a counter-reconnaissance screen west of the Saar River, and at the same time, holding part of the Army's front line.

This time, the elements, not the enemy, made the movement south one of the most difficult ever attempted by the Division. Rain and snow teamed up to send one Tiger vehicle after another off icy roads and into the ditches. Many Tigers will remember a particularly sharp left turn on the road to Falquemont. At this point, a Tiger sergeant brought his knowledge of physics into play. As each tank negotiated the treacherous 180° turn, it was assisted by him. By placing his hand on the side of the tank, he was able to create enough friction to permit it to make the turn. When accosted by Lieut. Col. John W. Sheffield, Division staff officer, as to the merits of his theory, the Sergeant pointed to two tanks already ditched, remarking, "Those two went off the road before I got here," adding, "but since I've used this system, they all made the turn." Doubtfully, Sheffield tried the experiment, and found that it worked. Apparently, just slight pressure was needed to overcome the lack of friction between the steel treads and the ice.

The Division's stay in the Faulquemont area was uneventful. Except, perhaps, for the unique arrangement which permitted one train a day to come from the German side to our area without having to suffer the indignity of being shelled by the Tigers. In this way, the Germans who worked on the German side but who lived behind American lines, could go to work every day and return in safety. And for once, the rear echelon found itself in surroundings far inferior to those which favored the front line Tigers. Nowhere, for example, was it possible to get a bath in the Division Headquarters area. But up front, all was serene as the Tigers there wallowed in hot water, thanks to the good condition of the area's water works.

BACK TO LUCKY FORWARD

Suddenly, on February 9, orders for movement north were transmitted from XV Corps to General Morris, and before dusk on February 10, after day-long travel, the entire Division was once again united with General Walker's XX Corps of the United States Third Army at Metz. This time, all identification was removed from the vehicles, and shoulder patches were put away. But despite this precaution and the secrecy which accompanied our movement to Metz, a French boy of seven bravely approached a Tiger staff officer and in perfect English said, "Welcome back to Metz, Tenth Armored Tigers."

Less than two months had elapsed since the US Third Army had concentrated on cracking the famed Siegfried Line north and south of Saarbrucken. The ill-fated German winter blitz in the Ardennes halted that effort when Patton's strength had to be transferred north to flatten the Bulge. Now once again Third Army divisions were to collide with the stone and steel of the enemy's Siegfried Line. This time, however, the Tenth Armored was the only division remaining which had participated in the November-December assault in the Saar-Moselle Triangle. And this time, the Division's drive was to set a model for tank-infantry teamwork, as

the Tigers were to race through an infantry division bridgehead
to seize important objectives deep in the enemy's rear area.

THE TRIANGLE

The Saar-Moselle Triangle is bounded on the west by the
Moselle, the east by the Saar, and the south by the east-west ad-
junct of the Siegfried Line. In order to overrun the Triangle, it was
necessary to capture Metz; and, by the same token, to capture
Trier, the Triangle had to be taken. The job given to the Tigers was
formidable. The Triangle formed a natural barrier at the outset,
but the efficient Germans improved on nature and erected strong
fortifications across the base and along their side of both rivers.
Nineteen miles long from apex to base, the Triangle was bisected
north to south by a long ridge line.

Tank-infantry team awaits orders to cross Saar River
near Ayl, Germany

TIGERS GET READY

To prepare the men of the Tenth Armored for the operation ahead, an intensive training program was begun. After a week of hard work, the Division was notified that General Walker planned to use the 94th Infantry Division in an attack on the Switch Line. To Tiger commanders this intelligence was of great significance, for they had known that General Patton had personally interceded in Walker's behalf at SHAEF to allow the Tenth Armored to be committed through the 94th's Saar bridgehead—if such a bridgehead could be clearly established. SHAEF permission was necessary, since, at the time, the division was in SHAEF reserve. At this juncture, too, Axis Sally began to refer to the Tenth as the "Ghost Division," on her entertaining broadcasts. For the duration of the war that title remained. . . . and was accepted by the Tigers as a mark of distinction.

At Metz, the Division's battalions, which had been shot up during the Bulge, were considerably strengthened with tough and experienced replacements. Almost all of these fighters came from an airborne division which had participated in a disastrous jump in Holland months before. After recovering from their wounds in hospitals, they were sent to the Tenth and proved to be superb in combat. Quickly the Division girded itself for combat, as it learned that both the Third Army and XX Corps were pressuring SHAEF to release the Division for use in clearing the Saar-Moselle Triangle. Ever confident, General Walker sent several plans to the Division which were translated into field orders to enable the Tigers to go into action in a moment's notice. These were known to General Morris's staff as plans A, B and C. In this way, Corps could set the Division into motion by designating either of the plans and zero hour simply by calling Tiger Headquarters. While the staff was busy with these plans, the rest of the Division was engaged in training the new replacements. And it was hoped that this time the impact of Tiger armor against the Switch Line at the base of the Triangle would be powerful enough to shatter the Line's reputation of invincibility.

TENTH ARMORED DIVISION

COMBAT ORGANIZATION
SAAR—MOSELLE TRIANGLE

CHART 3

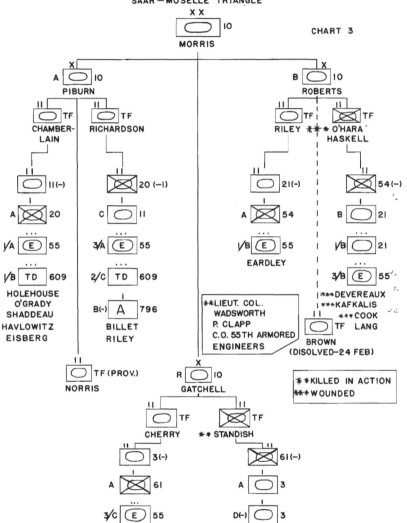

NOW OR NEVER

The Switch Line, completed in 1940, was two kilometers in depth. Its purpose was to deny access to the high ground overlooking Trier. Constructed in depth with obstacles such as concrete pillboxes, dragon's teeth and anti-tank ditches, it was intended to drain the attackers' strength to such a degree that the Germans waiting behind the fortifications could make short work of any troops who might be able to penetrate.. Despite this formidable array of defenses, General Morris marshalled the Tenth Armored in the new assembly area near Perl and Besch on the afternoon of February 19. Plan A was selected, and H hour was set for 07-00. Unfortunately, the Division was unprepared for the Corps' sudden directive.. Large numbers of Tigers had been favored with a visit to Paris at this time, for it was felt that sufficient time was available to grant them a well-deserved rest. Despite unbelievable difficulties in locating Tigers in that city, the Division moved out at about 1800 on February 19 and marched to the line of departure north of Metz in what is considered one of the war's most brilliant movements. Actually, the Armoraiders raced 75 miles that night and began the attack at 0700 on February 20 as scheduled. In front of them was the 94th Infantry Division, which had already battered a hole in the Switch Line to pave the way for armor's exploitation. At 1800 the day before, the crack 376th Regimental Combat Team of the 94th was attached to the Tenth Armored.

MAIN EVENT

Now the preliminary rounds were over. In the course of the next few days, the 10th Armored Tigers were to overrun the Saar-Moselle Triangle—one of the most heavily fortified areas in the world—and capture the important supply and communications center of Trier, oldest city in Germany. This battle operation was performed with magnificent skill and daring, and it brought praise to the Tigers from all quarters as General George S. Patton, in open admiration, termed this battle "one of the war's most audacious operations."

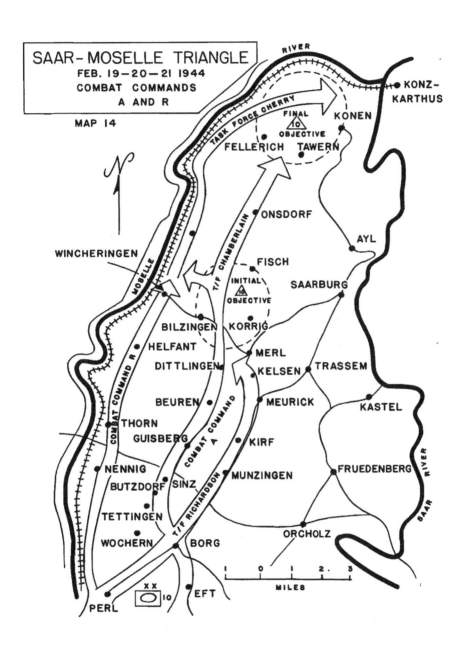

SAAR-MOSELLE TRIANGLE
FEB. 19-20-21 1944
COMBAT COMMANDS
A AND R

MAP 14

As outlined by General Morris, the Division attack was to proceed along two axes. While Colonel William L. Roberts' Combat Command B remained in reserve, Combat Command A under Brig. Gen. Edwin W. Piburn was to proceed on the right, and the Reserve Command led by Col. Wade C. Gatchell on the left. Promptly at 0700 on February 20, CC A launched a two-pronged thrust, utilizing Task Force Richardson on the right and Task Force Chamberlain on the left. Moving northeast, Richardson made contact with the Germans on the outskirts of Kirf. Temporarily stopped by minefields, this task force employed its attached engineers to clear a path for continued advance. Once through the fields, the column was hit hard by machine gun fire and assault guns, but this resistance was overcome, and Richardson's tankers captured Kirf. Then Team Billet was sent cross country on the left of Kirf to sock Meurick. For half an hour "Bud" Billet's Tigers were stopped by murderous anti-tank fire, which required that he bring his Headquarters Company mortars into position to reply to the enemy. Without further resistance, the town of Meurick capitulated. While this action was taking place, the remainder of Richardson's forces slammed into Kelson. There they overran and

Tankers pass burning building in Meurick, Germany while overrunning the Triangle

captured the command post of the enemy's 456th Infantry Regiment, the 256th Volkgrenadier Division and took almost 100 prisoners.

Meanwhile, Chamberlain and his Tigers, operating on the left of CC A, reached a position between Merschweiler and Eft. Here Team commanders were given final battle instructions to attack on the road from Tettingen to Sinz and take the high ground between Bilzingen and Korrig. After that, Chamberlain was to move north along the axis Fischonsdorf-Fellerick to grab the high ground near Tawern in the northern corner of the Triangle. Leading, from the line of departure, was Team Shaddeau. It was followed by Teams O'Grady and Holehouse. Flushing twenty enemy infantrymen out of their foxholes at the edge of the woods on the left and thirty - five more in the woods northeast of Bruen, Team Shaddeau methodically prodded its way to the high ground overlooking Dittlingen. On the way, it knocked out three enemy 75 millimeter artillery pieces, three halftracks, and eliminated small arms and mortar fire directed at it. However, Shaddeau did not get off lightly. Four of his tanks were put out of action, forcing Team O'Grady to move up from Dittlingen and take over. Then Team Holehouse darted away from Sinz and mopped up along the route cleared by the Tiger tankers earlier, in order to set up unobstructed movement along the road network for the Task Force supply trains.

While Shaddeau's Team overlooked the situation from an open field position, O'Grady's tanks rumbled along the road to Sost. Craters, roadblocks, unfavorable terrain and heavy enemy artillery fire slowed him, but in Tiger style, both he and Shaddeau took the Division's initial objective, the high ground in the vicinity of Tawern, by late afternoon. The third Team, commanded by Holehouse, rolled on by way of Sinz, and in a two-hour melee, cleared Dittlingen where they took 45 prisoners. Without pausing, they rolled on to Merskirchen and netted 30 more.

On the same day, Colonel Gatchell's Combat Command R,

fanning out on the left axis of the Tenth Armored's drive, drove to Wincheringen without meeting substantial enemy resistance. After a brief pause, the attack was resumed at 0700, against light opposition, and by evening CC R reached its target north of Tawern. It took the Tigers one day to smash the vaunted German defenses on the Switch Line, making it possible to overrun and destroy the entire Triangle. More important, it set the stage for the subsequent capture of Trier, one of the enemy's most vital communication centers on the western front. In a matter of 48 hours, the Tenth Armored blitzed 85 square miles of German soil and, with help from the 94th Infantry, captured 23 towns.

Previously, on February 21, General Patton visited the Division's Headquarters, located in an old schoolhouse at Ayl. After studying the situation and checking the maps, Patton turned to General Walker and ordered, "Johnny, cross the Saar and take Trier." With that, General Walker turned to General Morris and said, "Bill, cross the Saar and take Trier." The Tiger General then looked at his Assistant G-3 and declared, "You heard it, Sheffield; get busy." Perhaps this was the fastest transmission of battle orders from Army to Corps to Division on record. When Patton returned to his Third Army Headquarters that night, he phoned SHAEF and got permission to do what he had already done, in committing the Tenth Armored Division across the Saar.

CROSSING THE SAAR

The Saar River, averaging 150 feet in width and 15 feet in depth, could not be forded. For this reason, a bridgehead near Ockfen was to be established by the 376th Regimental Combat Team. The crossing would be supported by heavy protective fire from Combat Command B's tank destroyers. After the infantry crossing, that Command was directed to be ready to pass through the bridgehead. At the same time, CC A was ordered to provide covering fire for the doughs and to seize the bridges at Kanzem and Wiltingen. This important mission completed, the Command was then to follow CC B through the bridgehead, with CC R held

Smoke screen is generated by 81st Chemical Company
near Ayl to permit Saar River crossing

in readiness to back up its sister commands. The 90th Cavalry
Reconnaissance Squadron, commanded by Lt. Col. Cornelius A.
Lichirie, had been attached previously to the 3rd Cavalry Group
but was freed on the morning of February 20 to rejoin the Tenth
and provide a counter-reconnaissance screen, maintain patrols and
keep in contact with friendly forces along the line Saarburg-Mer-
tert between the Saar and the Moselle.

THE LOST BATTALION

After departing from Tenth Armored Headquarters at Sierck
on February 21, General Patton ordered a pontoon bridge battalion to move up from Army Reserve. Our own 55th Armored
Engineers were instructed to meet this battalion at the bridge
which spanned the Moselle at Tawern. At the designated hour, an
engineer officer sent by Lieut. Col. Wadsworth P. Clapp was at the
site to lead the pontoon battalion to Ayl. The engineer officer dis-
cussed the route to Ayl with the pontoon bridge battalion commander and then set out in pitch blackness as planned with the
battalion trailing behind him. When he pulled into Ayl, however,
only three of the pontoon trucks were still behind him. All the rest
were lost. Poor driver training, in this case, proved to be
extremely costly to the operation. And it was not until the next
morning that the trucks were recovered, too late to execute the
surprise river crossing at Ayl.

141

Though not at fault, Col. Clapp was severely criticized by XX Corps for the pontoon battalion's failure to arrive as planned. According to informed sources, this snafu also was responsible for the only critical remarks directed at the Division by General Patton during the war. In his memoirs, the rugged army commander recalled that "several days were lost here, as the Tenth Armored managed to get its boat train scattered all over the Triangle."

NEW PLAN

The loss of the pontoon bridge and the lack of sufficient assault boats forced postponement of the first attempt to cross the Saar, and a new plan had to be devised for the establishment of a bridgehead. This one called for the 3rd Battalion of the 376th Regimental Combat Team, attached to the Tenth Armored, to cross the Saar directly east of Ayl. The task of devising this difficult plan fell to Lieut. Col. Joseph A. McChristian, Division G-3. Observers noted that, at that time, everyone at Headquarters was exhausted. Worry and lack of sleep took its toll. Despite these handicaps, McChristian drew up the plans, issued the order, and saw to it that it was carried out. Thus while the 376th's Third Battalion occupied itself in getting across the Saar, the First Battalion was scheduled, at the same time, to cross a few hundred yards south of Ayl. Afterwards, both battalions were to converge in the area around Ockfen. This strategy was calculated to ease the task of getting the Tigers across the Saar. For the infantrymen of the 94th Division, however, the crossing was made under most difficult conditions. Enemy machine gun fire raised havoc with the doughs in the unprotected assault boats. To add to their woes, the boats got caught in partially submerged barbed wire. Nevertheless, the crack infantrymen managed to gain their assigned objectives to enable the Tigers to cross in their wake.

Task Force Richardson, under Combat Command A's guidance, had captured and outposted Tawern prior to the crossing of the Saar by the 376th doughs. Task Force Chamberlain was on its way to capture the bridges at Kanzel and Wiltingen. To speed their way, the roads were ordered cleared for them through Onsdorf by Division Headquarters. Chamberlain sent Team Holehouse at noon on February 21 to secure the bridge some 50 yards south of Wiltingen. Following Holehouse was Team Havlowitz, which had closed on Dittlingen from the south. His job was the job of taking the bridge at Kanzem. At the same time, Teams O'Grady and Shaddeau were instructed to perch on the original Division objective on the elevated position which overlooked Trier.

Enemy's troops are driven from Saarburg by 90th Recon Squadron

PRESS COMMUNIQUE

HEADQUARTERS 10TH ARMORED DIVISION
PUBLIC RELATIONS OFFICE
TELETYPE: PRESS CAMP
CODE A. O. D. THIRD UNITED STATES ARMY

21 February 1945

"The Tenth Armored 'Tiger' Division, commanded by Maj. Gen. William H. H. Morris, Jr., had practically cleared the Saar-Moselle Triangle of German troops, and had entered Saarburg by 1345 today. By 1900, organized resistance in the Triangle had ended, and the Tenth Armored was engaged in mopping-up operations.

"After patrols of the 90th Cavalry Reconnaissance Squadron of the Tenth Armored entered Saarburg at 1345, two armored infantry platoons of the Tenth were sent into the city to hold it. The city is surrounded on three sides. Tenth Armored troops hold high ground to the north, south and west, overlooking the city.

"Other developments in the second day of the Tenth Armored's smashing drive in Western Germany were as follows: Capture of the towns of Tawern, Mannebach, Onsdorf, Nittel, Temmels and Kahren; capture of approximately 500 additional prisoners; and penetration northward almost to the junction of the Saar and Moselle.

"During the two days, the 10th Armored Division has captured 23 towns and approximately 1250 prisoners, and has occupied approximately 85 square miles of German soil.

"Resistance encountered in the second day of the 10th Armored's drive consisted of mines, roadblocks, small arms fire, and craters in roads. End. Authenticated by G-3 10th Armored Division."

—Nichols

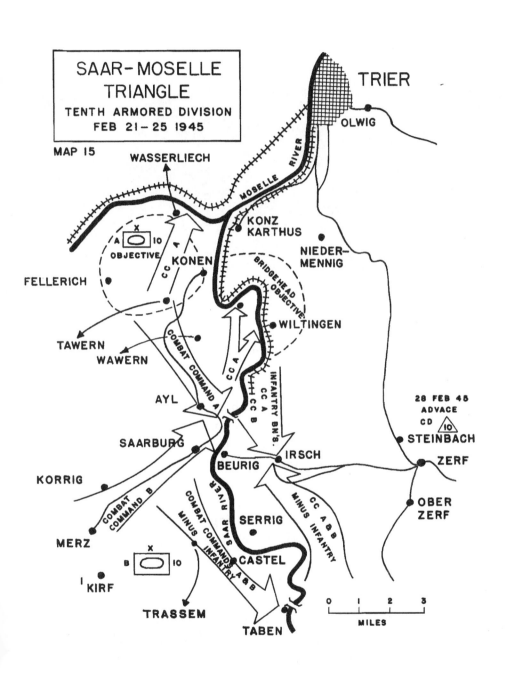

SAAR-MOSELLE
TRIANGLE
TENTH ARMORED DIVISION
FEB 21-25 1945

MAP 15

TRIER

OLWIG

WASSERLIECH

MOSELLE RIVER

KONZ
KARTHUS

NIEDER-
MENNIG

A ☒ 10
OBJECTIVE

KONEN

FELLERICH

BRIDGEHEAD
OBJECTIVE

WILTINGEN

CC A

COMBAT COMMAND A

TAWERN

WAWERN

CC A

INFANTRY BN'S.

CC B

AYL

28 FEB 45
ADVACE
CD 10
STEINBACH

SAARBURG

BEURIG

IRSCH

ZERF

KORRIG

COMBAT COMMAND B

CC A & B
MINUS INFANTRY

OBER
ZERF

MERZ

COMBAT COMMAND A & B
MINUS INFANTRY

SAAR RIVER

SERRIG

B ☒ 10

KIRF

CASTLE

TRASSEM

TABEN

0 1 2 3

MILES

Tigers' light tanks bolster lightning attack through Saar-Moselle Triangle

Small arms and anti-tank fire greeted Team Holehouse as it battled its way towards the bridge at Wiltingen. When it was within 400 yards of Ayl, it ran into a minefield which had been placed on both sides and on the road itself. Valuable time was lost as Lieut. Col. Clapp's 55th Armored Engineers frantically worked during the night of February 21 to clear a path through the minefields for Holehouse's Tigers. Finally, at 0300 it was breached, permitting the armored infantry to move through the gap. As they started through, a tremendous explosion on the river rocked them with the knowledge that the enemy had blown up their objective. Moments later, the bridge at Kanzem was blown too. Nothing was left for Holehouse now, except to patrol the river north of Ayl.

Team Havlowitz followed Team Holehouse. When the former reached the crossroads northeast of Mannebach, it ran into a German high-velocity 76 mm anti-tank gun manned by a crew of eight. This was the same outfit that had shot at Holehouse; but Holehouse had ignored them in order to close on his objective.

146

Havlowitz, however, decided to "get" the Germans and sent out dismounted doughs to do the job. A short time later, our Armor-aiders returned with all eight gunners and the 76mm gun, too.

Task Force Chamberlain was not involved in further action until February 24. The young officer and his men impressed Head-quarters greatly, as they smashed to their objectives in a style hark-ing back to the days of the charging cavalry. When Chamberlain raced through the 94th's bridgehead on February 20, he overran enemy horse-drawn artillery units. Acting quickly, to immobilize the German artillery, his Tigers killed almost all the horses. Since most of the big guns could not be moved by the Germans, they were captured by the 10th. The Germans angrily protested the slaughter of their horses but Chamberlain reasoned that "the guns immobil-ized could not be used in the future by the Germans to kill Ameri-cans."

Fighting over: Elder sons of the Wehrmacht wait for free ride to Tenth Armored's PW cage near Saarburg

At 1500 on February 20, Division Headquarters were moved from Apache to Winteringen. Shortly afterwards, General Walker of XX Corps stomped into the war room. He appeared impatient that the Division was not moving fast enough and barked at Col. Sheffield, "where's Chamberlain?" The assistant G-3 officer explained that Chamberlain was progressing very well and that he had heard from the latter about half an hour ago. "Get him on the radio again," Walker commanded. Immediately complying, Sheffield called, "Six, this is Three, over." Chamberlain answered, "This is Six, go ahead." At that moment the General grabbed the microphone from Sheffield and thundered "This is Walker, Over!" Thinking that Sheffield was still on the phone, the battle-weary Chamberlain cracked, "Walk over who, you S.O.B.?" Then as Sheffield tried to fade into the outer reaches, he heard the General boom, "This is General Walker, Commander of the XX Corps!" With that, Chamberlain's radio abruptly clicked off, and he was not heard from again until the Triangle was completely overrun.

Sherman's big guns dominate approaches to Trier

ENEMY PATROL CLAWED

On February 22, Task Force Richardson was busy moving its tanks up to the high ground south of Wasserliesch, located at the corner of the Triangle. There was no time to celebrate Washington's birthday as Richardson's Tigers scooted down the hill and captured Wasserliesch in the early hours of that morning. Opposite them, across the river, stood bristling fortifications. Concrete pillboxes backed up by heavy artillery gave the enemy a huge advantage over the attackers. For the time being, that Task Force watched over the enemy from high-ground outposts overlooking the river, and at night the observers crept down to the water's edge and in quiet darkness listened for signs of enemy activity. On the night of February 22, an enemy patrol ventured across the river and was promptly clawed by our outposts. For the next two days, Task Force Richardson maintained observation in this area.

NEW BRIDGEHEAD

Major General Walton Walker's XX Corps during this operation had planned a secondary effort in which he ordered the 94th Infantry Division to establish a bridgehead at Taben. This was calculated to serve as a diversionary action to help draw attention away from the Armoraiders' assault on the Wiltingen and Kazem bridges. However, the 94th doughs were so successful at Taben, that Walker now possessed a bridgehead of major importance. Rather than wait for a Tenth Armored bridge to be built at Ockfen, the stocky Corps commander decided to shoot CC A and CC B through the Taben bridgehead a few miles south to gain valuable time. To aid in speeding up the attack, General Morris decided to commit his armored infantry as a unit into the bridgehead set up by the 376th Regimental Combat Team of the 94th Infantry. At 0900 on February 24th, the change was effected, as the armored infantry battalions assembled at Ayl under the command of Brig. Gen. Edwin W. Piburn. In mid-afternoon that day, the popular and diminutive combat commander and his armored doughs began crossing the Saar near Ockfen. This maneuver served to bolster the 376th, as well as to place additional troops in the vital bridgehead area. At the same time, the tanks and halftracks of CC A—followed by CC B, minus their infantry,—began crossing the Saar at Taben on February 25. Riding in this column were General Morris, Lieut. Col. Sheffield, G-3; Lieut. Col. Eckles, G-2; and Major Hazen, assistant Division signal officer. They constituted the Division's Advance Command Post, the main CP remaining at Ayl. Once across, the commands struck north on the east bank of the Saar to mate up with their armored infantry which had fought its way to Irsch.

The day before, on February 24, all the combat commanders had assembled at Ayl to participate in the planning of the operation. In mid morning, and without warning, the Germans fired almost simultaneously, two 88's, one of which hit the front of the Command Post building, and the other, General Morris's jeep, parked in front. At the time, the writer was a short distance away on the way to the CP. Arriving there moments later, he found Major Walter Barnes, Headquarter's Commandant, dead, a victim of the second 88, which had hit the steel windshield of the General's jeep. It was the windshield itself, shattered by the enemy projectile which ended the life of the popular Commandant. Killed, too, were two Tiger military policemen on guard at the CP's doorway. The Division Chief of Staff, Col. Basil G. Thayer, was wounded. While working on the second floor of the CP, the latter was hit in the hand by shrapnel and was cut in the face from flying glass. After he had been evacuated to the rear, Lieut. Col. McChristian was made Chief of Staff, and Lieut. Col. Sheffield became G-3. Most of the Tigers had their share of lucky breaks at one time or another. The writer was no exception, for only hours before, he had been "requested" to remove his bedroll and person from the room which was most damaged by the first 88. The next occupant of that front room on the second floor was Col. Thayer.

General Morris, center, explains Tenth's situation to General Patton, left, and General Walker of the XX Corps

HOW IT WAS ACCOMPLISHED

To do the job set forth by General Walker, General Morris sent the 90th Recon to relieve Task Force Richardson, located north and east of Tawern. Col. Richardson then brought his armored doughs to Ayl for the Saar crossing at Ockfen. Meanwhile, the new bridgehead at Taben was established, enabling Richardson to proceed south to the new crossing site. At 1600 on February 24, Richardson's armored doughs, aided by a smoke screen generated by the 81st Chemical Company, supervised by Lieut. Col. Harry B. Feldman, Division chemical warfare officer, began the ordeal of an assault boat crossing under intense enemy fire. Continuous machine gun and artillery fire raised havoc with the unprotected Tigers, who carried their mortars, automatic weapons and ammo by hand. Despite continuous enemy fire, the crossing was made without heavy losses. Also crossing at Ayl was CC B's Task Force

151

Heavy pontoon bridge supports artillery unit crossing Saar. Note wine vine yards across River

O'Hara made up of three infantry companies of the 54th Armored Infantry Battalion. With enough rations and equipment for two days of combat without resupply, O'Hara's Armoraiders crossed the Saar in assault boats and were hit in the same fashion as their sister battalions. Twenty men were casualties when the Battalion reorganized on top of the hill directly opposite its crossing site. From here O'Hara led his Tigers to Ockfen in the wee hours of the morning of February 25.

PILLBOX PROBLEM

By noon on the 25th, all the armored infantry battalions of the Tenth Armored had crossed the Saar north of Ockfen. After careful reorganization they pushed on into that town, and, after a brief stop, continued on to mount an attack through the lines of the 376th RCT. Task Force Standish, which consisted of the 61st Armored Infantry Battalion, veered off sharply toward Scharfenburg Hill as Task Force Riley, made up from the 20th Armored

Infantry, battled its way south towards Irsch. The 54th Armored Infantry Battalion under O'Hara was held in reserve. The Tiger doughs' big advantage was speed. To keep the upper hand, they fought through the night. Though he was able to penetrate the German lines of resistance, Standish found himself cut off on the Scharfenburg Hill, and Riley was held up continuously by the enemy pillboxes to the south.

PRESS COMMUNIQUE

25 February 1945

"One combat command of the Tenth Armored 'Tiger' Division, commanded by Major General William H. H. Morris, Jr., crossed the Saar River below Saarburg Sunday afternoon, and by early evening had smashed northward six miles in a drive to effect a junction with armored infantry units of the Division in the vicinity of Ockfen.

"The crossing was made over a pontoon bridge. Tanks, half-tracks, armored artillery and trucks were transported to the east bank of the river in this fashion, while supplies were simultaneously ferried across. Earlier attempts to lay a bridge north of Saarburg had been defeated by enemy artillery, mortar and machine gun fire.

"This operation opened the second phase of the Tenth Armored's smashing drive into Germany in the upper Saar region. Earlier this week, the Tenth had rolled over more than 100 square miles of German soil, taking 35 towns and capturing some 1500 prisoners, as well as large quantities of enemy equipment.

"Towns, captured by the Tenth Armored included: Thorn, Palsem, Kelsen, Sudlingen, Meurich, Dilmar, Beuren, Kirf, Bilzingen, Fisch, Wehr, Esingen, Merzkirchen, Helfant, Korrig, Kreuzweiler, Dittlinge, Tawern, Mannebach, Onsdorf, Nittel, Temmels, Kabren, Oberbillig, Wasserliesch, Konen, Kanzem, Wawern, Niederleuken, Fellerich, Portz, Kelsen, Hamm, Ayl and Wellen. The Tenth also made first advances into Saarburg.

"The Tenth Armored completely cleared the Saar-Moselle Triangle in four days of slashing attacks, thus setting the stage for new offensives east of the Saar.

"Halted temporarily at Ayl, above Saarburg, where enemy fire repeatedly prevented construction of a pontoon bridge, the Tenth Armored nevertheless resumed its offensive. Elements of the Tenth were ferried across the Saar Thursday night, under heavy artillery, machine gun and sniper fire. Earlier that night, one complete infantry regiment attached to the Tenth had been transported across in assault boats. During the late afternoon and night on Saturday, three armored infantry battalions of the Tenth had been transported across to the vicinity of Ockfen. It was these units toward which the tanks of the Division were rushing Sunday night. Authenticated G-3"

—Nichols

HOW TO REDUCE A PILLBOX

A total of eleven pillboxes blocked the way for the infantry's advance. To knock them out, a detailed plan was developed which called for minute coordination. Since the concrete fortifications were staggered in a line south of Ockfen, it was decided that TF Riley would clear the pillboxes southeast of Ockfen, while TF O'Hara would proceed east in the path followed by TF Standish. Then O'Hara was to turn south and fight abreast of TF Riley to clear all the pillboxes in its zone along the road leading to Irsch. Dusk was counted on to aid the Tiger infantry, which dismounted, and set out methodically to reduce each pillbox to rubble.

A Company of the 54th Armored Infantry moved out towards the first two pillboxes as the sun dipped below the horizon. Once artillery and machine gun fire was placed on them, resistance ceased. Then C Company passed through A Company and took the next two pillboxes with heavy fire support. To light the area for targets, the Germans sent up flares and battled the Tigers at every step of the way. They were soon forced to surrender when artillery fire was increased on their positions and two tank destroyers, ferried across the Saar earlier in the day, fired directly on them.

The job of C Company was made more difficult as the Germans brought additional machine guns to fire on the attackers from the slope to the east of the second two pillboxes. Despite this measure, C Company reached the two boxes and set off satchel charges. Unshaken by the detonations, the Germans continued to fight, necessitating withdrawal of C Company so that Col. Bernard F. Lubbermann could direct more artillery fire on the positions. Two hours later, the enemy signified that he'd had enough. The tank destroyers of the 609th continued to aid the Tiger doughs in eliminating the remaining pillboxes, whose occupants, in observing the fate of their comrades, decided that it was better to surrender. They did so in a hurry!

Armored infantry flush snipers from fields on east bank of the Saar beyond Ockfen, Germany

Most of the night was spent in this operation, and the result spelled victory at small loss for the armored Tigers. The Germans lost twenty killed and fifty-four captured, as compared to C Company's total casualties of four.

THE TANKERS ARE COMING

Task Force Riley, of Combat Command B, like Richardson, was ordered to move its tanks and halftracks to Freudenburg for crossing the Taben bridge. Though beset by enemy artillery fire, Riley's forces crossed the bridge with slight losses. With them was A Company of the 21st Tank Battalion, which was reinforced by a light tank platoon of D Company. They were followed by Headquarters Company and the infantry's empty halftracks.

By this time, Serrig was in our possession, and here Riley received CC A's orders to push through the 94th Infantry's bridgehead to Irsch. He was to meet the 61st Armored Infantry commanded by Lieut. Col. Miles L. Standish, where both forces were to join in the attack east to relieve the rugged 5th Ranger Battalion and to take over the high ground west of Zerf.

On their way to Irsch, Riley's attackers ran into elements of the 94th Infantry engaged in a fire fight with the enemy at the outskirts of the bridgehead near Beurig. Not wishing to deviate from the assigned objective, Riley steered clear of this encounter by utilizing secondary roads. Since only M-4s could get over the muddy roads, cables were attached to the light tanks and the mediums pulled them through safely. By late afternoon of February 24, the column pulled up to the outskirts of Irsch from the West. It was thought that Task Force Standish had cleared Irsch. But unknown to TF Riley, Standish was in serious trouble trying to spin out of the trap on Scharfenburg hill and had not been able to reach that town.

HIT HARD

As A Company's 1st Platoon Leader, Lieut. Hanover, rumbled into Irsch, he noted a roadblock to his front. His two lead Sher-

Tank retrievers cross Saar on pontoon bridge at Taben

mans slammed a few rounds of 76's into the block and then by-passed it to the west and continued on through the town. The Germans let the first two tanks pass the roadblock, but the third was hit by a hidden enemy 88 mm ground mount gun. Our fourth Sherman was knocked out by a bazooka team on the right, and the fifth tank was hit by still another enemy bazooka team. While the German bazookas and the 88 were systematically eliminating our Mediums, a German Tiger tank moved up and hit two of our Second Platoon light tanks, which were further back in the column.

To rally support, Captain Eardley, A Company commander, contacted the Rangers at his rear. They came forward immediately and helped to uproot the enemy. They then went on to contact our first two tanks to protect the flanks as the Shermans rejoined the main column. At dusk, Task Force Riley's B Company of the 20th Armored Infantry barged into Irsch from the northwest and began cleaning up that troublesome town. They captured about 300 members of the 416th Volksgrenadier Division and knocked out five German Panzer Tanks. In the fighting there, we lost five killed and twenty wounded, in addition to the loss of five tanks.

At 2300 in the evening, Captain Holehouse, commander of A Company of the 20th Armored Infantry, came into Irsch from Ockfen to help clear the town. His men took 250 prisoners, some of whom started to take off when one of their own Tiger tanks opened up. They were held in tow by a machine gunner of an A Company halftrack. Fifteen were killed trying to escape. Shortly afterwards, the 20th Armored's C Company arrived on the scene to help finish the job there. The three armored infantry battalions, with the help of the 376th, succeeded in reaching Irsch. Later the 94th Infantry doughs made their way south to meet with their own 302nd Infantry and captured Beurig on February 26. The capture of Beurig permitted construction of a heavy pontoon bridge at Saarburg, located opposite that newly-taken town. Completion of this bridge on February 27 enabled the Tenth Armored to send all of its units across the Saar. A continuous bridgehead was now a reality in the area from Ockfen to Taben.

TEMPORARY TEAM A

To complete the mission of relieving the 5th Ranger Battalion west of Zerf, all Tenth Armored elements in Irsch were formed into temporary Team A. They took off in a hurry and, as their leading tanks edged up on the eastern part of Irsch, a German Tiger tank knocked out the two lead tanks and three halftracks which followed. This havoc halted our column temporarily while dismounted doughs of B and C Companies of the 20th Armored cleared the Irsch-Zerf road for about 2500 yards beyond the town. Once again the Tigers were on the move, and by February 26, the Armoraiders reached Biedchen, halfway between Irsch and Zerf. There the column was exposed to point-blank fire aimed down the road from a point west of Zerf. Undaunted, our tanks continued up the road while our armored doughs maneuvered to a draw which offered protection from the enemy artillery. Here, first contact was made with the Rangers who were entrenched in the woods. Their most pressing desire was for evacuation of the wounded. Five halftracks were immediately dispatched by Col. Richardson to help them.

Meanwhile, enemy artillery fire continued to plaster the road with direct fire from a 75 mm gun. Fortunately, a fog rolled in, permitting the Tigers to advance with greater security. B Company of the 20th Armored hooked southeast from a point slightly west of Zerf to attack and take Ober-Zerf while C Company went on to capture Nieder-Zerf. Ober-Zerf was in our hands by dusk, but Nieder-Zerf was abandoned by C Company in the face of six German Tiger tanks which menaced that town.

PRESS COMMUNIQUE
26 February 45

"The Tenth Armored 'Tiger' Division, commanded by Major General William H. H. Morris, Jr., drove four miles deeper into Germany Monday and enlarged its bridgehead on the east bank of the Saar River in preparation for further offensives. By 1300, leading tanks of the Tenth had rolled to the town of Zerf, on the Ruwer River, where they coiled for the night. Zerf is an important railhead from which German troops were sent to participate in the Ardennes offensive of mid-December. Enemy troops removed from the Western Front to meet the Russian offensive in the east also entrained at Zerf.

"Earlier in the day, one combat command of the Tenth Armored had effected a junction with armored infantrymen of the Tenth who had been ferried across the Saar several days ago and had fought their way southeast. Halftracks picked up these troops Monday morning in the vicinity of Irsch and, augmented by tanks, rolled east through hilly terrain to Zerf.

"Irsch and Beurig, on the east bank of the Saar opposite Saarburg, both fell to the Tenth Armored on Monday, increasing to 36 the number of towns taken by the Fighting Tigers since the division jumped off, February 20, in a drive to clear the Saar-Moselle Triangle—a drive that has now carried across the Saar. In the fighting Monday, the Tenth Armored destroyed 15 pillboxes and captured 500 additional prisoners, increasing its total bag of prisoners to approximately 2000.

"Towns captured by the Tenth Armored since February 20 are: Thorn, Palzem, Kelsen, Sudlingen, Meurich, Dilmar, Beuren, Kreuzweiler, Dittlingen, Tawern, Mannebach, Onsdorf, Nittel, Temmels, Kahren, Oberbillig, Wasserliesch, Konen, Kanzem, Wawern, Nieder-leuken, Fellerich, Portz, Hamm, Ayl, Wellen. Irsch, and Beurig.

"As of 2100 Monday, the Tenth Armored Division was consolidating in the vicinity of Zerf, preparing for new drives. End Authenticated by G-3, Tenth Armored Division."

—Nichols

The remainder of Task Force Riley's vehicles, consisting of 54th Armored Infantry halftracks, tanks of the 21st Tank Battalion, and two platoons of B Company of the 609th Tank Destroyers, began to assemble west of Zerf. Teams were organized from these units by Richardson, who sent one to the high ground on each side of Ober-Zerf, another to capture Nieder-Zerf and the high ground around it, and a third team into Zerf to grab the high ground east of the town.

German PW is put to work repairing road at Saar bridge site

ZERF ASSAULTED

Richardson's Armoraiders took off at 1800 but ran into mine-fields in front of Zerf which stalled their efforts for a few hours. While the removal of the mines was being accomplished, a platoon from the 609th Tank Destroyers moved up on high ground some 600 yards from Zerf. For ten minutes the platoon slammed 76 mm high explosives on targets within the town. They halted their fire to permit our walking doughs to enter. A Tiger tank was seen on the outskirts of town and was pursued by Tenth Armored bazooka teams which scored hits but were not able to knock it out. The big Tiger withdrew, however, and Zerf was entirely cleared by 0100 on February 27. At this time, Team A was disbanded, and new missions were worked out by Tiger commanders now intent on the big prize—Trier!

CUT OFF

Just one week later, after having plunged into the Saar-Moselle Triangle on February 20, the Tiger Division was poised for the kill on the heights overlooking Trier. One important reason for the lightning advance may be attributed to the highly-developed combat skill of the Tigers. In particular, the initiative of Colonel Roberts and his CC B to locate and make passable a cut-off just west of Ober-Zerf made possible the saving of many lives as well as speeding up the attack. It is difficult to imagine the havoc caused by the murderous anti-tank fire of the Germans who domin-ated the high ground north of Ober-Zerf. As Combat Command B's Tigers pushed down the hill to that place, they had to negotiate a sharp left turn and go uphill—all in the face of withering anti-tank fire. In the corner at Ober-Zerf, Tiger vehicles, wrecked and burning, were mute testimony to enemy marksmanship. But after the 55th Armored Engineers bulldozed a road through the cut-off the advance for the rest of the column was made easier. Then too, the sudden switch in direction employed by the Tenth Armored— from attacking to the east, then suddenly making a 90 degree turn northwards—completely fooled the Germans who had massed in the Ober-Zerf area, expecting the Division to continue east towards the Rhine.

In all probability, the officers who trained Tiger tacticians at the Command and General Staff School at Fort Leavenworth would have regarded with utter disbelief the manner in which orders were planned and executed for the successful drive that led to the capture of Trier. For, while Division Headquarters were still located back at Ayl, the Advance Command Post was holed up miles away across the Saar. At the Advance CP were Lieut. Colonels Sheffield and Eckles, Major Hazen and the Division's Commanding General. Later, to add to the "flexible" situation, the final plans for attacking Trier were made in Combat Command A's Headquarters. Assembled there were Generals Morris and Piburn, Colonels Roberts and Raymond, Lieut. Colonels Sheffield and Eckles, and Major Jack Balthis, the S-3 of Combat Command A. The attack order was written up by Balthis' men, making this perhaps the only time in Tiger battle operations that a division order was written and issued by one of its combat commands.

TOO CLOSE

After the Trier attack order had been issued at noon on February 27, Tiger task forces pushed out towards that city at sundown. Later, in darkness, the Division's Advance CP was moved to Steinbach. This CP was also the advance command post for all the combat commands, too. Located about 100 yards away were the Germans, who, had they known of the Advance CP's location, could have easily destroyed it by firing a few well-directed rounds from their concealed position in a narrow ravine nearby. As the first messages arrived, reporting progress, they signalled the departure of the combat commanders, who made a beeline for their task force commanders.

Earlier, when the Division's Advanced Headquarters utilized the school house at Zerf for its point of operations, it was heavily shelled by the Germans. Lieut. Col. Sheffield hurriedly telephoned

Lieut. Col. William W. Beverly, commander of the 423rd Armored Field Artillery Battalion. "Bev", he shouted, "For God's sake, do something about counter-battery fire. The Germans are about to blow us right out of this town." After a brief pause, the artillery commander replied, "Hell, you're not any more anxious than I am," adding, "By the way, do you know where I'm located?" Sheffield said, "No, I haven't the slightest idea." At this juncture, Beverly yelled, "You damn fool, I'm in the classroom right next door to you!" Conversation completed, the cannoneers silenced the enemy battery, and the building and its occupants were spared.

COMBAT COMMAND B CONTINUES ATTACK

The mission of deféating any attempt of the enemy to mount a counter-attack on Zerf was assigned to Task Force Richardson, while the rest of Combat Command B rolled out of Zerf towards

Sharpshooters of the 609th Tank Destroyer Battalion convince residents of Wiltingen to surrender

Trier. Now TF Chamberlain assumed the lead. In column, Chamberlain's Tigers were protected by Company A, 20th Armored Infantry, which moved in front of and on the flanks of Teams O'Grady and Shaddeau. On the left flank, the enemy put direct fire on the Tigers from the woods. For two hours, the Task Force battled the Germans to a depth of 1000 yards and at 0400 decided to rest until dawn. Promptly as the sun edged its way over the horizon, Team Eisberg's infantry stalked out to attack. Waiting for them around a bend in the dimly-lit road was a self-propelled 88 mm assault gun and a hulking German Mark V. But they were eliminated in short order as the Task Force rolled forward. Later, its speed was slowed again by stout German resistance in four pillboxes and a heavily inhabited troop shelter which had to be given a thorough shellacking before progress could be resumed. As soon as the woods had been skirted, Team O'Grady rumbled on through Tiger doughs and deployed across country. After they passed Steinbach, O'Grady's tankers hit a minefield and lost two tanks. Heavy mortar and artillery fire pounded the Task Force from a ridge a quarter of a mile to the front, forcing our armored infantry to hop off their halftracks and use the ditches for cover. Moreover, our doughs could not deploy because of the heavy direct-fire shelling thrown at them. In mid-afternoon, Chamberlain sent the Third Platoon of Company A of the 55th Armored Engineers to clear the minefield. By 0100 on February 28 the minefield, some 300 yards in depth, was cleared, thus allowing Chamberlain to employ his tanks on the flanks of the enemy position.

GET LOST

Pvt. Charles P. McDowell of Bridgeport, Conn., underwent an experience during this phase that was "one for the books." Pinned down by enemy fire, he was captured with several buddies and spent one long, endless afternoon as a prisoner. Toward evening, when American artillery made the Germans' position untenable, the Jerries began retreating and for a while kept their prisoners with them. Then a German officer walked up to the Americans and, in perfect English, said "We can't possibly take you with us, and we have one of two choices, either to shoot you or let you go free. We have decided to let you go." Scarcely able to believe their ears, McDowell and his buddies took off. Enroute to their own lines, they picked up 35 weary Germans who had had enough of war. They reached safety at 2200 that night with their prisoners.

FORWARD THE TANKS

Team Shaddeau was instructed to remain on the ridge overlooking Pellingen, and Team O'Grady was sent along another ridge on the right where its fire-power could assist the infantry attack along the road north into Pellingen. As planned, the assault started at dawn. In no time at all, the infantry slashed into Pellingen with help of the 75's of the tankers who had plastered the town. The Germans pulled out to high ground positions about half a mile northwest of that place. By 1000, they were routed from this position, too. And an hour later, Team Eisberg had forced the Germans off their elevated perch. Orders were transmitted immediately to Chamberlain, altering his mission. Now he was to clear Konz-Karthaus and protect the left flank of the Tigers' drive into Trier. Combat Command A sent Task Force Norris, which had been in reserve, through Chamberlain, in the middle of the afternoon, to drive on north to Trier. At this juncture, General Morris commented, "The speed with which the 10th Armored moved seventy-five miles in one night to attack a surprised enemy the next morning was magnificent." The Tiger commander added, "In ripping through one of the most heavily fortified areas in the world, the 10th denied to the enemy a stable, continuous line of defense and made it possible to launch a successful assault on Trier." Important, too, was a successful operation in which Tigers and their vehicles were brought together east of the Saar, after having crossed separately at Ayl and Ockfen on February 25, in one of the most intricate problems of coordination ever faced by the Division.

HINGE BROKEN

Most important, the seizure of the Saar-Moselle Triangle and the subsequent capture of Trier smashed the hinges of the Siegfried Line and permitted large-scale operations to the north and south for the breakthrough to the Rhine. Captured documents indicated that the Germans had been certain that the Tenth Armored was trying to break through to the Rhine. An enemy withdrawal toward Zerf was ordered, which left the remaining troops at Trier to face the rampaging tanks and infantry of the Tiger Division which, at this moment, were moving in multiple columns on the city. With a pre-war population of some 77,000 inhabitants, Trier offered the Tigers a rich prize.

THE COST WAS GREAT

Taking the important communications center was to be costly. The loss of scores of fine Tiger officers and men dealt a heavy blow to the Division. Two key battalion commanders were killed in action at Ayl and Ockfen in the early stages of overrunning the Triangle. On February 21, Lieut. Col. Wadsworth P. Clapp was killed by mortar fire while helping to direct the infantry crossing on the Saar at Ayl. The rugged commander of the 55th Armored Engineers had provided valuable information to General Morris on possible crossing sites at the Saar River. His loss was keenly felt by the engineers who continued to play an important role in Tiger history under Major William Geiler. Killed in action, too, was Lieut. Col. Miles L. Standish, eleventh direct descendent of his illustrious forbearers. The 61st Armored Infantry Battalion did not take the loss of their popular and respected commander lightly, and fought with increased fury. He was replaced by Major "Red" Hankins.

The supreme sacrifices made by these two commanders, along with so many other valued Tigers in the Triangle, made possible the saving of many lives. Their superb battle performance in helping to break through an almost impenetrable defense line

166

made possible the headlong rush of the United States Third Army to the Rhine River later in March.

SURRENDER BY SUGGESTION

The manner in which the town of Wiltingen, in the Saar-Moselle Triangle, fell to the Tenth Armored Division during the drive on Trier was like something a Hollywood director might have dreamed up. By-passed in the blitz offensive of the Tenth, Wiltingen, on the east bank of the Saar River, was effectively sealed off and remained only to be mopped up. This was a job for the Psychological Warfare Branch, aided and supported by the 609th Tank Destroyer Battalion, attached to the Tenth.

Leaflets informing the Germans that they would be permitted to surrender peaceably were showered on the garrison. Doughboys stood on the alert just outside the town, ready to move in when the rush to surrender began — or if the enemy troops decided to fight it out.

The stage was set. Using a public address system, a Psychological Warfare announcer told the Germans that they would not be fired upon if they proceeded quickly to a designated point. Almost immediately, figures could be seen leaving pillboxes on the river bank and elsewhere in the town, moving toward the collecting point. Suddenly, however, two running Jerries appeared in an open field, travelling in the opposite direction. One of the tank destroyers opened up. One shell left the big gun, and when the smoke cleared in the distance, the two figures were no longer moving.

From this point on, the operation proceeded quickly and smoothly. Approximately 250 "supermen" decided to give up the fight, and another town was added to the Tenth Armored's growing collection of war prizes.

HEADQUARTERS XX CORPS

Office of the Commanding General

5 March 1945

SUBJECT: Commendation

TO: Commanding General, 10th Armored Division,
            APO 260, U. S. Army

"1.   The workmanlike manner in which your division assisted in the clearance of the Saar-Moselle Triangle and in the accomplishment of the capture of the fortified city of Trier is an outstanding military achievement.

"2.   The aggressive and efficient manner in which your missions have been carried out reflects credit upon your division in keeping with the high traditions of the service and upon you as its Commanding General. Your ability to take immediate advantage of fleeting opportunities contributed substantially to the successful accomplishment of your mission.

"3.   Please convey to the officers and men of your command my personal thanks and appreciation for the splendid accomplishments and devotion to duty."

WALTON H. WALKER
Major General, United States Army
Commanding

1st Ind.

HEADQUARTERS 10th ARMORED DIVISION, U. S. Army,
TO: Officers and Men of the 10th Armored Division

"Your splendid work during the operation set forth above which the Corps Commander mentions in his commendation resulted in the capture of one of the great fortified cities of Germany — Trier. This was the military base captured by Julius Caesar with his famous 10th Legion. The 10th Armored (Tigers) captured in one night what it took several days for the 10th Roman Legion to take. I extend to you my congratulations along with those of the Corps Commander. We are now going forward with our spearhead to the Rhine."

W. H. H. MORRIS, Jr.
Major General, United States Army
Commanding

VII

THE CAPTURE OF TRIER

ON FEBRUARY 27, Combat Command B was ordered by General Morris to begin the attack on Trier. Task Force O'Hara, following Task Force Chamberlain on the move from Irsch to Zerf, was shelled by the Germans continuously. And as the columns wheeled north on the road west of Zerf, they were hit hard by an enemy 88 which had zeroed in on the corner. This menace was eliminated, and the column pushed on. For Combat Command B, the main road along the high ridge was their assault avenue against Trier. Task Force Chamberlain moved out ahead of O'Hara's Force and bolted down the main route. The latter's mission was to protect the right flank, capture the town of Paschal, Hill 508, and then work its way along the ridge road on the right of the line of attack. To accomplish this task, O'Hara sent Team Devereaux, dismounted, along the road in late afternoon to Paschal, where the Team took over without opposition. Moving out quickly, Devereaux and his Tigers forced their way up to Hill 508 and silenced a German crew manning a battery of direct-fire weapons. Along with the two objectives, a total of 158 prisoners was bagged.

That same night saw a new commander of the Task Force take over, as Colonel William L. Roberts ordered Major Warren B. Haskell, executive officer of the 54th Armored Infantry Battalion, to lead CC B's attack on Trier. Shortly before midnight, Haskell, who had been carefully briefed by Richardson's staff, directed Team Kafkalis to attack Obersehr. From the high ground to the south, the town was subjected to a determined Tiger infantry advance, while to the southeast, a platoon of Tenth Armored tanks crawled forward towards the town. The Germans put up a sizzling fight by setting up a battery of 80 mm mortars and machine gun positions in the houses. Despite these measures, Kafkalis overpowered 80 Germans and captured the town, aided by tank and artillery fire. Immediately the enemy plastered the Team with 105 mm mortars and artillery fire from the northeast and east. This appeared to be a last-ditch effort on the part of the Germans to hold back the invaders' attempt to capture Trier. In the early hours of the morning of February 28, Kafkalis sent out reconnaissance from Obersehr to take a look at the enemy situation. After a while they returned with the information that the town was protected by a mine belt which, in turn, was covered by artillery and machine gun fire. From south of Pellingen to Ollmuth and over the high ground north of Niedersehr, the entire area was covered with mines. Kafkalis put his infantry under cover. Then he set out with his attached 55th Armored Engineers platoon to free a pathway along the road through the mines.

Tankers go "over the hill" in the big assault on ancient Trier.

BURSTS IN AIR

As they approached the field, the Germans covered them with heavy machine gun fire and filled the air with artillery air bursts. Despite strong opposition, the platoon cleared a path through the minefield, but not without severe losses. Both Kafkalis and the engineer platoon leader were wounded, along with 40 per cent of the platoon. After that, Lieut. Cook took over and forged ahead to establish a bridgehead through the minefield. The area finally was breached in the afternoon, although Lieut. Cook was wounded and had to be evacuated.

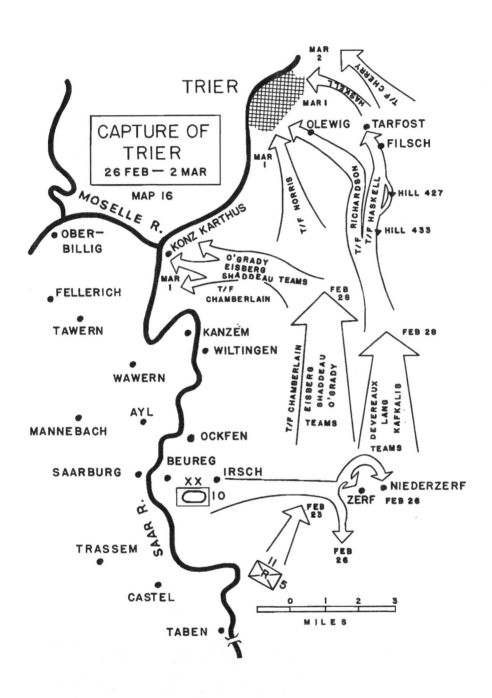

CAPTURE OF
TRIER
26 FEB — 2 MAR

MAP 16

Now that the big obstacle had been surmounted, the mission of Task Force Haskell was to move on Trier. Team Lang rumbled through the minefield and led what was left of the Task Force along the road to Trier. However, from east and west, this route was under constant observation and artillery fire, and the going was rough all the way. Not to be stopped, Lang's Tigers moved out along the ridge line on the evening of February 27. As they reached a point just south of Hill 433, the head of the column lost a tank and several halftracks to strong German artillery fire from the east. Doggedly the column pushed on and finally reached a position opposite Hill 427, where it pulled in for the night for much-needed rest and to lick its wounds. Unknown to Lang, the position was but a scant hundred yards from a hidden German gun battery position. At 0300 the battery suddenly opened up on Lang's position. Luckily, the enemy position was in defilade, and their guns could not be depressed sufficiently to bring direct fire on his vehicles. Sensing this, the Germans set their fuses for artillery air bursts and wounded 15 Tigers. The Task Force held its fire to locate specific targets. Two appeared in the form of machine gunners who sent a steady stream of hot lead straight down the road at the Tigers. At the same time, the enemy unleashed an attack from the east. Lang's riflemen took care of the German infantry, as two halftracks trained their 50 cal. machine guns on the enemy positions and wiped them out. However, in the morning, our two halftracks were knocked out by German 88's, which apparently sighted on them during the night and waited until daylight to finish the job.

Recon cars traverse "Cut Off" west of Ober Zerf

Major Haskell hurried in to get the enemy battery on Hill 427. He sent B Company of the 54th Armored Infantry to circle to the right in order to get behind the hill. At the same time, two tank destroyers stalked in behind the battery's south flank. As the Germans poured their fire to the west, the tank destroyers surprised them with some of their own medicine. The result was 30 prisoners, four 88's and 12 automatic guns.

During the night, urgent orders were transmitted to Haskell by Colonel Roberts of Combat Command B to drive toward Trier as quickly as possible. At daybreak, February 28, Team Lang led the Task Force out of its position. While the main body travelled along the ridge road, the Task Force teams peeled off to the right into Filsch and Tarforst to prevent the occupants of these towns from threatening the flanks. On their way, the Teams and the main body were hit hard by direct fire from the northwest. The shooting came from the high ground east of Trier. Within minutes, the enemy 105's destroyed five halftracks and an armored car. Nevertheless, the column continued smashing its way towards the big objective ahead. Both Filsch and Tarforst were captured, and B Company of the 54th Armored hauled in five 88's and 40 prisoners on the slopes of the terrain east of Tarforst. Here Captain Devereaux and his executive officer were wounded by artillery fire.

After this action, Haskell had only four tanks and five halftracks in operation. Infantry losses were severe, and ahead was the main objective—Trier. To bolster his force, Haskell converted wire men, platoonmen from the assault guns and Headquarters men into infantry. What was left of B and C Companies and the Headquarters Detachment was reformed as infantry support under Captain Lang.

PRESS COMMUNIQUE

28 Feb. '45.

"Tonight the Tenth Armored "Tiger" Division stands on the threshold of Trier—leading elements at a late hour were less than two miles from the city—with four task forces moving steadily along the high ground overlooking this important communications and supply center. Behind the imminent capture of Trier lies a story of bold tactical operation. Eight days ago the division was given the sole mission of clearing the Saar-Moselle Triangle — a mission that was accomplished in two days, catching the Germans so completely by surprise that orders were suddenly issued for the Tenth Armored to cross the Saar. On the fourth day, Feb. 23, the 376th Regiment of the 94th Division, attached to the Tenth, was put across the river in assault boats under heavy artillery, machine gun and sniper fire and seized high ground around that area, in the vicinity of Ockfen. On Feb. 24, three armored infantry battalions of the Tenth crossed in assault boats at the same point and moved on foot toward Irsch, which they attacked from the northwest. Meanwhile, the division's CC B crossed the river on a pontoon bridge built by the 94th at Taben— earlier attempts to lay a bridge in the vicinity of Ayl had been blocked by heavy enemy fire—and drove northward, attacking Irsch simultaneously from the south. In a striking demonstration of the flexibility of an armored division, the armored doughboys then jumped into halftracks other than their own, since speed was of utmost importance. Some of the infantrymen were then rushed to the heights dominating Irsch, and dropped off to protect the advance of CC A—following close behind CC B—toward Zerf. CC B went on to Zerf, took the town and placed a task force on the high ground around it so that CC A could make its all-important turning movement to the north, toward Trier. When CC A had turned northward at the Zerf elbow, CC B then followed closely behind, making a parallel drive. The headlong drive of the two combat commands, eastward into the enemy defenses and then suddenly northward, thereby exposing both flanks, was an exceptionally daring act which has proven to be well worth the gamble. Tonight CC R was moved up under cover of darkness behind CC A and CC B, and the entire division is now moving up the southern approaches within striking distance of Trier. Authenticated: C. H. King, Major, Asst. G-3."

—Nichols

TASK FORCES TEE OFF

On February 27, the tanks and vehicles of the Reserve Command crossed at Saarburg. Task Force Cherry moved forward on the right flank of the zone of advance and during the next day cleared the area of the Ruwer River and provided cover for the flank.

While the battle was smoking around Trier, Combat Command A's Task Force Richardson was freed from protecting Zerf from possible enemy counter-attacks and joined the assault on Trier. Using the valley road through Olewig, the Task Force threaded its way between Task Force Haskell and Task Force Norris. In the afternoon of March 1, Richardson moved to the crossroad west of Lapaden from Zerf. Here the Task Force paused momentarily while waiting for further orders from Combat Command B. Soon Richardson was told that Trier was to be hit that night by the entire Division. Further, he was informed, "get into Trier tonight and seize intact, if possible, the two key bridges over the Moselle." At 2200 on March 1, Richardson uncoiled his Armoraiders and darted towards the city.

Digging in prior to the flaming battle for Trier

PRESS COMMUNIQUE

28 Feb. '45.

"Four task forces of the Tenth Armored "Tiger" Division, commanded by Major General William H. H. Morris, Jr., seized high ground south of Trier Wednesday night, overlooking the city which at some points was less than three miles away. Elements of the Division supporting these task forces ran a gauntlet of intense enemy crossfire the past two days on the road from Irsch to Zerf, already famed as "88 Alley." Despite murderous enemy fire on this alley, the entire division is moving in for the kill at the important communications and supply center of Trier. The slashing attack of the Tenth Armored, first to the east to Zerf and then, suddenly, to the north toward Trier, brought high words of praise for the Division from Lieut. Gen. George S. Patton, who visited the division command post today. Summing up the operation, which gave the Germans a new destructive version of their vaunted Blitz-Krieg, General Patton declared: 'Daring Operation, well executed.' The 3rd Army Commander had reference to the strategy whereby the Tenth Armored's CC B first crossed the Saar River in the vicinity of Saarburg Sunday afternoon and fought on to capture Zerf the next day. On Monday, CC A followed behind CC B and passed it at Zerf, which became the pivot, or "Elbow", for the entire division's drive northward toward Trier. CC B, after providing security on the high ground overlooking Zerf for CC A, then shot to the north and the two combat commands are now making parallel drives two miles apart, on a line stretching from north of the town of Pellingen and north of Ollmuth. These elements banged headlong eastward into the enemy, and then turned at Zerf to the north, an exceedingly dangerous operation which exposed their flanks on both sides. Pellingen fell to the fast-advancing tanks of Task Force Chamberlain today. Four other towns fell to Task Force Haskell: Hertern, Lampaden, Obersehr, and Niedersehr. This increases to 50 the number of towns taken by the Tenth Armored since Tuesday, February 20. In the past 24 hours, nearly 1000 additional prisoners have also been captured." —Nichols

TRIER APPROACHED

On February 28, "Steve" Lang's Tigers under CC B control, pushed their way to the hill east of Trier. Enemy barracks there were filled with allied prisoners and impressed laborers. By nightfall, the area was in our hands, and a big ammunition dump in the vicinity was fired. The big, efficient Lang, impatient to be moving, made up his mind to wait no longer. Lining up his tanks, he raced down the hill and struck the city from the northeast in a night blitz despite the threat that the city was heavily mined. At the edge of the town, the Team ran into a roadblock which was dismantled piece by piece. All of this was accomplished in the quiet of the darkness to enable the Team to maintain an element of surprise.

TANKERS CRASH INTO TRIER
WITH THE 10TH ARMORED DIVISION IN GERMANY,

March 1 (INS)by Larry Newman—"Rampaging tank and infantry fighters of the U. S. Third Army's 10th Armored Division crashed into the historic German city of Trier from three directions and swept ahead to cut off hundreds of Wehrmacht soldiers northeast of Saarburg.

"Armored and infantry combat teams under Lieut. Col. Henry Cherry of Macon, Ga., Lieut. Col. Raymond Riley of Danville, Va., and Major Warren Haskell of Lee, Maine, brought to a climax one of the most daring assaults of the war. Engineers under Major William Geiler, Flushing, L. I., N. Y., led the engineers who cut out a forest road with bulldozers to allow the American armor to by-pass the heavy German artillery fire."

TRIER ENTERED

By 0400 on March 1, Lang's Tigers were inside Trier. The entire northeast section was deserted, and by 0730 the northern section of the city was in our hands.

In the meantime, Teams O'Grady and Shaddeau of Task Force Chamberlain, Combat Command A, were perched at 0800 on March 1 on the twin peaks that dominated Konz-Karthus on the eastern banks of the Moselle. That place was blasted for an hour, after which Team Eisberg's doughs sliced into and captured Konz-Karthus. After that feat, the Task Force guarded the left flank without further trouble.

From the vicinity of Niedermennig, Task Force Norris rolled out towards Trier. During the afternoon, the force reached the outskirts of the important rail and communications center. For the rest of the day, Norris held his Tigers in check there. On March 2, the Norrismen charged into Trier to help Richardson clear the area.

PRESS COMMUNIQUE

1 March 1945

"The Tenth Armored "Tiger" Division entered Trier today at 1250 when task forces fought their way into the southern section of this important communications and supply center, which is the oldest city in Germany. Meanwhile, the Tenth Armored also cut the main highway at the junction of the Saar and Ruwer Rivers in the vicinity of the town of Ruwer, little more than a mile northeast of Trier. Thus the main avenue of escape for the enemy to the north and northeast has been cut off by the Tenth. Other task forces are at this moment fighting in the outskirts of Trier, rapidly moving into the city. Today at 1200, the main power cable leading from Zerf to Trier was severed by the 150th Signal Company of the Tenth Armored. Over 800 prisoners were captured today by this division up until 1700 this afternoon, and the towns of Wiltingen, Oberemmel, Krettnach-Obermennig and Tarforst were captured by the Tenth this afternoon. Total numbers of towns now taken in this operation by the Tenth Armored is 54, and the total bag of prisoners has been swelled to 3900. End. Authenticated by G-3, Tenth Armored Division."

—Nichols

Artillery's M-7 gets firing data for bombardment of Trier

RICHARDSON ROLLS

Task Force Richardson, in the meantime, had left its position at the crossroads west of Lampaden in the early hours of March 1. Leading the column of Tigers was Captain "Bud" Billet. Following him were Team Riley and Headquarters Company. A full moon provided excellent visibility on February 28, as the column raced on to Irsch where an unusual roadblock faced them. Three big 88's loomed ahead, causing the lead tank to belch two rounds of 75's at the site. However, by this time, the Germans wanted no part of the Tigers and left the 88's unmanned. In the village, the German garrison readily surrendered and was put to work dismantling the roadblock which it had erected only a short time before. Off again, the column swung through Olewig and burst right on to the city limits of Trier. A company of German infantry and four anti-tank guns were captured without firing a single round at a railroad crossing within the city limits. It was readily apparent that the Americans were not expected in this area, and fortunately, this factor enabled the Tiger Teams to nab the careless enemy infantry in the nick of time. In addition, one of the prisoners taken confessed that he had neglected to notify a German demolition detail on the far side of the railroad bridge of the Tigers' arrival. Things were looking up for the attackers as they gained valuable time at the expense of the loafing Germans.

179

NO REST

Staff Sergeant Don Jerge and his halftrack crew have long memories of Trier and the long, bloody road leading to its capture. His outfit had just got the call again to "Load up; we're pulling out in ten minutes," and in the platoon every man had the same reaction: "Can't they let us have any rest?" But, automatically they shrugged into their coats and rifle belts and piled into the halftracks. The moon had come up, and it was growing dark as the column started off. Each man experienced the same feeling every GI had when he went into battle, whether it was for the first or the 100th time: "What will it be this time?"

The column moved along without event until, suddenly, the whine of shells was heard in the distance. The Germans had found the range, and as usual, had the road zeroed in. Shells began landing all around the column, and a tank got a direct hit. Jerge received a radio message telling his platoon to move up to the head of the column, and the platoon pushed ahead, firing everything it had. Then a shell hit the left track of Jerge's vehicle, and all the occupants piled out.

Someone shouted for the medics, and a squad leader asked Jerge if he thought he could get back to the track and radio for help. Jerge and four of his buddies started for the vehicle and had almost reached it when a sixth sense told Jerge to hit the dirt. As he hugged the ground, a shell landed close by, wounding two of his buddies and killing a third. The radio was forgotten as Jerge helped load the two wounded men onto a tank.

The platoon was widely scattered by this time, and the survivors dug in for the night. Next morning the doughs rode on tanks to a high ridge overlooking the town of Pellingen while the rest of the Command fought a bitter battle on the main road to town.

Next afternoon they headed for Trier. Not a shot was fired at them as they descended the steep hill leading into the ancient city. The phase was ended.

ROMER BRIDGE CAPTURED INTACT

When Col. Richardson entered Trier on March 1, he had already made up his mind to go after the northern bridge first rather than risk having the nearer southern bridge blown upon arrival. Team Billet was designated to stab at the northern bridge. Following was Team Riley whose job it was to try and grab the southern span. "Bud" Billet reported at 0200 that the northern bridge was blown, whereupon Richardson dispatched Team Riley post haste to get the southern bridge. Riley raced on the road along the Moselle, hardly daring to hope that the bridge would 'still be standing. When he got to the site, he saw that the structure was still intact. Hurriedly, he radioed Richardson, "Bridge intact. Am receiving small arms fire." Richardson gave quick instructions to Riley, dropped the phone and dashed to the span to direct its capture. He sent a platoon of tanks and a platoon of dismounted doughs led by Lieut. Wilbur Beadle, Jr., speeding across to the western side of the bridge. These hardy Tigers knew that they were treading over momentary death. They expected the structure to blow up in their faces. But death took another holiday, fortunately, and they safely reached the other side where they grabbed a German major and five helpers who, too late, were hurrying with detonator caps and an exploder. The great 2000-year-old Romer bridge was ours!

West side of Romer Bridge used for assembling Nazi PW's

BACCHANALIAN BOOB

STARS AND STRIPES - WITH THE TENTH ARMORED DIVISION—"A Nazi hero, who sat in a barroom while forces smashed toward the bridge he was to protect, fiddled just long enough with his glass to enable the Tenth Armored "Tiger" Division to capture intact the strategically located Romer bridge across the Moselle at Trier. Before the drunken officer could give the order to blow the bridge, Task Force Richardson of the Tenth had taken it—and him—and established a bridgehead from which later offensives were to be launched. When Colonel William L. Roberts, commander of Combat Command B and his Task Force staff, planned its capture, they had not counted on an ally in the ranks of the enemy."

Not included in the Stars and Stripes story was the interesting information that the German major, remorseful that he had failed in his duty, and wishing to hide this fact, led his captors to seventeen other German officers who were revelling in another house. All were taken in tow. Never were prisoners apparently in so happy a frame of mind as this group of inebriated Nazis as they were led to the Tenth Armored PW cage.

Snipers routed by Armoraiders

FLAG RAISED

By James Cannon, Stars and Stripes Staff Writer

WITH TENTH ARMORED DIVISION, Trier, Germany, March 2—"The Porta Nigra arch, built in 275 A.D., was in better shape than most of Trier, which fell today to this armored division.

"Attacking with five columns of infantry and tanks, the Tenth reached the outskirts of Trier yesterday at noon, and 24 hours later Capt. Robert Wilson raised an American flag that his wife had sent him from Newark, N. J., over the Porta Nigra hotel.

"Ignoring snipers, Lt. Col. Jack Richardson, of Athens, Texas, led a task force through the town to take one of the two bridges over the Moselle intact. Lieut. Wilbur Beadle, Jr., led a force of armor and infantry across the bridge to secure it."

DYNAMITE BELOW

After the bridge was taken, the 55th Engineers cut all the wires and removed two tons of dynamite from underneath the structure. Then Task Force Richardson turned its attention to clearing the city to the east from the Moselle. More than 800 German troops were scooped up as they came out of the houses in the morning ready to defend a city that had already been overrun! Richardson's command post was set up in the center of the city at dawn. Just across the street from the CP, a group of Germans sauntered out of a house to help defend Trier. They, too, were much too late to help.

SCRANTON TIMES

WITH THE TENTH ARMORED DIVISION IN GERMANY—"Sgt. Vernon Smith and Cpl. Eugene M. Dutchak of Co. B, 21st Tank Battalion, hated to seem rude and break up the little party—but, this is war, they reasoned. The two tankers were busily engaged in the pleasant task of flushing out Germans from houses in Trier. They opened the door to a room in one house and caught three very surprised Jerries—who were having breakfast in bed."

183

CLEAN UP

While Task Force Richardson held the Moselle River line within the city limits and the bridge it had seized, Haskell and Norris tooth-combed the town in a house-to-house search which ended all further resistance. At this juncture, General Morris summoned the 376th Infantry to help occupy the city and evacuate prisoners.

OLDEST CITY

Tenth Armored Division troops who fought into Trier found a city rich in historical and religious lore. The city, known to the French as Treves, is considered Germany's oldest and contains more important Roman remains than any other place in northern Europe. Its oldest and best-known remains include piers and buttresses of the bridge over the Mosel said to date from 28 B.C.

One of the most successful and spectacular battles of the war was over. The Tenth Armored's combat performance in this operation was eminently successful. Detailed planning, high morale and fighting ability all contributed to the significant victory in the Saar-Moselle Triangle and in the capture of Trier. Few of us realized at the time that the Tenth Armored had a leading role in one of the three most important phases of the entire war. In a signed statement at Nurnberg later, Marshal Herman Goering and Field Marshal Jodl declared that, "the capture of Trier was other two, they believed, were the successful Normandy invasion and the speedy crossing of the Rhine.

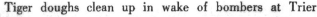

Tiger doughs clean up in wake of bombers at Trier

Adolph Hitler Platz and
Porta Nigra Arch

EISENHOWER VISIT

While the Tigers battled their way north towards Wittlich, after capturing Trier, the Division Headquarters occupied a large modern building which shortly before had served as an SS headquarters for the Germans in Trier. During the morning of March 7, Sergeant "Herb" Dynan of the G-3 Section, while standing at a window, noted the approach of Major General Walton Walker. Turning quickly to Lieut. Col. John W. Sheffield, he announced, "Colonel, here comes the Corps Commander." Then, observing the arrival of additional vehicles in the courtyard, he exclaimed, "The Army Commander is with him." By the time Sheffield had joined Dynan, the latter let out a whoop and proclaimed, "Believe it or not, here comes the Supreme Commander too."

Moments later, the three distinguished Generals entered the Headquarters, and before Sheffield knew it, Colonel Joseph A. McChristian popped into the room with the visitors. Without a moment's hesitation, the Chief of Staff said, "Colonel Sheffield, tell the Supreme Commander how the Tenth Armored took Trier." After getting his wits collected, the G-3 outlined the Division's brilliant combat operation to General Eisenhower. When he had finished, General Patton, with a twinkle in his eye, turned to his Corps Commander and told him, "Johnny, if it hadn't been for the Tenth Armored Division, I would have relieved you." Not knowing whether to take his superior seriously or not, the diminutive

185

Corps Commander heard General Eisenhower remark, "Well, Georgie, if it hadn't been for the Tenth Armored, I might have done a little relieving myself." When the good-natured by-play ended, the Supreme Commander shook hands with everyone and complimented the entire staff for its masterful planning.

Trier rout completed

By the time the visitors left Tiger Headquarters, word had quickly gotten around of the Supreme Commander's visit. Though he was in a hurry, General Eisenhower stopped to talk with the Tigers. He asked if any were from Kansas and posed with two Tigers from that State who stepped forward. To a man, everyone was impressed with his unpretentious and warm personality. His visit to Trier brought to mind a rumor which had been widely circulated. Eisenhower supposedly sent a directive to Patton on March 2. In it, Patton was ordered to "By-pass Trier to the south . . . it will take four divisions to capture it." The Third Army Commander immediately radioed General Eisenhower with the news that he had just taken Trier with one armored division, adding, "What the hell do you want me to do . . . give it back to the bastards?"

VIII

SWEEPING THE WITTLICH CORRIDOR

ORIGINALLY, THE TENTH ARMORED'S battle plan called only for clearing the Saar-Moselle Triangle. However, the blazing speed with which the Tigers achieved their objectives in the Triangle made it possible for the Division to go a step further to include the capture of Trier. At first Corps and Army commanders had not considered crossing the Moselle at Trier. But because of quick thinking on the part of Colonel Richardson and his battle teams in capturing the Romer Bridge just before it was to be destroyed, the Tenth's combat operation was extended to include crossing the Moselle to launch an armored drive north to Wittlich.

To this end Task Force Cherry and another Tiger force led by Major Curtis L. Hankins rumbled over the "Romans Bridge," wheeled eastward, and by March 8, had battled their way to within six miles of the Division's objective at Wittlich. Churning ahead, Tiger combat units led by Major "Red" Hankins sealed off Wittlich from the east, as Lieut. Col. Cherry's tankers fought their way into that city on March 10. From Wittlich, Task Force Cherry barrelled ahead an additional ten miles to Bullay, in an effort to seize the bridge there. Thwarted in this attempt because Germans had already blown the objective, the Task Force had to content itself by clawing a 50 vehicle enemy convoy near the Mosel. On March 12, the mission was ended, allowing Cherry and his Tigers to join the remainder of the Division for the race, four days later, across the Palatinate to the Rhine. Swift battle movements such as these had previously earned for the Tigers the name "Ghost Division" by the Germans.

Before the Tenth Armored unleashed its Tigers eastward to the Rhine, it completed the task of sealing off a 44 mile pocket on the west bank of the Moselle. While Cherry and Hankins ground their way to Wittlich, Combat Command B and the Reserve Command rumbled over the centuries-old Romer Bridge built by Augustus Caesar's Tenth Legion. Here the Moselle becomes the Mosel. Unconcerned with the River's change of spelling, Tigers of the Tenth with tremendous force of impact drove the Germans across the Kyle River, a Mosel tributary, near Ehrang, which was located about three miles north of Trier. Covering the attack of the two combat commands was Task Force Haskell, which trailed the fast-moving Piburn and Gatchell Armoraiders as the latter's command banged through the 76th Infantry's bridgehead across the Kyle some six miles above Ehrang and the former's tanks and doughs circled behind Combat Command B, streaked across the Kyle River and headed for Wittlich.

Two white rabbits fared better than the Germans as the Tankers push along the Kyle River to capture Ehrang

PRESSURE RELIEVED

In the south the bewildered enemy folded like an accordian before Colonel Roberts' savage attack, permitting both Combat Command B and the Reserve Command to wheel back to the Kyle at Ehrang. Here the Division lost another fine Tiger combat leader in the person of Captain Holehouse. When the initial crossing via foot bridge was made at the Kyle near Ehrang, Holehouse's Company A of the 20th Armored Infantry Battalion pushed into that town to establish a bridgehead to give the engineers time to repair the main bridge. Waiting to cross on the far side were our tanks—desperately needed to back up Holehouse and his Tigers in the bridgehead. But work progressed at a snail's pace on the bridge, giving the Germans time to mount a terrific attack against the doughs in Ehrang. Captain Holehouse was killed, and his Company suffered heavy casualties as a result of the enemy attack. Shortly afterwards, Task Force Haskell of the Reserve Command crossed the Kyle and knocked the Germans from the hills. Proceeding to the high ground overlooking Schweich, the Command swept the enemy there too and looked down into the town from the heights to see Task Force Chamberlain enter it on March 10.

"OPEN CITY"

Colonel Luebberman's big guns were silent as a result of the German declaration that Schweich was now an "open city." The enemy message to the Division stated that the town was "undefended and sheltered 3,000 wounded Germans." But when Task Force Chamberlain entered Schweich, they found a devastating array of 88's, mined streets, and instead of 3,000 wounded—they found but two German casualties. Nettled by the big lie, the tankers quickly seized Schweich. Shortly afterwards, the acerbic Germans rained a steady stream of shells into that "open city." Enemy treachery resulted in heavy Tiger casualties there as the bombardment took its toll. Later in the day, Colonel Wade C. Gatchell's Reserve Command Headquarters moved into Schweich.

189

Then, after two days of fighting, the Germans were encircled and neutralized, allowing the task forces to return to Trier on March 11 in advance of Cherry's raiders. In eight days, four task forces had spearheaded some forty miles over terrain completely unfavorable for armored operations. In addition, the pocket created by Combat Command A was sealed tightly. When Cherry's command retraced its steps to Germany's oldest city on March 12, the cycle was complete. Four days later, on March 16, the Tiger Division sprung into action once again in a drive from the Saar to the Rhine in the area known as the Palatinate.

Tiger Recon forces roll past enemy roadblock on their way to Ehrang, located three miles above Trier

During this interim, Colonel Roberts was summoned to General Patton's Headquarters in Luxembourg. Upon arrival, Patton lauded the genial Roberts for his outstanding leadership in the Tenth Armored. Then the surprised Roberts was informed of his promotion to the rank of brigadier general and of his new assignment to the Fourth Armored Division. The veteran commander returned to Trier, where he decorated Lieut. Col. "Jack" J. Richardson with the Silver Star. Several bottles of choice Moselle wines were produced by Colonel Roberts for the occasion, which was attended by all of Combat Command B's battalion commanders. At the affair, one of the G-3 liaison officers related an incident which took place only a few days before when Combat Command B was fighting to get across the Kyle River. When

the officer reached Colonel Roberts' command post, located halfway from the Romer Bridge to Ehrang and about 1200 yards from
the front lines, he delivered a note to the Commander from General Morris. Its contents suggested that Roberts move his headquarters to the front lines. The latter raised his eyes from the
map he was studying and told the young liaison officer, "You go
back and ask Bill Morris if he wants my posterior shot off—or
my brain back here to run this operation." Fortunately, the Division Commander's attention was diverted to other more pressing
battle problems, and Colonel Roberts answer was never delivered
to him.

GREATEST FIGHTERS

Before he left for his new command assignment, Brig. Gen.
Roberts, in salty fashion, described the Saar-Moselle-Trier-Witt-
lich battles. He recalled, "Keeping track of the task forces and
trying to coordinate them was difficult. It was nothing but confusion, chaos, killing, loss of equipment, patching up units—and
getting along somehow with what we had left." He added, "We
were lucky that Richardson escaped serious losses on the roads
as he rolled in darkness, but then, that's one way to get by the
enemy's guns and troops." As for Trier, he continued, "When
Lieut. Col. Roberts and I went forward to Task Force Riley's
Headquarters, we found it completely shot. Only one lieutenant
was left, as Jack Riley was knocked out with battle fatigue, and
his executive officer had been killed the night before, and we
took command and stayed there in the rain.

Tenth Armored machine
gunners and riflemen push
forward to the Kyle River
near Ehrang

"Pressure on us to keep the heat on the Germans mounted steadily, and by early evening, General Morris radioed me to push my units into Trier. About this time, Richardson reached my location at Riley's CP, hoping to knock off for a time to rest his bedraggled command. Instead, I was forced to direct him to continue his attack to the heart of Trier." Then, Roberts noted that "after a two-hour briefing, Jack Richardson shoved off with a plan to split his column after entry into Trier in order to reach the bridges simultaneously." Roberts recalls that at 0500 "a faint radio message reached him with the astounding news that the Romer Bridge was captured." "General Morris," Roberts concluded, "came into Trier with me, the next morning, and set the Division into motion across the captured bridge to exploit our good fortune. After a few days' operations in the north, Combat Command B returned to Trier, where I left the greatest fighters I've ever seen, for service in the Fourth Armored."

Tiger doughs stalk enemy troops hiding in wrecked building at Fohren

IX

RACE TO THE RHINE

ON MARCH 12, 1945, after having clawed German troops in the Wittlich Corridor north of Trier, Tigers of the Tenth Armored returned to that ancient city for a much-earned four day rest. During that time, the Armoraiders visited the old Roman Coliseum, the Porta Nigra Arch and other historic Roman remains in and around the once-beautiful city of Trier. One building in particular proved to be more popular than all the rest and was visited many times by almost every Tiger. This was the building that contained many thousands of bottles of fine champagne—left behind by the Germans in their hurry to avoid being trapped by the Division at Trier. Unfortunately, an unthinking Air Corps bombardier was responsible for a gaping hole down through the middle of the building as one of his bombs fell straight and true some days before. The damage to the building, however, did not deter the Tigers in their search for unbroken bottles of champagne. The writer, wishing to become a "big shot" with the war correspondents of the U. S. Third Army at Luxembourg, sent ten cases of the stuff to their press camp as a gift from the Division. In anticipation of the prized loot, the war reporters arranged an elaborate party at their hotel in Luxembourg. Some days later, the writer visited the press camp there expecting red carpet treatment but instead was ushered to the street in a fashion not befitting one who had been so thoughtful only a few days before. Moments later, the awful truth was learned by the writer. The party was a dismal failure. The gift champagne was "green" and tasted worse than the very strongest kind of calvados.

On March 16, the Tigers' brief vacation was ended. From the area south of Trier at Zerf, the entire Division was catapulted in a new drive to the Rhine. The area between the Saar and Rhine Rivers comprises Germany's vast Palatinate belt. In the region were two powerful enemy armies of about 100,000 men. To get to the Rhine, Tigers of the Tenth Armored were to be called upon to deal with an endless series of enemy pillboxes, barbed wire, anti-tank ditches, dragons' teeth, roadblocks and, toughest of all, well-trained German troops.

By mid-March, 1945, the Palatinate constituted Germany's only sizable holdings west of the Rhine River. Their vital coal and steel industrial centers were soon to change hands, at least what was to be left of them. Most important, from the Tenth Armored's viewpoint, was the fact that despite enemy entrenchment behind natural defensive positions, the enemy no longer could take cover for long, behind formidable defenses as in the case of the heavily fortified Saar-Moselle Triangle.

RACE TO THE RHINE

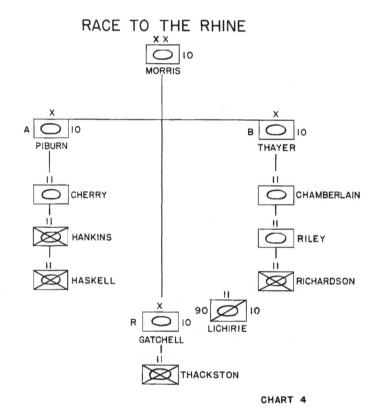

CHART 4

From Zerf, southeast of Trier, the Tigers burst out into the open and, almost without stopping, were to eat up the kilometers all the way to the Brenner Pass.

First objective for the Tenth Armored's rampaging tanks and infantry was St. Wendel, important communications center some 30 miles from southeast of Trier. Led by Combat Command A, the Division attack got under way at 0300 on March 16. Following Piburn's command was Combat Command B which rumbled ahead half an hour later. As darkness closed in, both spearheads were 20 kilometers from Trier.

On March 17, Task Forces Cherry and Hankins of CC A knifed their way to the Prims River. Here the Tigers were hit by strong enemy small arms and artillery fire, but pushed on after the 55th Engineers had spanned the small river. They slammed forward all the way to Castel, some eight miles northwest of St. Wendel, where they captured a bridge intact.

In the meantime, the 90th Cavalry, led by Lt. Col. Cornelius Lichirie, pushed south to protect Tiger flanks and to contact the 26th Infantry Division. To the north, CC B's Task Forces Chamberlain, Riley and Richardson ground their way to within four miles north of St. Wendel. As Chamberlain pushed eastward, Riley and Richardson wheeled south toward the Division objective at St. Wendel.

SEARCHLIGHT ATTACK

A few minutes after midnight, on March 17, both combat commands struck out in a coordinated assault, utilizing searchlights to light up the battleground. Against very stubborn resistance, the advance was slowed during the day, but by dusk on March 18, Cherry managed to reach the outskirts of St. Wendel. At this time, the other task forces had knifed their way to within three miles of the city. Teams from Task Force Hankins ploughed forward towards the Division's first big objective at St. Wendel. Before they reached that place however, they had to clear Castel.

RACE TO THE RHINE
MARCH 21, 1945

MAP 17

Here, Team Hyduke of Company A, Third Tank Battalion and Team Holland of Company B, Sixty-First Armored Infantry Battalion entered with little resistance. But, as if at a given signal, four enemy tanks bolted out of barns and other hiding places to knock out three Tiger Mediums. Lieut. Edward of Team Holland assisted by Sergeant Oscar Messer destroyed three German tanks with the aid of bazookas and the fourth escaped in a hail of fire. Then Team Hyduke was ordered to push the attack on to St. Wendel, some ten miles away. At 2300, with Lieut. Bernard Connolly leading, Team Hyduke shoved off on March 17. This drive was aided greatly by large anti-aircraft searchlights which were just as effective as bright moonlight. At dawn, the Team by-passed a roadblock and entered Guttan. Shortly afterwards, as Connolly led his Tigers out of the eastern end of the town, a German tank, hiding behind a barn, opened fire at a distance of only 15 yards but missed its target. Gunner Stanley Wisniewski immediately retaliated and destroyed the Mark V. Later as the column rolled down the road toward St. Wendel, the lead tank almost ran into an enemy anti-tank position. Before the Germans could man their gun, it was knocked out by a well-placed shot. At Harthien, Team Havlowitz of Company C, Sixty-First Armored Infantry, took over the lead. And when it reached the outskirts of St. Wendel, this Team lost its two lead tanks as a result of enemy anti-tank fire. At this point, Team Holland was directed to flank the enemy guns, but in so doing, it too, lost two of its Mediums. Then Team Hyduke initiated a reconnaissance to locate the enemy strongpoint. After brief probing, it located four murderous enemy 88's which were soon destroyed by Lieut. Connolly's platoon. After this action, Team Hyduke barrelled on to St. Wendel.

Give up—or be burned up!

On March 19, the combined power of our assaulting forces drove the Germans out of St. Wendel. Without stopping, Cherry and Chamberlain raced on twenty miles to the east. Supporting them on the flank was Colonel Gatchell's Reserve Command. CC R's Armoraiders kept pace with the other two attacking commands as all three blasted aside everything in their path in their headlong race to the Rhine. By March 20, the attack was fast producing a rout as the enemy fell or retreated before the savage Tenth Armored drive which propelled itself through Kaiserslautern. The big industrial city was in the path of Patton's streaming tank and infantry divisions. Formerly a supply center for the German army, its population of 100,000 was left for the doughs of the 80th Infantry Division which mopped up after the Tiger Division.

Tigers push through burning Geiselhardt

Tankers make good use of Hitler's famed autobahn

Before Kaiserslautern was captured however, forces of both the Tenth Armored and 80th Infantry Divisions raced eastward on all four lanes of Hitler's famed Autobahn in an effort to be the first to enter that city. Separating the superhighway's lanes was a broad grassy area which was utilized by the retreating enemy who waved little white flags at the doughs and the tankers as they streamed past them. First to reach Kaiserslautern were the Tigers of the Tenth who slammed through the city and continued the attack to the east. The Division's G-3 at this time prepared a message for Corps stating that the Tenth had captured Kaiserslautern. However, General Morris insisted that the message be destroyed so that the 80th Infantry would be credited with its capture. The Division Commander felt that since the doughs had done the dirty work of mopping up the city, they ought to be given recognition for its capture.

199

After racing through Kaiserslautern, Combat Command A banged eastward to the Rhine, while Combat Command B and the Reserve Command struck south to Annweiler, some twenty miles, to sever enemy escape routes to the Rhine. South of Kaiserslautern, the 90th Cavalry caught a German column on the road and with the aid of the Air Corps promptly wrecked everything in sight. Trucks, wagons, supplies and enemy were left in smoking ruins on the road which was so congested that for hours later it was virtually impassable. In this area, the Tiger's Recon Squadron held in check the entire German army which had been cut off by the Third Army drive to the Rhine, on the Tenth Armored's southern flank. Constant attacking by Lieut. Col. Lichirie's cavalrymen kept the retreating enemy from threatening the Tiger flanks.

Battering ram is used to drive enemy snipers from house

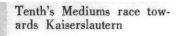
Tenth's Mediums race towards Kaiserslautern

Combat Command A's doughs catch retreating enemy in hail of fire while crossing open field

GERMANS RESIST

On March 21, the enemy paused to try to hold the onrushing Tigers. Again, they were unsuccessful. Task Force Cherry rumbled southward to Neustadt, where in an effort to knock out several of the enemy's biggest tanks, Lieut. Col. "Hank" Cherry was wounded and had to be evacuated. Fortunately, a medical officer was nearby to render immediate aid to Cherry who had been shot in the leg by a sniper. The bullet had severed an artery and probably would have caused the battalion commander's life were it not for the expert medical attention given him on the spot. Known as "King Tigers", the German tanks packed a terrific punch and it is believed that the Tenth Armored Division was the first to fight these iron monsters. In the area, one enemy tank was found which mounted a 120 millimeter gun. After a brief encounter, that tank was put out of action. At Neustadt, Cherry's forces operated beautifully as they outsmarted the enemy who preferred to defend that city from the east. Actually, Neustadt lies at the eastern end of a very deep valley and is located on the Rhine Plain and might have been held by the Germans for considerable time, had they chosen to defend it from its western approaches in the valley instead of falling back into the city itself to fight Cherry's Tigers.

Germans' supply column wrecked at Bad Durkheim
Right: Bulldozer clears path through wreckage for tankers

Elsewhere, the doughs and armor of Task Force Hankins bottled up an entire German army's supply trains at a point 15 miles west of the Rhine. Here, Hankins' Tigers destroyed 300 vehicles, five tanks and 15 artillery pieces. The devastation was fantastic. For days afterward, ammunition continued to explode and bulldozers had to clear a path through the wreckage on the road to permit further advance. Hearing of the unbelievable destruction, General Patton decided to visit the scene. Afterwards he commented that this was the most terrible destruction he had ever seen of a military column.

To the south, CC B and the Reserve Command moved steadily forward, reducing roadblocks and eliminating small arms and artillery fire on the way. Near Bad Durkheim, Task Force Haskell joined Task Force Hankins and together, they wheeled south on March 22 and raced to the Rhine on the north flank of the 12th Armored Division. Following the same route, a third task force, commanded by Major Wheeler M. Thackston, of the Reserve Command, bolted all the way to Landau, ten miles south of Neustadt. Thackston's Tigers assaulted the city from the north as Combat Command A's Chamberlain, Riley and Richardson slammed in from the west. On March 22, Landau was captured by the four attacking task forces.

TANKERS TRAVEL MINED ROAD

Sergeant Amos B. Danforth was in charge of an outpost after the capture of the city of Landau and the Sergeant decided that a little reconnaissance was in order. His little force reconnoitered to, and captured, the town of Offenbach. The Team commander received a message from the Sergeant advising that the road to Offenbach be cleared of mines before the tanks were brought there. Puzzled by how the Sergeant could report a road to be mined that he had already travelled, Lt. Henry E. Curtis sent out his engineers to verify the report.

The engineers found and cleared fifteen American anti-tank mines that had been captured and laid by the Germans. The half-track in Sgt. Danforth's column had run over one of the mines which had failed to explode. The engineers rendered their expert opinion in one word, "Miraculous."

Top: 61st Armored Infantry eliminate Germans in woods
Bottom: Downcast Germans return to their homes

Forty-eight hours after the capture of Landau, the giant trap set by the Tenth was closed. Against light resistance, the Division streaked out of Landau to the south to set up radio contact with the Fifth French Armored Division in General Patch's Seventh Army on March 23. On the following day, contact was made with the Seventh Army's 14th Armored and 36th Infantry Divisions which were driving north. All during the Tenth's lightning drive across the Palatinate, the missions of the Division were constantly being changed and each succeeding objective took the Tigers further south. Within gunshot of the Rhine, we found ourselves completely out of the United States Third Army boundary and in the Seventh Army area.

In the dwindling pocket, six armored divisions chewed up the retreating Germans and the Sixth Armored Division, driving north, crossed paths with the Tenth Armored just east of Kaiserslautern. This movement so intrigued "Time Magazine's" war correspondent that he wrote, "Armored divisions sometimes perform feats that would be textbook nightmares. Two Patton armored divisions once crossed each other at a right angle road junction in the midst of combat, but only the enemy were confused." Now that the Tenth was completely out of the United States Third Army's boundary zones, it was evident to higher commanders that steps would have to be taken to straighten out the situation. Consequently, on March 23, the Tenth was attached to the XXI Corps of the United States Seventh Army. In the big switch, the Third Army got General Patch's Sixth Armored Division. So imbued was General Patton in his intense desire to eliminate the enemy that he occasionally ignored boundaries. In this case he saw a golden opportunity to inflict heavy losses on the enemy by sending the Tenth Armored south into Seventh Army territory

"CONGRATULATIONS"

At this time it was rumored that General Patch had wired Patton the following note: "Congratulations on completely surrounding the entire United States Seventh Army". The reason why the Sixth Armored crossed Tenth Armored lines east of Kaiserslautern may be found in the factor that their objective was Worms—east and north of the Tenth's front. General Grow, who commanded the Sixth Armored, was formerly commander of the Tenth's CC A. At Kaiserslautern, he stomped into the Tenth's Command Post and collared Lieut. Col. Sheffield demanding, "What the hell is going on here." The latter explained the situation and showed the General the Tigers' plan of attack. As a result, the Sixth Armored was ordered off the road by General Grow for a well-earned rest. It was this unique situation which "Time Magazine" noted in its dispatches from the front.

In little more than a week, the Armoraiders kicked the Germans up one hill and down another through the 100 miles of the Hunsruck and Hardt mountains to the Rhine Valley and in the process, grabbed 8,000 prisoners from 26 different enemy divisions. Now the narrow escape corridor was sealed, cutting off the one avenue of retreat that the Germans had hoped to travel. The giant trap was now closed as the two American armies closed in at the Rhine River for the final phase of the long and costly struggle against the German armies.

Storied Frankenstein entered by Tenth's tank-infantry team

MISSION REVERSED

In XX Corps' initial planning, the Tenth was scheduled to lead Third Army's drive on its southern flank. The first objective was Mainz. But even as the Division rolled halfway across the Palatinate, its objective was changed. Now, Ludwigshaven became our target. However, our orders were revised for a third time as the Tenth was now assigned to capture Worms. This too, was altered as the Tigers' next goal was Speyer. But instead of Speyer, the Tenth wound up at Landau—only a few miles from the French border—and at the right flank of the U. S. Seventh Army! At this juncture, a wild-eyed Division staff officer noted that the Tenth had captured every immediate objective of the Seventh Army during the execution of our encircling movement. Despite the continuing changes in the battle plan however, the Tenth Armored managed to capture 8,000 enemy and cut off the escape routes for more than 50,000 additional Germans.

Now the Tigers had a brief four-day respite as they assembled near the summer palace of Ludwig, Bavaria's insane seven-foot former monarch, to wait for the call to roll across the Rhine. Later in the month, when they were to shove off to the attack again, the Tigers were to spearhead General Alexander Patch's Seventh Army drive all the way to the Bavarian and Austrian Alps. They were not to rejoin the Third Army again until the occupation of Southern Bavaria, three months later.

FAST-TALKING TIGER

One of the neatest bits of fast talking on record saved the day for Sergeant Robert Hedtke, of the Engineer Rcn Platoon, 55th Armored Engineers, and his companion, Tec 5 Howard C. Roper of the same unit.

It was during the drive on Kaiserslautern when Hedtke, then attached to Troop C, 90th Cav Rcn Sq, was driving his amphibious weasel to CCB headquarters carrying engineer reports. As he and Roper roared through a town en route, they were struck by the singular quiet and deserted aspect of the place.

Tiger doughs utilize woods to bypass enemy strongpoint

Suddenly, from windows and cellars and from behind a stone fence, came a stream of small arms fire. From the flank a baby panzerfaust flew across the road and struck the gas tank of the weasel. Miraculously, the tank did not explode, but the concussion broke the track and scattered body wheels in the ditches.

Hedtke and Roper jumped from their knocked-out vehicle and attempted to escape the vicious hail of Schmeisser fire. Roper returned fire with a full clip of carbine. Hedtke ran across town while Roper took cover in a cellar.

After clearing two or three fences, it became obvious to Hedtke that his position was hopeless. Fire was directed on him from the part of town to which he was attempting to escape. And so he did the sensible thing and stood still with his hands raised.

From both sides of the nearest house came four German infantrymen. Hedtke and Roper were taken prisoners. They learned that they had run right into the middle of a full company of German infantry.

The two prisoners were taken to the Company CP where they were brought before the captain and a 1st lieutenant. The German commander and his aide inquired as to the name, rank, serial number and unit of the prisoners. Hedtke, fluent in German, told the captain his name, rank and serial number.

After the interrogation Roper and Hedtke were placed under guard and were surrounded by an inquisitive group of enlisted men. Hedtke decided that this was an ideal opportunity for a little subtle persuasion.

Hedtke's little pep talk did its work well and the Germans were almost demoralized. They had not eaten or slept for three days and were ready to believe the worst. When the order came from the CP to fall out for a march they responded listlessly.

The column moved out and Hedtke began to talk to the Germans around him, urging them not to be fools but to surrender. The lieutenant at the head of the column overheard the Sergeant's remarks and called out, "If that man says another word, shoot him." Hedtke dropped back a little farther down the column and continued his talking.

During the march, the German column was turned back and detoured several times by American armor passing along the roads, and once Hedtke and Roper were forced to lie down in some bushes by the roadside while a platoon of American light tanks passed within fifty feet.

As the march stretched to about two miles, it was apparent that Hedtke's arguments were telling on the Germans. Finally one of them turned to him and said, " Listen, I'll do it."

Seven other Germans made the same decision, and little by little the group dropped back in the column and finally out of it altogether. They started in the other direction and then circled and headed for Rohrbach where the two engineers were being classified as "missing in action" by their friends.

Finally, at 0200 on March 21, Hedtke, Roper and their eight prisoners moved into the town and to safety with C Troop. The prisoners were turned over to CCB, and the engineers were welcomed back by the Troop Commander, Capt. John J. D'Orazio.

A few hours later, seven of the frantic Germans who had been Hedtke's and Roper's captors attempted to infiltrate through the outpost of C Troop. They were cut down by cannon and rifle fire.

Surrender flags are displayed at captured Saint Wendel

RHINE

23 March 1945

TO: Officers and Men, 10th Armored Division.

"The following message has been received from General BRADLEY, Commander, 12th Army Group:

" 'My congratulations on the magnificent accomplishments of your Division.' "

" 'Let's Go Tigers.' "

W. H. H. MORRIS, JR.,
Major General, United States Army
Commanding, 10th Armored Division
27 March 1945

TO: Commanding General, 10th Armored Division

"1. I desire to commend you and your command for the outstanding manner in which you and they have accomplished all your assigned missions while a part of the XX Corps. Your recent operations west of the Rhine were undertaken and completed in a superior manner.

"2. The efficient manner in which you carried out your appointed tasks reflects great credit upon your division and upon you as its Commanding General. Your sound judgment, keen foresight and the highly effective manner in which you employed your command contributed materially to the operational success of the XX Corps.

"3. Please convey to the officers, warrant officers and enlisted men of the 10th Armored Division my personal thanks and those of the XX Corps for their fine fighting spirit, their untiring efforts, their skillful performance of duty and their effective teamwork which contributed so greatly towards the successful accomplishments of all their vital missions."

WALTON H. WALKER
Major General, United States Army
Commanding, XX Corps

Terrify and destroy: Alert doughs quit burning German village

27 April 1945

TO: Commanding General, 10th Armored Division.

"It is with deep appreciation and a sense of humility that I transmit to the officers and to the enlisted men who have served in the VIII Corps since December 16, 1944, this letter of appreciation from General Patton.

"As we review the picture, since Bastogne, we see performance of feats by officers and men of the Corps which in normal times one would have believed to be impossible of execution. It is however doing the impossible which marks the leader and returns the winner in war.

"My sincere thanks to those members of the Corps now living and my humble reverence to those now deceased who by devotion to a cause and a duty made this letter of appreciation from our Army Commander possible."

TROY H. MIDDLETON
Major General, United States Army
Commanding, VIII Corps

25 April 1945

"My dear General Middleton:

"Again the exigencies of war have separated the VIII Corps and the Third Army. We are all most regretful.

"None of us will ever forget the stark valor with which you and your Corps contested every foot of ground during von Rundstedt's attack. Your decision to hold BASTOGNE was a stroke of genius.

"Subsequently, the relentless advance of the VIII Corps to the KYLL River, thence to the RHINE, your capture of KOBLENZ and subsequent assault crossings of the RHINE at its most difficult sector, resulting in your victorious and rapid advance to the MULDE River, are events which will live in history and quicken the pulse of every soldier.

"Please accept for yourself and transmit to the officers and men of your command my sincere thanks and admiration for the outstanding successes achieved.

May all good fortune attend you."

Very sincerely,
G. S. PATTON, JR.,
Lieut. General, United States Army,
Commanding, 3rd Army

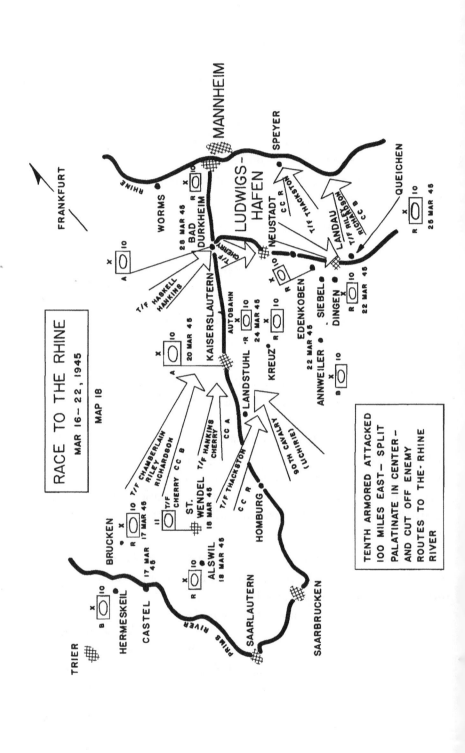

RACE TO THE RHINE
MAR 16 – 22, 1945

MAP 18

TENTH ARMORED ATTACKED
100 MILES EAST – SPLIT
PALATINATE IN CENTER –
AND CUT OFF ENEMY
ROUTES TO THE - RHINE
RIVER

X

RHINE TO THE NECKAR RIVER

IN THE LAST DAYS of the Saar-Palatinate fight in which the German 1st and 7th Armies were badly mauled, the Tenth Armored overran Seventh Army boundaries and was traded to General Patch for the latter's Sixth Armored Division, which went to General Patton's United States Third Army. By March 28, the Seventh Army engineers had completed two bridges across the Rhine at Worms and on that date, the Tigers rolled over the pontoons in anticipation of the final clean-up drive that was to carry them to the Austrian and Bavarian Alps in late April of 1945. Though on the run, the German war machine still packed a lethal punch as it opposed the Tenth's entry into the Wurttenburg area. In the next, and final six weeks of battle, the enemy was to extract a heavy toll in American lives. On March 30, the crack Forty-Fourth Infantry Division, commanded by Major General William F. Dean, was in its final stages of sweeping the Wehrmacht out of Mannheim to permit the spearheading Tigers to swing through the infantry's bridgehead there and scramble ahead to the Neckar River at Heilbronn. Because General Dean's infantry were in one corps and the Tenth in another, close coordination was necessary. Especially since one division had to pass through another in the midst of combat. Tiger staff officers who were delegated to work out details for the operation, found General Dean very cooperative and were not surprised to learn much later that the General distinguished himself in the Korean Conflict and that he won the coveted Congressional Medal of Honor, the nation's highest battle award.

Before the Division propelled its way to the Neckar from the Rhine on March 31, it was brought under control of VI Corps. On April 1, the Tenth hardly noted its completion of six months of rugged combat but it clearly showed wear and tear. At the start of its new campaign it was far below par. It had not received combat replacements since February 20, 1945 and actually was 50% below strength. This dangerous situation was to be a vital factor in the Division's rapid drive into the heart of Hitler's Nazi Germany later. At this time, too, high command strategy dictated that troop priority was to be given to American armies to the north which had the difficult task of reducing the Ruhr Valley. For this reason, the Seventh Army was unable to launch a large-scale offensive of its own. Instead, it sent its Sixth Corps southeast, on the right flank, to pave the way for the coming offensive into Southern Bavaria and the National Redoubt area just as soon as more troops were made available. The Sixth Corps possessed only three divisions at this time. They were, in addition to the Tenth Armored, the 63rd and 100th Infantry Divisions. The Corps' plan included sending the Tenth Armored out in front to be backed up by the 100th on the right and the 63rd on the left flanks. As a result of the Corps' decision, the Tenth planned to attack southeast astride the Neckar River by sending out its three combat commands abreast. Colonel Wade C. Gatchell's Reserve Command, and the 90th Recon were to fan out north and south of the Neckar, as Combat Command B led by Colonel Basil G. Thayer initiated a drive south along the Rhine until contact was made with the First French Army and then wheel east to meet up with the Tenth again. Brig. Gen. Edwin W. Piburn's Combat Command A prepared to sweep southeast towards Heilbronn.

Instructions are given German Red Cross Nurse at Warden, Germany

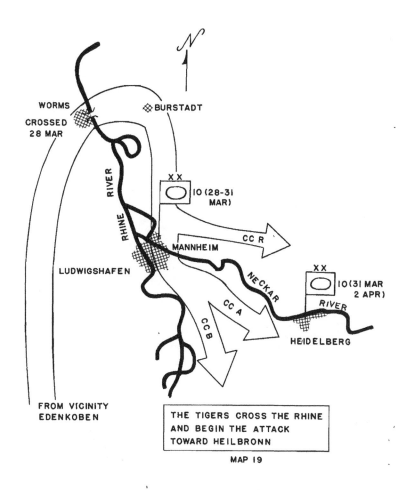

WORMS
CROSSED
28 MAR

◈ BURSTADT

RHINE RIVER

RHINE

XX
10 (28-31 MAR)

CC R

MANNHEIM

LUDWIGSHAFEN

NECKAR

XX
10 (31 MAR 2 APR)

RIVER

CC A

CC B

HEIDELBERG

FROM VICINITY
EDENKOBEN

THE TIGERS CROSS THE RHINE
AND BEGIN THE ATTACK
TOWARD HEILBRONN

MAP 19

ON TO HEIDELBERG

At 0530, on March 30, the 55th Engineers bridged the Neckar at Mannheim permitting the tanks and infantry of Combat Command B to cross. At first rapid progress was made by Task Force Chamberlain, which led the Division's drive through Rheinau to Schwetzingen six miles south of Mannheim against sporadic enemy resistance. But at Schwetzingen, the Tigers ran into fanatic civilian resistance—in addition to the 198th German Infantry Division. Task Force Richardson, in the meantime, had pushed to the Mannheim-Stuttgart superhighway and continued south in

215

a parallel route. Further north, Combat Command A's Task Forces Hankins and Riley sped across the Neckar and slammed east toward the university city of Heidelberg. On March 31, Red Hankins cleared Friedrichfeld and Riley's column, led by Team O'Grady, passed through Heidelberg, nine miles east of Mannheim. That city had already been taken with comparative ease by

World's largest tank, the German Jad Tiger, is destroyed by Team O'Grady near Heidelberg, Germany.

the 63rd Infantry Division. Heidelberg had been declared a "free city" and consequently, not a shot was fired as a patrol of the 63rd Infantry waded across the River and walked into the city. A few minutes later, the Tenth rolled in and established its Headquarters in the city but caused no damage. When the armor rumbled into Heidelberg, almost the entire populace turned out to cheer the Tigers on and to strew flowers in the path. During the same afternoon, Lou Lochner, veteran Associated Press correspondent, enlisted the aid of the author in uncovering a gigantic marble plaque which had been erected years before on the American wing of that venerable educational institution known as Heidelberg University. When the Nazis rose to power they had ripped it from the main building and dumped it in one of the cellars because the plaque honored several "non aryans" whose money was responsible for the erection of the wing in the first place.

Farther to the south, task forces of Richardson and Chamberlain careened into one of the enemy's most powerful divisions but the resultant fight effectively screened the French First Army crossing of the Rhine south of Speyer, allowing the two allied forces to link up on March 31. Among the many Tiger losses was that of Captain "Bud" Billet, popular and capable young officer, who was killed here.

Carving a wide arc above the Neckar some 30 miles east of Mannheim, Lichirie's Recon Squadron and Task Force Thackston now were in a position to wheel south and outflank the fortress city of Heilbronn. The first big dent in the enemy lines however, was made by Task Force Riley when it penetrated 16 miles on April 1. Then Combat Command B enjoyed similar success on the extreme right flank as it broke through to its initial objective 23 miles south of Mannheim. In the center of the Tigers' spearhead, however, Hankins and Roberts fought forward slowly against mounting resistance.

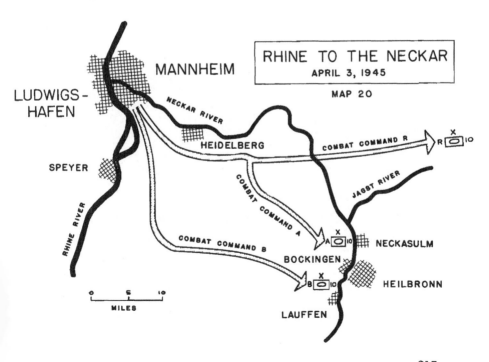

Tankers and doughs press forward to the Neckar River

BREAKTHROUGH

On April 2, Task Force Riley ground forward 22 miles to reach the Neckar just north of Heilbronn, and 30 miles to the west, CC B's Tigers pivoted, captured Bruchsal and took 300 prisoners, then rolled eastward to join CC A on the latter's objective—the west bank of the Neckar at Heilbronn. But the Reserve Command and Combat Command B advanced more slowly against stubborn resistance that day. On the other hand, Chamberlain and Richardson ploughed ahead on April 3, exploiting the breakthrough to the maximum. Each rumbled on more than 25 miles to converge on Heilbronn. The Reserve Command and Recon forces closed at the Jagst River about 11 miles north of that city. To cross the Jagst, the doughs swam the River in a search for boats on the opposite shore, but returned empty-handed. In the meantime, Combat Command A assembled for the crossing of the Neckar to assault Heilbronn, which VI Corps had ordered to be captured by the Tenth.

Enemy is flushed from the woods by Tenth Armored Mediums

219

Now the entire Division was poised along the line of the Neckar and Jagst Rivers ready for the assault on Heilbronn. And in the course of its sweep south and east, the Tigers destroyed 100 dual-purpose anti-aircraft guns, a most unusual feat for a speeding armored division. On April 4, Combat Command B mopped up small enemy groups west of the Neckar River, then sent a task force south of Heilbronn in an attempt to seize a bridge at Lauffen, reported intact by air observation. At this juncture, the 3rd Battalion of the 398th Infantry from the 100th Division was attached to Combat Command A and was immediately dispatched across the river to set up a bridgehead. The doughs, though strongly counterattacked by the enemy's crack 17th SS Panzer Grenadier Division, managed to widen their foothold. Though initial plans

The infantry, for a change, get a ride on a Sherman
as Tenth's spearhead rolls on to Heilbronn

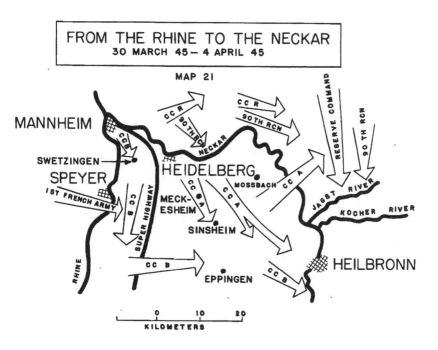

MANNHEIM

SWETZINGEN
SPEYER
1ST FRENCH ARMY

HEIDELBERG
MECK-
ESHEIM
SINSHEIM

MOSSBACH

RESERVE COMMAND
90TH RCN
JAGST RIVER
KOCHER RIVER

HEILBRONN

EPPINGEN

NECKAR

RHINE

SUPER HIGHWAY

CC R
CC R
90TH RCN
90TH RCN
CC B
CC B
CC A
CC A
CC A
CC B
CC B

0   10   20
KILOMETERS

called for the infantry to consolidate the bridgehead, so that Combat Command A could pass through and go on to take Heilbronn, it was quickly apparent that it would require more than a combat command to do the job. For this reason, the mission was altered and instead, the 100th Infantry was designated to assault the fortress city. In the north, pressure exerted by the Reserve Command made possible the crossing of the Neckar by the 63rd Infantry Division, which brushed aside weakening enemy resistance. Finally, the Tenth, except for Combat Command B, crossed the 63rd's bridge near Mosbach and thundered on to the east while Combat Command A sent its recon units as far south and east as Crailsheim. Combat Command B was left behind to support Maj. Gen. Burress' 100th Infantry at Heilbronn in the hope that the doughs might effect a breakthrough. The stage was set now and the curtain was about to go up for the Division's newest exploits as Company A of the Third Tank Battalion led Task Force Hankins' probing movement all the way to Crailsheim, some 70 miles east of Heilbronn.

Dazed Hitler Youth are lined up prior to departure for
PW camps

TEXAS TIGER

One of the most dramatic episodes of the Rhine-Neckar phase
was the wild night battle on the main street of the town of Roth
between squads of infantry and one medium tank under the command of Capt. Thomas E. Griswold, Jr., of Marshall, Texas, of the
3rd Tank Battalion and about 100 Germans. The battle ended in
an overwhelming victory for Griswold & Co. When the shooting
stopped, there were 42 dead Nazis, an equal number of prisoners
—and not a single wounded Jerry. Griswold's casualties were six
wounded.

The Germans descended on Roth without warning, and before long there was a battle with all the characteristics of a six-
gun western thriller. The doughboys roamed up and down the
street, flushing out the enemy, while Griswold rode his tank like
a cowboy, his hand glued to the handle of the 50 cal. machine gun.
Before the fight ended, he had fired 1300 rounds of ammo, and
dead Germans were strewn everywhere.

222

XI

THE BATTLE FOR CRAILSHEIM

IN EARLY APRIL, 1945, General Brooks ordered all fighting units of the VI Corps to search for a weak spot in the German defense line. It was Corps' intention now to swing the Tenth away from the strongly defended city of Heilbronn towards Nurnberg, birthplace of Nazism.

This sudden change of plans was the result of the enemy's last-ditch build-up of its defensive lines at Heilbronn. Elements of five powerful German divisions dug in to prevent the capture of that important key city in the enemy communications network. Connecting main highways between Heilbronn and Stuttgart also linked with Munich and Nurnberg. Heilbronn was, then, the gateway to Bavaria and Austria. Realizing this the Germans put up a ferocious defense against any American attempt to break through into the area. In addition to heavy enemy troop concentrations facing the Tigers, the terrain posed a real problem. Favoring the enemy defensive units, the area was hilly, wooded, and cut by rivers. Many small towns and villages served as strong defensive centers. These factors, Corps decided, were sufficient to free the Tenth Armored from its assigned task of taking Heilbronn. Instead, the new plan of attack, as outlined to General Morris by VI Corps, was to attack to the east through the 63rd Infantry Division's zone and seize and hold the line Rothenberg-Wettringen-Crailsheim-Schwabisch Hall. The purpose of the new operation was to seal enemy escape routes from Heilbronn, cut the Nurnberg-Stuttgart railroad and outflank and surround the crack 17th SS Panzer Grenadier Division defending the Neckar-Jagst river line.

THE TIGERS PROWL

To put his armored Tigers into motion, General Morris directed Colonel Wade Gatchell and his Reserve Command to attack east, General Piburn to send CC A across the Neckar, north of Heilbronn, and attack east; and Colonel Thayer, after supporting with fire the 100th Infantry's crossing the Neckar at Heilbronn on April 6, was to order his CC B units to seize the bridge at Lauffen and also attack east. Supporting the Tenth Armored in its new drive were the 100th and 63rd Infantry Divisions whose job it was to back up Tiger armor to the east and south and permit the Armoraiders to exploit the elements of speed and surprise, with the knowledge that they were protected in the rear and on the flanks by the reliable doughs.

Specific orders on April 4 were for the Reserve Command to loop through the 63rd Infantry the following day and crash eastward to seize the line Rothenberg-Wettringen. Simultaneously, the 90th Cavalry was designated by General Morris to reconnoiter in force to the line Rothenberg-Crailsheim after it was relieved of its task of protecting Tiger flanks on the north and east.

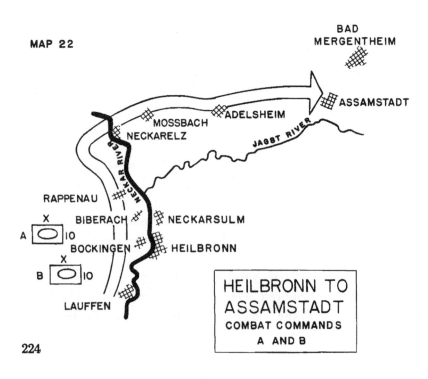

MAP 22

HEILBRONN TO
ASSAMSTADT
COMBAT COMMANDS
A AND B

Three bridgeheads were planned in the area which would permit construction of bridges for an armor and infantry crossing of the Neckar. General Piburn's Combat Command A got priority on bridge #2, if completed, for the purpose of darting across and swinging a haymaker at the enemy to the east and seizing the line Crailsheim-Wettringen. In the event that this bridge did not materialize, the 63rd bridge near Mossbach, was to be used for the crossing. And Thayer's Combat Command B prepared to speed across a third bridge, if available, to fight eastward and control the line Schwabisch Hall-Crailsheim. Like CC A, this command too, had to prepare alternate plans for using one of the other two bridges, should the third bridge fail to materialize.

On the morning of April 5, the CC A CP was located at Biberach, Task Force Hankins at Kirchenhausen, Task Force Roberts at Frankenbach, and Task Force Riley at Biberach. By the end of the day, it was expected that all of Piburn's units would close at Assamstadt. Morris told Piburn, "continue your attack southeast and take Crailsheim, then turn southwest and secure the line Crailsheim-Schwabisch Hall-Backnang."

TIGERS HELD IN CHECK

The day before, our task forces had suffered losses from the enemy who fought desperately to hold back the onrushing Tenth Armored Tigers. Combat Command B probed west of the Neckar in a search for crossing sites. Units in the Command were the Fifty-Fourth Infantry, Eleventh Tank Battalion and attached medics, ordinance, artillery, engineers and tank destroyers. Commanding these units were Lt. Col. Richardson and Lt. Col. Chamberlain, who were locked in battle near Lauffen and Klingenberg. Both forces suffered heavy casualties as a result of heavy enemy shelling from east of the Neckar. After two days, CC B crossed the Neckar near Neckarelz and rumbled on to Assamstadt through Frankenbach, Kirchausen, Bonfeld, Rappenau, Huffenhardt, Wollenberg, Bargen, Helmstadt, and Aglaster Hausen. It was almost midnight on April 6, when the last CC B unit crossed the bridge. When the Command pulled into the Assamstadt area, it found that not enough space was available to accommodate it. Furthermore, the rain-soaked fields did not permit passage of the medium tanks and forced Thayer's men to fan out beyond the assembly area limits during the night. Later, at the time Tiger Headquarters were located at Assamstadt, the Division Trains were pulled into an area near Osterburken. Here, as customary in the past, training was given for replacements while the combat units were engaged in battle. At the time that the Division crossed the Rhine, new replacements were brought into the Division. Colonel Thomas M. Brinkley and Major Floyd Walters were now busily indoctrinating these men for future combat. In one of the small towns near Osterburken, Major Walters was conducting a class in how to mop up a town to get all the snipers and stragglers. One particular day, while demonstrating proper ways of doing it, he captured 19 German troops. Back at Assamstadt, the Tiger CP was bombed by a single enemy plane but no real damage was done. On another occasion, two enemy planes zipped down the main street giving Division Headquarters personnel a rare opportunity to demonstrate their marksmanship. Both planes were shot down by the wild firing as every machine gun available was put to use. Each one of the gunners was certain of course, that he had made the kill.

NIGHT RAID

Meanwhile, Task Force Hankins rolled over the 63rd's crossing site to lead the CC A attack towards Crailsheim. Following them were Task Forces Riley and Roberts which were intent on grabbing Schwabisch Hall while Hankins hung on to the shoulder at Crailsheim. The latter, after barreling 45 miles, met up with Lichirie's 90th Cavalry and Gatchell's Reserve Command near Rengershausen by dinnertime on April 5. Two hours later, after refueling and coordinating their movement through the Cavalry, Hankins' raiders pushed on in darkness towards Crailsheim. Their progress was impeded at the outset by poor road

THE BATTLE FOR CRAILSHEIM

APRIL 4-10 1945

CHART 5

COMBAT COMMAND A

```
          X
      A  [ O ]  10
         PIBURN
```

TASK FORCE HANKINS	TASK FORCE RILEY	TASK FORCE ROBERTS	CC A CONTROL	SUPPORT
61 AIB (-COA)	21 TANK BN	54 AIB (-CO A&C)	TR A, 90 CAV RCN BN	419 AFA BN
COA 3RD TANK BN	CO. A, 61 AIB	CO B 21ST TK BN	CO. A, 55 AE BN (-)	(D/STF. RILEY ROBERTS)
I PLAT. COB, 609TH TD BN	I PLAT. COB, 609 TD BN	I PLAT. CO B, 609 TD BN	CO. B, 609 TD BN(-)	420 AFA BN
IST PLAT. CO. A, 55 AEB	2 PLAT CO. A, 55 AEB	3 RD PLAT. CO A, 55 AEB	CO. A, 80 MED BN	(D/S TF HANKINS)
				634 TA BN
				(G/S CCA, I BTRY)

nets and a roadblock south of Rengershausen. Forced to stay on the roads because of the heavy bordering woods, Hankins had to pull his vehicles from the mire every time the unit by-passed a roadblock. By daybreak, the force reached Hollenbach. Worried by the slowness of the attack, Piburn dispatched Task Force Roberts on April 5, to find a way through to the west of Hankins. Like the latter, Roberts was beset by a strongly defended roadblock north of Dorzbach and the rest of the night was lost as Roberts attempted to by-pass this block. Back at Assamstadt, Piburn waited for an opportunity to push Task Force Riley through either Hankins or Roberts—depending on which unit could open a way to speed the attack to Crailsheim. The wiley General didn't have to wait too long. Hankins finally captured Hollenbach just before darkness on April 6. By noon the next day, the unit overran Gutbach and the rat race was on as a breakthrough was accomplished. With pulverizing speed, Hankins raced through Laufelden, Brettenfeld, Rot am See, Wallhausen, Croningen, Sattweiler, Satteldorf, Neidenfels, Burleswagon to Crailsheim. For 22 miles, every step of the way was hotly contested by the Germans. Resistance mounted as the 420th Armored Field Artillery, commanded by Lieut. Col. Willis D. Crittenberger, Jr., leapfrogging its batteries, was forced to occupy 18 firing positions in this one day's advance.

DEFENSE ORGANIZED

Major Curtis L. Hankins immediately organized a defense of Crailsheim to offset the enemy's use of darkness to disorganize his forces there. Three hours later, Riley's forces joined Hankins' in the city, destined to become for the Tigers, a miniature Bastogne.

During the night, both units resupplied and, on their own initiative, planned carefully to defend the city as radio contact with CC A's CP was lost. All of Hankins' men plus one of Riley's teams remained in the city while two additional teams of the latter's force were dispatched to Satteldorf and Sattweiler. More

THE BATTLE FOR CRAILSHEIM

COMBAT COMMAND B

B ⬭ 10
x
THAYER

CHART 6

TASK FORCE CHAMBERLAIN

II TK BN (-CO C 3/4, I/D)
CO.C, 20 AIB
3 PLAT CO.A, 20TH AIB
I PLAT CO.B, 55 AEB
I PLAT CO.A, 609 TD BN

TASK FORCE RICHARDSON

20 AIB (-CO C 3/4)
CO.C, II TH TK BN
3 PLAT CO.A, II TK BN
3 PLAT CO.B, 55 AEB
3 PLAT CO.A, 609 TD BN

CC B RESERVE

HQ'S & HQ'S CO, CCB
CO.A, 609 TD BN (-)
CO.B 55, AEB BN (-)
IST PLAT CO.D, II TK BN
I PW TEAM NO. 113
CO.C, 31 ENGR (C) BN
CO.A, 31 ENGR (C) BN (RPL B CO)
CO.B, 2287 ENGR (C) BN (RPL A CO)
2 PLAT CO.A, 90 RCN BN

SUPPORT

423 AFA BN
CO B 80 MED BN
CO A 132 ORD BN
405 FA GP
93 AFA BN
141 FA BN
B BTRY 976 FA

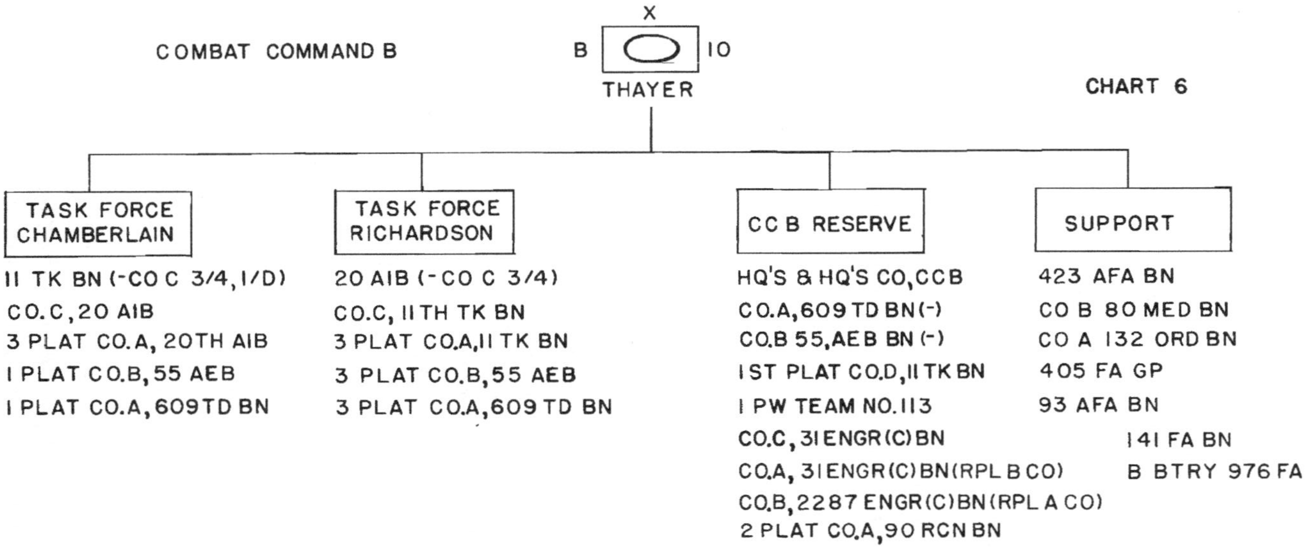

than 200 Germans were bagged by Hankins on April 6. But in the north, Task Force Roberts was hit hard by anti-tank, artillery and small arms fire at Dorzbach which held it in check all day. By evening though, Roberts managed to force his way into that town.

At 2030, CC A was told by Headquarters to keep going and to protect its flanks and hold the shoulder at Crailsheim until the Reserve Command could be sent in to relieve it. To do this, Piburn sent word to Hankins to block at Crailsheim while Riley wheeled through and drove westward toward the Tigers' objective. Piburn's directive, unfortunately, did not reach Hankins as radio contact between the two command posts had been broken. Moreover, the Germans were unaware that American forces were in Crailsheim. This was borne out by the enemy who were surprised to find our troops already there. At Sattendorf, too, a German busload of troops was stopped in front of Riley's CP and relieved of its mission which was to pick up its division's laundry! And at the local airfield, several enemy planes landed even as a German train churned into the town from the east. They were all unaware that the Tenth Armored Tigers were already established in the area. But not for long.

General Morris had planned to send the 90th Cavalry and the Reserve Command in support of CC A, but because of heavy enemy pressure in the area, the mission was altered and both units were told to hold the northeast corner of the Division zone. At Stuppach, for example, about 150 SS troops infiltrated the town, where they captured some of our forces there. It took most of the day of heavy fighting to retake Stuppach. At this time 35 enemy prisoners were captured and another 75 were killed, while the remainder beat a hasty retreat to Bad Mergentheim. At this time, Thayer was told by General Morris to relieve CC R and the 90th Cavalry and to keep open the main supply routes between Mergenshausen and Crailsheim and Dorzbach and Crailsheim. On the night of April 7, CC B sped 70 miles in darkness over poor roads and smashed into the enemy.

THE MEANING OF THE TIGER ATTACK

It took less than 36 hours to streak some 70 miles and get the Division 35 miles behind German lines. More than 300 of the enemy were captured and many more killed. A large amount of enemy equipment was destroyed or captured. All this was accomplished at a relatively small loss to our own forces. Crailsheim was the high-point of our rampaging tank and infantry attack—for this town was the key to a triangle formed by Heilbron, Bad Mergentheim and Crailsheim. Our successes here in effect, caused the Germans to drastically alter their tactics. We were now less than 100 miles from Munich and only 40 miles southwest of Nurnberg. The surprised Germans reacted quickly and threw planes and ground forces at the Tenth in their greatest display of strength since the Ardennes in an effort to halt the dangerous threat to the rear. So important was the defense of Crailsheim, that they committed their newest weapon, the ME 262. Heavily armed and able to fly at blinding speed, this jet undoubtedly would have made considerable difference in the course of the war if the Germans had been able to get it in the air before now.

On CC A's front, the Germans on April 7, sent a number of attacking forces to cut the road between the forward elements of Task Force Roberts and rear elements of Task Force Riley.

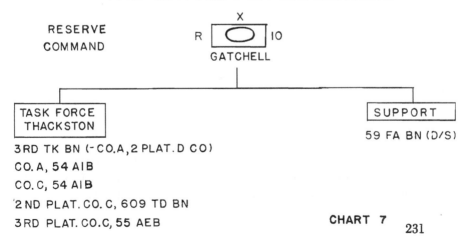

THE BATTLE FOR CRAILSHEIM

RESERVE COMMAND

R [O] 10 X
GATCHELL

TASK FORCE THACKSTON
3RD TK BN (-CO.A, 2 PLAT.D CO)
CO. A, 54 AIB
CO. C, 54 AIB
2 ND PLAT. CO. C, 609 TD BN
3RD PLAT. CO.C, 55 AEB

SUPPORT
59 FA BN (D/S)

CHART 7

Tiger Recon troops slug away at German infiltrators
on "Bowling Alley" between Assamstadt and Crailsheim

Thus, for the first time the main supply route from the area of
Hollenbach to Crailsheim was cut. And for all practical purposes, it was to remain that way throughout the rest of the operation. The only traffic along the road was that of task force supply trains struggling to get through to Crailsheim, and the author,
who along with Associated Press war correspondent, Robert Goldberg, managed to reach Crailsheim before dark of April 7. Speeding along at 60 miles an hour, and armed with but one automatic
and carbine, we ran into one road block after another. About 15
miles from Crailsheim, we sighted a four-truck convoy carrying
gas for the beleagured Tigers in Crailsheim. As we rolled up behind the trucks, an 88 boomed out from a corner of the woods
some 400 yards away. The German gunners scored a direct hit
on the convoy as we rolled into a protective ditch and watched
exploding gas cans sail over our heads into the fields on either
side of the road. When things quieted down, we took off again
and raced into the town. Met there by Major Hankins, we learned
that we were the only ones to have gotten through in the past two
days. It was an unhappy Hankins who was told that his expected
gas supply now consisted of burnt cans strewn along the road to
the north. While Goldberg got his press story from the Commander, the Germans threw a hail of Nebelwerfer into the town and

sent the slate on the rooftops hurtling to the streets. Two hours after we departed along the "bowling alley" for Assamstadt, Hankins and his men were attacked for the third consecutive night by a battalion of SS infiltrators.

During the same day, on April 7, General Morris flew into Crailsheim in a cub plane to reestablish contact with forward elements. Prior to this flight, the General ordered Task Force Roberts and the CP of CC A to the Crailsheim area. When he got to Crailsheim, the Tiger Commander sent word to Riley to pass through Hankins and set up a forward CP with Task Force Hankins. It was not until late in the morning of April 7, that Riley was able to send Team Felice towards Schwabisch Hall. On the way it captured Rossfeld. By afternoon, the Force had gone on to take Ilshofen and Wolpertshausenn. At Ilshofen, Riley was bombed and strafed by a squadron of ME 109's. Here Team Felice of Task Force Riley had a field day as it waited for an approaching German train to roll opposite its positions. Tanks of the unit sent a few point-blank rounds at the train and its surprised occupants and then wrecked it with machine gun and cannon fire. Then by 1400, the Team had moved on to capture Maulach. Later a liaison plane reported to Riley, when he reached Wolpertshausen, that it had sighted a bridge intact across the Kocher River at Croffelbach. Riley's Team Felice attempted to capture the bridge but it was blown up before the Team got there. The Germans plastered the bridge site with mortar fire. They followed this with an attack of small arms and panzerfaust at the armored column from the elevated area around the bridge. With no place to turn, the team had to back out, but not before it lost a Medium from a direct panzerfaust hit on its engine compartment. Finally the team was able to withdraw and go on to capture Wolpertshausen. The attack was to be the deepest penetration that the Tenth had made in the west during the entire operation. Meanwhile at Crailsheim, Hankins was able to better his defenses by clearing the area surrounding the City. Lieut. Hill's team captured Ingersheim on April 7, and at the same time, Team Havlowitz at 1130 captured the enemy's airfield west of Crailsheim, destroying an 88 and 14 grounded planes. Team Holland was busy clearing Altenmunster to complete the job of providing an area of safety around Crailsheim.

OBJECTIVE IN SIGHT

In less than four days, the Tigers had managed to get within striking distance of the objective—to seize and hold the line Rothenberg-Wettringen-Crailsheim-Schwabisch Hall. During this period, the Tenth Armored had disengaged from contact with the enemy near Heilbronn, made a 90-degree change in direction and barrelled a distance of 59 miles from the vicinity of Heilbronn to Assamstadt. Pausing only to plan its attack, the Division rolled on in darkness, collided with the enemy and completed a 180-degree turn from the direction it had followed during the move from Heilbronn and drove 31 miles behind enemy lines to Crailsheim. Now the Tigers were 40 miles from the nearest VI Corps units and, though unsupported, captured more than 300 Germans. More important, Crailsheim offered its captors a chance to seize a vital link in the German military communications system connecting Heilbronn with Nurnberg.

HIT THE ROAD

At dusk, April 7, General Piburn directed Task Force Roberts to take Kirchberg. Lt. Col. Roberts decided that in order to accomplish this task quickly, Team Riley would be sent to Wallhausen and Team McIntosh to Hornberg. Both towns were captured, but Team McIntosh was forced to remain in Hornberg overnight because it could not find a suitable route to Kirchberg.

On April 7, Colonel Gatchell's Reserve Command, at the request of General Morris, pulled away from the Germans during the morning in order to swing out towards Crailsheim. The new mission was to block the approach of the enemy from the south and southeast to Crailsheim and to relieve Task Force Hankins. Blocking for Gatchell's Tigers was to be done by the 90th Cavalry

Mediums roll cross country to strike at enemy's rear

which extended its positions to include those formerly held by CC R. Before taking off for Crailsheim, however, Gatchell's men had to set fire to part of Roth and disengage from the counter-attacking Germans. Under cover of the flaming buildings, they withdrew and headed for their next destination at Crailsheim. By 1830 on the evening of April 7, the cavalrymen had covered the Reserve Command's withdrawal, and the men of the 90th were fighting everywhere in the area. Their headquarters and Troop B were in Hachtel. Troop A slugged away at the enemy in Crailsheim. At Roth, Troop C withstood a German assault. Troop D was at Hollenbach. Headquarters and Service Troop were to be found in Schwabhausen. Small groups of enemy harrassed the blocking forces all day, but for the most part, Germans were unwilling to risk a pitched battle with the 90th Armoraiders.

Meanwhile, northeast in the woods near Hollenbach, the Reserve Command, following the same route used by Combat Command A, ran into strong enemy resistance. The Germans threw 88's, automatic weapon and small arms fire at the relief column and managed to split the command. To offset this action, Gatchell sent his tankers into the woods to wipe out the Germans hidden

235

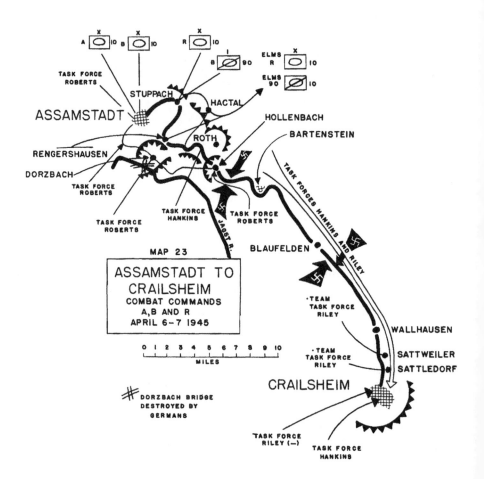

A ⬭ 10   B ⬭ 10   R ⬭ 10

B ⬭ 90   ELMS R ⬭ 10

ELMS 90 ⬭ 10

TASK FORCE
ROBERTS

STUPPACH

ASSAMSTADT

HACTAL

HOLLENBACH

BARTENSTEIN

RENGERSHAUSEN

ROTH

DORZBACH

TASK FORCE
ROBERTS

TASK FORCE
HANKINS

TASK FORCE
ROBERTS

TASK FORCE
ROBERTS

TASK FORCES HANKINS AND RILEY

JAGST R.

MAP 23

ASSAMSTADT TO
CRAILSHEIM
COMBAT COMMANDS
A, B AND R
APRIL 6-7 1945

BLAUFELDEN

•TEAM
TASK FORCE
RILEY

WALLHAUSEN

0 1 2 3 4 5 6 7 8 9 10
MILES

•TEAM
TASK FORCE
RILEY

SATTWEILER

SATTLEDORF

⌗ DORZBACH BRIDGE
DESTROYED BY
GERMANS

CRAILSHEIM

TASK FORCE
RILEY (—)

TASK FORCE
HANKINS

there. The action was successful, but two Tiger light tanks were lost. As the Reserve Command broke through the woods and swung out across open areas, it was bombed, strafed and slowed by one roadblock after another. Despite heavy opposition, Colonel Gatchell led his Command into Crailsheim later in the day. Unfortunately, it was unable to fulfill its mission of relieving CC A, because of lack of supplies—especially ammunition and fuel. Accordingly, CC R was placed temporarily under Piburn's operational control. Thackston sent the Third Tank Battalion's Team Connolly to Wolpertshausen to set up a defensive position. At the same time, CC A's Team Felice protected the south and west as Team Griswold moved to the vicinity of Maulach where it cut the east-west railroad to Crailsheim. The main forces of the latter Team looped into Ilshofen to augment the defense established there by Task Force Riley. The Headquarters of Colonel Gatchell's Reserve Command set up a CP at Crailsheim.

After fulfilling their blocking mission, the 90th Cavalry assembled for movement to Crailsheim where they were to hold secure the line Crailsheim-Schwabisch Hall, already established by CC A.

On April 8, it was readily apparent that the Germans had recovered from the Tigers' initial shock assault. At dawn they unleashed the first of many violent attacks. From the northeast, southeast and east, some 600 SS engineers slammed against CC A and CC R after flattening the area with an intense rocket and mortar barrage. However, the enemy column striking from the northeast was cut to shreds by Task Force Hankins which surprised the blundering Germans. The two other Nazi attacks were better organized, though, and they steamrollered over Tiger outposts and barged into the outskirts of Crailsheim. It was not until noon that Hankins' Armoraiders were able to shove the attackers back and inflict heavy casualties on them. To keep them reeling, Team Holland put heavy pressure on the retreating foe, stopping only to capture Altenmunster for the second time. Here the Team set up day- time defenses, then hurried to Crailsheim for the night. Team

Hill searched Ingersheim for enemy infiltrators as Team Havlowitz swept out to the airfield for the same purpose. Crailsheim was in our hands again by noon, as all enemy attacks on the town had been successfully repulsed.

To carry out orders from Tiger Headquarters, General Piburn notified Task Force Riley to step up its attack to the west. As soon as Task Force Hankins could be spared from Crailsheim, it too, would support Riley's efforts. As events proved, Hankins' defenders had to remain in position because of the weakened status of the Reserve Command. Without reinforcements, Gatchell's units could not relieve Hankins and, as it was, CC R had its hands full to keep the road open between Wolperthausen and Crailsheim. This factor deprived Riley of needed support as he ran into heavy small arms and bazooka fire beyond Croffelbach. With only one armored infantry company for support, Riley was in no position to risk his tanks on the road.

ROBERTS' RAIDERS

A few miles north of Crailsheim. Task Force Roberts, which had spent a sleepless night in the Wallhausen-Hornberg area, set out after dawn on April 8. In a period of four hours, Teams Riley and McIntosh took over the Force's objective at Kirchberg. In this vicinity, the entire Task Force sharpened its defenses and waited for the expected enemy surge on its positions. But it never materialized. However, on this date, Colonel Bernard F. Luebberman, the Division's veteran artillery commander, was killed by a sniper as he neared Crailsheim. He was the highest ranking Tiger commander killed in the war.

Meanwhile, in Crailsheim, Task Force Hankins loaded up some 500 enemy prisoners for evacuation to the rear, after Tiger units had defeated German attacks on that city. Troop A of the 90th Cavalry was given the task of escorting the PW's to Assamstadt. Since the road between Assamstadt and Crailsheim had been severed by the enemy, it was anticipated that the convoy would have to force its way through the enemy pockets along the road.

When the column reached Blaufelden the expected happened. A strong enemy force ambushed the column and inflictd heavy losses in both vehicles and personnel. In the ensuing fight, many of the PW's were killed as others escaped. The battered convoy was forced to turn back to Crailsheim with 200 prisoners who elected to remain with the convoy. Included in the convoy was Corporal Richardson of the 61st Armored Infantry Battalion. The mild mannered Mississippian had made his third attempt to reach the rear area in order to take advantage of a pass to gay Paree. But this time Richardson in utter disgust turned in his pass and blithely said, "to hell with Paris."

SUPPLY ROUTE CUT

Supplies were running low and, to make matters worse, the road was cut. Now Crailsheim was assuming all of the characteristics of another Bastogne. At this juncture, General Piburn requested resupply by air. He sent Major Geiler's 55th Armored Engineers to prepare the airfield for the big C-47's bringing in fuel, food and ammunition to the beleagured Tigers. Upon their return, the planes were to evacuate our wounded. Among the first to be flown out was Lieut. Col. "Ned" Norris, who had been hit near Crailsheim.

It was impossible to get help from the 9th Troop Carrier Command on April 8th, but in the succeeding two days, fifty transports, protected by blunt-nosed P-47 fighters brought in 20,000 gallons of gasoline, 7,000 rations, 100,000 rounds of small arms and 1,000 rounds of 105mm ammunition. The operation was magnificently timed and though the airfield was subjected to steady pressure of enemy small arms and artillery fire, only one transport was destroyed. But before his Command was resupplied by air, Piburn pushed Task Force Roberts to the northwest between the Jagst and Kocher Rivers at the request of Division Headquarters. Roberts assembled his fighters in Kirchberg before dark on April 8th and rolled on to Ilshofen via Allmerspan. At Ilshofen, Lt. Col. Robert C. McCabe of the 419th Armored Field Art-

illery Battalion, gave up enough of the Battalion's fuel and ammo
to supply Roberts for his attack. Battery C of the 419th joined
Roberts to provide needed artillery support. By midnight, the Task
Force was ready to begin its mission.

ROCKETS, BOMBS AND SHELLS

Further south, at Crailsheim, CC A's forces were hit by a
dawn barrage of rockets and artillery on April 9. This was fol
lowed by an enemy bombing and strafing attack by ME 109's and
jets. With the exception of German air attacks, both Ilshofer
and Wolpertshausen got the same treatment as Crailsheim. Des
pite the ever-increasing intensity of the enemy attacks, Hankins
dispatched Team Holland to Altenmunster where, for the third
time, it mopped up that town and took prisoners. As before, Hol
land held the place all day and returned to Crailsheim at night
Of tremendous help were our supporting fighter planes which
bombed and strafed the roads east of Crailsheim. This served to
lighten enemy pressures on the Crailsheim defenders. While Task
Force Hankins fought off enemy patrols and prepared for night
infantry attacks, Task Force Roberts attacked northwest of Ilsho
fen. Here it halted to receive much-needed supplies made possi
ble because of Combat Command B's successful breakthrough to
Crailsheim. Later Roberts assaulted and captured Ruppertsho
fen with the aid of his supporting artillery. In the meantime, Riley
left Wolpertshausen to back up the Armoraiders near Rup
ertshaufen. The two forces then struck out at Ruppertshaufen
from Dunsbach. At 0700, both columns were hit by 25 enemy
aircraft, and suffered serious losses. Then, after the Luftwaffe
swoop, the Germans plastered them with mortar and artillery fire
During the chaos precipitated by this air and ground enemy action
the rear elements of Task Force Roberts advanced, by mistake, to
wards Leofels, while the head of the column moved through Duns
bach. When the rear approached to within a quarter of a mile of
Leofels, it was hit hard by heavy weapons fire. Thinking it was fol
lowing the lead elements of Roberts' column, the unit instead was

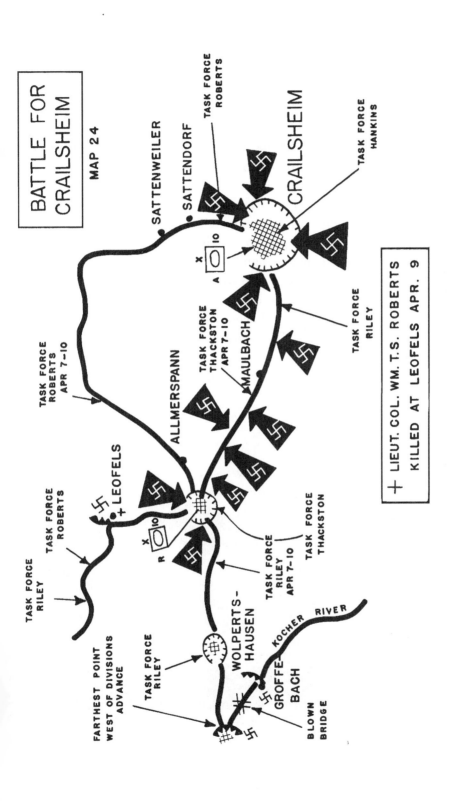

BATTLE FOR CRAILSHEIM

MAP 24

+ LIEUT. COL. WM. T. S. ROBERTS
KILLED AT LEOFELS APR. 9

TASK FORCE ROBERTS

TASK FORCE HANKINS

CRAILSHEIM

SATTENWEILER

SATTENDORF

TASK FORCE ROBERTS APR 7-10

TASK FORCE THACKSTON APR 7-10

ALLMERSPANN

MAULBACH

TASK FORCE RILEY

LEOFELS

TASK FORCE ROBERTS

TASK FORCE RILEY

TASK FORCE RILEY APR 7-10

TASK FORCE THACKSTON

FARTHEST POINT WEST OF DIVISIONS ADVANCE

TASK FORCE RILEY

WOLPERTS-HAUSEN

GROFFEN-BACH

KOCHER RIVER

BLOWN BRIDGE

greeted by a raking enemy fire and thrown into confusion. At this point, Lt. Col. William T. S. Roberts hurried to untrack his disorganized rear. While getting the column off in the right direction, he was forced to expose himself and was killed by a sniper's bullet. The loss of the veteran Tiger officer was felt deeply by everyone. He was replaced by Captain Richard Ulrich, S-3 and senior remaining commander. The new leader had been in Nesselbach, captured minutes before. When he learned of Roberts' death, the stunned young commander quickly outposted the town and returned to Ruppertshaufen where he was ordered by General Piburn to assume command of the Task Force. His first decision was to attack Leofels. Led by light tanks, the vindictive operation was completed in short order. After that action, the Task Force regrouped in Nesselbach and smashed its way through Lassbach to Buttelbronn. Task Force Riley pushed ahead, taking a route parallel to and west of Ulrich. By mid-day, the unit had taken Hassfelden. At the same hour, Ulrich's Tigers were slowed

Baby-faced young Nazi surrenders to tanker

by a road washout near Hermuthausen. Here they eliminated harrassing enemy small arms fire but were endangered by mortars of the 63rd Infantry Division. Now that a meeting with friendly doughs was imminent, Ulrich held up the attack and pulled up on the high ground overlooking Berndshausen and Wolfsolden to prevent the escape of the enemy which had been driven in front of the 63rd's push.

For the rest of the day elsewhere on the Tenth Armored front, Task Force Thackston kept the supply routes open between Tasks Forces Riley and Ulrich, in addition to maintaining control of the airfield. Team Griswold also moved to the airfield on April 9 to make certain that further air resupply could be accomplished if necessary. And Team Connolly swept up and down the main road between Crailsheim and Ilshofen and Riley-Ulrich forces. Part of Task Force Thackston of CC R stayed in Ilshofen to protect it from enemy thrusts originating from the south and west.

RECON MEN PROWL

During the night of April 8, the 90th Cavalry entered Crailsheim and, the next day, troops commanded by Lieut. Col. Lichirie fanned out to nearby towns to assist the other teams in patrolling the area. During the entire Crailsheim operation, the 90th proved exceptionally capable in every task it was called upon to perform. Despite constant enemy resistance, the Cavalry successfully accomplished its mission.

For the Tenth Armored Division, the night of April 9 signalled the end of offensive operations in the Crailsheim area. When Task Forces Riley and Ulrich pulled into the Berdshausen area, it meant the end of these operations. Crailsheim had been captured but for lack of supplies and sufficient troops and because of the strong enemy air-ground showing, the remaining mission of capturing the Schwabisch Hall-Backnang line had to be abandoned. "At no time except when the Germans controlled the air in Africa, have I ever seen so many German planes as over the Crailsheim area," General Piburn told the writer. Further, "the threat of continued attacks on Tiger positions by some three thousand enemy troops," he said, "caused Colonel Thayer to withhold Task Force Richardson, newly-arrived in Crailsheim, from offensive action." For VI Corps and the Division too, it was disheartening not to be able to make use of the immense tactical advantage gained in the surprise capture of Crailsheim.

THAYER'S MARAUDERS

The battle activity of Combat Command A and the Reserve Command have been reported in full. Turning now to Combat Command B, it will be noted that General Morris ordered Thayer's marauders to head for Crailsheim when Task Force Richardson pulled into the Assamstadt area. Lieut. Col. John Sheffield, Division G-3, asked that CC B establish a "chain of armor" between Bad Mergentheim and Crailsheim. Thayer obliged by setting strong points at every possible enemy approach. He supplemented this device by sending out light patrols to sweep between the strong points. The purpose of this plan was to keep the main supply route to Crailsheim free and clear. To the Tigers and Germans alike in the days to come, this was to be known as the battle of the "Bowling Alley" as the main route to Crailsheim was so aptly named. Task Force Richardson began this phase by charging down the road from Stuppach through Wachbach and on to Herbsthausen. Though other Tiger units already had travelled this road, the enemy surged back to dispute our control of the MSR. Task Force Chamberlain looped in behind Richardson and maintained continuous contact in the town of Wachbach. The next day, Chamberlain rumbled south, trailing Richardson as he did the day before. Team Maher, following orders, established four strong points on the northern section of the road while Team O'-Grady outposted the southern section. Meanwhile, Task Force Richardson had the vital task of wheeling south to make sure that the supply vehicles included in his column would reach Crail sheim to aid the beleagured troops there. However, the shrewd Germans allowed Richardson to proceed almost to Bartenstein, then cut the MSR behind him and attacked the column, using small arms and mortars to impede the Force's progress. Heretofore, the Luftwaffe had bombed and strafed the main supply route, but now it was held in check by our supporting P-47's.

Behind Richardson, Chamberlain's command was busily eliminating small pockets of stubborn Germans dug in in the woods north of Bartenstein. Team Maher routed some 200 enemy troops there as O'Grady prowled south to make contact with Richardson's rear. South of Machbach, the enemy infiltrators sliced in behind the head of the Combat Command B column to slow down its speed. At one point, the longest tree abatis yet observed was strewn for a hundred yards across the main road. Before the column could continue south this obstacle had to be cleared. During an intense enemy artillery barrage the "tree block" was pushed aside. During the night, Chamberlain established prearranged strong points and patrolled the sector of the MSR against light enemy activity. During the night, Task Force Richardson

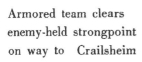

Armored team clears
enemy-held strongpoint
on way to Crailsheim

German infantry routed from woods by lone Tiger Sherman

managed to charge through the thin crust of enemy resistance and whipped into Crailsheim before daylight. After delivering badly-needed supplies, Richardson established a series of strong points from Crailsheim north to Blaufelden. For the rest of April 9, Combat Command B continued faithfully to carry out its assigned mission of outposting and patrolling the "Rollenbahn." Continued infiltration by the enemy was halted, for the most part, though in the northern sector the Germans continued to throw in artillery fire to prevent full use of the main route to Crailsheim. In the meantime, friendly doughs continued to press in from the north to take over that area of responsibility from our units.

On April 9, Team O'Grady was subjected to heavy strafing by 36 enemy fighter planes, but luckily escaped without serious losses. On the same day, units of the 90th Cavalry passed through Combat Command B and rolled down the "Bowling Alley" all the way to Crailsheim, arriving at midnight. In the afternoon of April 8, Colonel Thayer alerted all units in the area to desist from shooting at low flying aircraft unless hostile action was indicated. This order was designed to protect our own planes from damage às they flew in supplies for the hard-pressed Tigers at Crailsheim.

Though the details of the Tigers' resupply by air have already been outlined, it is important to mention the vital role of the Air Force in delivering badly-needed supplies to Combat Command A in Crailsheim. The sudden and devastating advance of the Tenth Armored in the Crailsheim area, threw the Germans off balance for a time. Their rapid recovery, however, enabled them to cut the important main supply route to cut off our task force units there. In doing so, the Germans regained the necessary strength to offset our tactical advantage. Were it not for the timely air supply at the Crailsheim airfield, Tiger prospects for escape would have been slim indeed.

CRAILSHEIM GIVEN UP

Throughout the night of April 10, the Germans stabbed constantly at the Crailsheim defenses with patrol actions. It was soon apparent that they were aware of the strength and locations of our defenses, for they put together a rugged attack against Tiger units there. About 600 troops of the enemy's Alpine Regiment forged in from the south, east and northeast, hitting Task Force Hankins with heavy impact. Teams Hill, Havlowitz and Holland bore the brunt of the German assault. The 420th Field Artillery Battalion, commanded by Lt. Col. Crittenberger, in support of Havlowitz, plastered the on-rushing enemy and, with the Team, helped to break up the attack. But Team Hill on the southern side of Crailsheim was less fortunate and was overrun by the enemy assault. Penetrating the main line of resistance, after having broken through the outposts, the Germans fought a pitched battle in the streets with Hill's defenders. The situation was becoming more critical by the minute as Major Hankins hurriedly committed a reserve platoon from Holland's team into the fray. Together, the two reserve platoons and Team Hill systematically chopped up the enemy penetration as Tiger artillery denied avenues of approach for enemy reinforcement from the

247

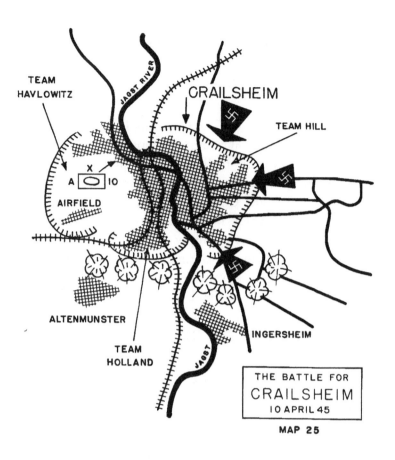

TEAM
HAVLOWITZ

JAGST RIVER

CRAILSHEIM

TEAM HILL

X

A ☐ 10

AIRFIELD

ALTENMUNSTER

INGERSHEIM

TEAM
HOLLAND

JAGST

THE BATTLE FOR
CRAILSHEIM
10 APRIL 45

MAP 25

south. During the attack on Lieut. Hill's unit, he requested artillery fire directly on top of his position. Upon verification of his request the fire was promptly delivered. Frantic attempts by Task Force Commander Hankins to get a report on the effects of the fire were negative. Later, an inspection of the area by Major Blair, Executive Officer of the 61st Armored Infantry Battalion, revealed that Lieut. Hill had snatched up a rifle and personally killed eleven enemy in and around his command post. Hankins says, "Lieut. Hill was probably the outstanding junior officer in the operation and as fate would have it, he was killed in action while attempting to free a stalled tank."

For the fourth time, Team Holland cleaned out Altenmunster. Not only was the German attack thrown back by noon on April 10, but their troops took a frightful beating in the process. Once again all defenses in the Crailsheim area were soundly reestablished. During the Battle of Crailsheim a constant effort was made to strengthen the defenses by means of position changes. One such change was debated by Captain Max Schoenberg, Headquarters Company commander of the 61st. Though he considered moving his Command Post to the Crailsheim city bank, for a reason known only to himself, he decided against the change of location. From that day on he was tagged as "Stay Put Max". Fortunately, he and his men were not present when the bank building was leveled to the ground by enemy artillery fire the next morning.

THACKSTON BATTERED

While enemy troops lashed out against Hankins at Crailsheim, other Germans in the northwest, at dawn on April 11, slammed in on Thackston at Ilshofen. Here some 200 enemy doughs were held in check by the Task Force, aided by the 419th's artillery. By 0900, this attack too, was beaten back and, as elsewhere, the Germans suffered heavy losses: 50 killed, 17 wounded and 65 captured—including the enemy commander. After destroying an assault gun, Thackston's men reorganized their newly-won positions.

Despite our ability to beat off one attack after another, it became increasingly evident to General Piburn that his Command could not continue for long to absorb additional losses and still maintain supremacy in the area. He requested more infantry support and made it clear to VI Corps that he could not guarantee holding the area against growing enemy strength without substantial increases in personnel. Corps could not meet his demand, for no additional troops were available. After consulting with General Morris, General Brooks decided to accomplish his Corps mission by making a closer envelopment with the Tenth Armored by withdrawing the Division and having it follow the 63rd Infantry Division across the Jagst River and attack towards Heilbronn. Orders were then issued to

Combat Command A to withdraw to the line of Steinkirchen-Langenburg-Blaufelden. A plan was devised in which Task Force Thackston was to slip out of Ilshofen to Dorzbach. It was to be followed by Task Force Hankins and both forces were to use the route taken by Task Force Ulrich. To cover CC A's and the Reserve Command's movements, Combat Command B and the 90th Cavalry stayed behind to block enemy attempts to disrupt the operation. Before Task Force Thackston closed in the assembly area in the vicinity of Hohebach on the afternoon of April 11, it had to disengage from combat. Thackston's Tigers of Combat Command R established an enviable fighting record during the Crailsheim operation, their losses of 17 killed, 77 wounded and 13 missing in action provided grim testimony to the rough-going encountered there. The Tigers of Task Force Hankins also suf· fered heavy losses in the operation. When the unit assembled near Dorzbach, it had lost 26 killed and more than a hundred wounded. This great unit bore the brunt of the enemy assaults against Crailsheim. Finally, Task Force Ulrich was attached to Task Force Riley for control purposes during the withdrawal. Both units were detached from Combat Command A at this time and placed under direct command of General Morris. When the units arrived in the vicinity of Dorrenzimmer in late afternoon, the Tiger Commander sent them out to reconnoiter crossings over the Kocher River near Weissbach in accordance with the Tenth Armored's new plan to drive to Heilbronn and assist the 100th Infantry Division fighting there.

COMBAT COMMAND B ENDS OPERATION

On April 10, Task Force Chamberlain busied itself patrol· ling the "Bowling Alley" between Bartenstein and Blaufelden while Task Force Richardson held the Wallhausen-Gaggstadt area. The latter had alerted Team Lordwood earlier to prepare for the movement to Crailsheim to lend a hand to Piburn's forces there. But the movement never materialized because of a change in Division plans.

Tenth Armored doughs swing across footbridge and push on into Forchtenburg, Germany

At 0730 the next day, Colonel Thayer directed Chamberlain to bring his command to Blaufelden for movement to the new assembly area near Kirchberg. Three hours later, as they neared that town, they were subjected to bombing and strafing by the Luftwaffe, but this failed to destroy the column. At 1500, after having closed in the assembly area, the Task Force was notified that its new mission was to help cover the withdrawal of CC A from Crailsheim. From Kirchberg, after an all-night march —during which time the unit was continually plagued by enemy action—it assembled near Bartenstein in order to carry out its new assignment. Meanwhile, Lieut. Col. Richardson, from his CP at Wallhausen, proceeded to Thayer's Command Post at Rot am See to get further orders for the withdrawal of Combat Commands A and R from the Crailsheim area. Shortly after 1400, Richardson left Thayer's Headquarters armed with orders to block, while Combat Command A quit the Crailsheim sector. After that operation, Richardson was to assemble his men in the Mulfingen area. After an all-night march, Richardson's Tigers rumbled into Mulfingen without incident, at breakfast time, on April 11. Its mission was completed.

TRIPLE MISSION FOR THE CAVALRY

On April 10, Lichirie's 90th Cavalry was occupied in providing its efficient mobile power to aid Hankins in Crailsheim, guarding the bridge across the Jagst River at Kirchberg and patrolling the road between Crailsheim-Ilshofen-Berndhausen. Troops A and D, reinforced, helped to back up Task Force Hankins while C Troop, reinforced, cruised up and down the "Rollenbahn". Squadron headquarters and headquarters of Troops E and F were located at Wollmerhausen. Troop B, in reserve, protected the Kirchberg bridge until 1800, when it was switched over to Rossfeld to patrol the line Rossfeld-Maulach. Of the Cavalry units engaged in action, only Troop C found heavy opposition from the enemy which constantly sniped and fired dreaded panzerfaust at them on the MSR between Ilshofen and Crailsheim. On the afternoon of April 10, Lichirie was told to assist in covering CC A's withdrawal, in cooperation with Thayer's CC B. Small groups of the enemy did their utmost to prevent the Cavalry from doing its assigned job. But they were unsuccessful from the outset, in preventing an orderly withdrawal by Combat Command A. "Operation Crailsheim" ended before dark on April the 11th when the squadron safely established itself at the Tenth's assembly area near Steinkirchen and Blaufelden.

GOOD RIDDANCE

One of the most frustrating battle operations in the Division's brilliant combat history was now concluded. Begun with promise of sweeping victory, the battle instead ended in a bitter deadlock. With adequate infantry support in the early stages of the operation, the Tigers of the Tenth would have been able to sweep the Germans from the Crailsheim area. On April 12, however, the enemy was once again in full possession of the contested city, a city retaken by default.

Despite the severity of our losses, the seizure and retention of Crailsheim for four days by the Tigers netted 2,000 prisoners, disrupted enemy rear communications, killed more than 1,000 Germans, diverted large enemy forces from main efforts elsewhere and shot down 50 of the Luftwaffe's few remaining fighter planes. Without question, this was one of the most spectacular and successful battles in the Division's history. In the opinion of several key Tiger staff officers, a definite breakthrough had been achieved by the Tenth—a breakthrough which might have been carried all the way to the Alps—had higher headquarters taken quick advantage of the situation. However, this thinking was a matter of individual judgment at the time as it is entirely possible that Seventh Army's lack of sufficient infantry support would have denied VI Corps' bid for further exploitation of the breakthrough. At any rate, by the time Army was aware of the breakthrough, it was too late. The Germans knew it too, and had taken immediate steps to prevent further penetration in the area by the Division.

Former Staff Sergeant Donald Jerge, Company A, 54th Armored Infantry Battalion, provides the following "eye witness" account of the Crailsheim operation: "When we started towards Crailsheim", he said, " we expected little opposition because another task force had already rolled down the highway. An anti-tank gun hidden in a straw pile on the outskirts of a tiny

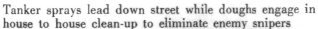

Tanker sprays lead down street while doughs engage in house to house clean-up to eliminate enemy snipers

village suddenly belched lead at the column. There was an awful explosion as the shells hit the halftrack behind us. Amid screams of the wounded, we saw Tigers spilling out of the halftracks. Everyone ran like hell for cover. Our vehicles became mired in the field as we tried to bypass the roadblock. The outfit was in a jam as the Jerries threw a heavy artillery barrage. They followed this with a smoke screen which was intended to hide the enemy attack coming up. The Germans fell before our machine guns when the wind suddenly removed the protective smoke screen from in front of them. Some stood, others ran, but they were all caught in a crossfire and cut down.

"The column got out of the mud and raced across a big field. The purpose of this assault was to clear out the German gunners from the woods to our front. Tanks and halftracks spread out in a line—then surged forward, firing every gun. Everyone was cheering and yelling. When we got near the woods we ran

Tiger teams push forward past empty German houses

onto a road and the ditches on the sides were filled with Germans. The entire column raked the ditches, killing most of the enemy before they could fire their rifles and panzerfaust. At this time, our sergeant got a bullet through his neck and his buddy, who was helping him, was wounded when a bullet went through his helmut, grazing his skull. We stopped and left the two men to be picked up by the aid men and then took off again. As we came within gunshot of Crailsheim we picked up an unusual signal on our radio. The operator asked for the message again. When I asked him what it was, he said, 'It's nothing that concerns you.' At that moment an M-E 109 swooped down and strafed the column. Later we learned that the message was from headquarters warning us to be on the lookout for enemy planes strafing the area. When we entered Crailsheim, we found that the city was being bombed and strafed constantly by the new jets of the Luftwaffe. We thought at last we would get a chance to rack up some sack time, but instead we were sent on our way again.

ON TO ILSHOFEN

"We traveled a helluva long way after we left Crailsheim, and it got cold and dark. Up ahead we finally saw a light and knew that this was to be our destination. It was Ilshofen, a town lighted by burning buildings . . . the fires were out of control as the Germans' antiquated fire department struggled in vain to douse the flames. However, we managed to find a place to sleep for the night, but not before we fried every egg we could find. Before we turned in, we posted two men to listen behind a barn in back of our house for the approach of the enemy. During this time too, we released some of the villagers so that they could return home. This was a big mistake, we found, for later that night, a tremendous explosion rocked us out of bed. The villagers apparently had informed a panzerfaust team of the whereabouts of our CP and the location of one of our tanks. However, in the darkness, the enemy gunners missed the targets and hit the side of the barn instead, blasting a hole big enough to drive a truck through.

"At another town, my platoon had the job of guarding the approaches. We dug a deep foxhole and put our machine gun in it and were ready for an expected attack. It came, but not from the ground; the enemy's Luftwaffe bombed and strafed us mercilessly. Luckily, we escaped being hit. We ran into a windfall when one of our guys found a meat packing plant—so between the bombing and shelling, we cooked a big steak for ourselves! Later while we were occupying another house, a German shell zoomed in one side and out the other. Since it didn't explode, no one was injured.

"After two days of this rat race we learned that the Command was badly needed at Crailsheim.

THE BIG SQUEEZE

"By the time we started to roll down the "Bowling Alley", the Germans had pushed to within a mile of either side of the road. For this reason, it was necessary to keep our tanks swinging up and down the highway in order to keep it clear. Then, when we got into Crailsheim we found the city wrecked. The Germans had bombed, strafed and shelled the city so much that it looked like St. Lo and other badly damaged French towns. Later, American planes landed under fire to deliver gas, oil, ammo and food and to evacuate our wounded. By this time, the long finger of our attack was broken. We had to move back into Crailsheim to join up with the other units there. It was a miserable trip back through the woods at night as we foundered in ditches a couple of times.

"We used a white cloth so that the tank behind could avoid ramming into us, and the pitch blackness was filled with sparks and the roar of the tanks and the clink of the halftracks as we rolled past knocked-out German and American vehicles on both sides of the road where we had fought only a few days before. This is what it was like at Crailsheim. When we left on April

Tigers' tank is ditched

11, we took 2,000 prisoners with us and left another 1,000 enemy dead behind."

The Battle of Crailsheim is now history but to the men who were there and to the wounded who were tended by the tireless and valiant medics it will remain an indelible mark on their memories.

The supporting medical company for the attack had been cut off and medical aid was needed badly, so Section A, Company A, of the 80th Med. Bn. received orders to leave for Crailsheim at once. The column started out at once, led by Capt. James Curbo, and the reconnaissance was furnished by the 90th Cavalry. Sniper and small arms fire harrassed the column continually, finally forcing it off the road onto an overland route. Air activity was also heavy and the column was forced to dig in several times. But despite these difficulties the column reached Crailsheim safely at 0500, April 9.

Upon their arrival, the medics selected the local theatre as the treatment station and they were greeted by those in charge with broad smiles, expressing their sense of security to see their own medics on the scene. The wounded men received immediate attention and were billeted for the night in the local post office,

257

and those needing surgical attention were put in the lobby of the theatre, later being transferred to the basement. Great quantities of plasma and whole blood were given, with the whole blood being flown in along with other medical supplies by C-47s that were landing under constant enemy mortar fire. Surgery was continuous from 0530, April 9, until the last case came off the table at 1500, April 10. With each passing hour the town became hotter and hotter, and all night long the screaming meemies kept coming in but true to medical training, the patient came first and their safety last.

On the morning of April 10, a convoy of ambulances was formed to evacuate the casualties to a zone of safety, and medium tanks were offered as an escort but Capt. Curbo decided to run the gauntlet of enemy fire without them. The order to evacuate Crailsheim came at 1600, April 10, and it was a tired group of medics that loaded their equipment against time, happy in the knowledge that every last case had been treated. CC A led the column out and, drawing enemy fire, the medics were protected from any rear action by the bristling armor of CC B. Rising over the knoll that marked the exit of the town the tired medics could watch the efficient 419th Field Artillery systematically destroying the once beautiful city of Crailsheim for which the enemy was so stubbornly fighting.

To the ever adventurous unarmed medics Crailsheim was a little Bastogne. Those medics who were present at Crailsheim should not go unmentioned and they are as follows: Capt. James R. Curbo, Capt. Charles Pruitt, Capt. Thaddeus Slomkowski, Tec 3 Woodrow Lucroy, Tec 3 Jack Bradican, Sgt. Henry R. Gooley, Tec 4 Eldredge Welton, Tec 4 Arthur Starbird, Tec 5 Alton L. Aldridge, Pfc Joseph Brame, S-Sgt Henry Humphries, Pfc Granville Taylor, Pfc Timothy Keenan, Tec 5 Eulon Brasel, Pfc Joseph Maguire, Pvt George Paro, Tec 5 Charles F. Black, Pfc Floyd Duignan, Pfc Laverne Zlomke, Tec 5 Peter Pamianco. Pfc's Smith Coombe, Robert Figireroa, John Howard, Melvin Kolessa, Robert Duerr and Clause Peterson.

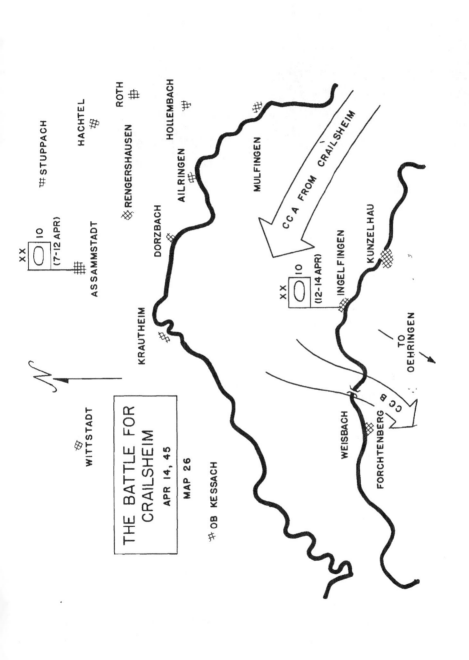

THE BATTLE FOR CRAILSHEIM

APR 14, 45

MAP 26

Sherman's armor is implemented with layer of rock

by Richard J. H. Johnston
New York Times

"With the 10th Armored Division in Germany, April 9. The German Air Force and ground forces cooperated today to press dawn-to-dusk attacks on the constricting band of steel being drawn by the Tenth Armored Division of the United States Seventh Army around German troops in the Heilbronn-Bad Mergentheim-Crailsheim triangle.

"While German ground troops continued their furious attempts to cut the Tenth's supply route from Bad Mergentheim to Crailsheim, twenty-five miles to the south, the Luftwaffe followed up an early-morning dive-bombing and strafing attack by thirty-six planes on Crailsheim with reckless, low-level slashes through the day on American positions and supply columns.

"The German Air Force sent twenty-five additional fighters into an attack on leading elements of Major General William H. H. Morris' Tenth Armored Division units stabbing westward from Crailsheim at a point six miles from this pivotal town.

"The ferocity and costliness of these attacks indicated high value that the German High Command placed on the troops whose position in the triangle offered strong potentialities for entrapment and the mounting danger of new drives for Nuremburg and Munich by Lieut. Gen. Alexander M. Patch's Seventh Army.

CRAILSHEIM "BASTOGNE NO. 2"

"Crailsheim, forty miles southwest of Nuremburg and 100 miles northwest of Munich, seized two days ago by a task force of the Tenth Armored Division, was described today by members of General Morris' staff as "Bastogne No. 2".

"The town got its worst beating in last twenty-four hours, during which the only supply route leading into the town was cut a number of times at a half dozen places between Bad Mergentheim and Crailsheim.

"Reopened time after time by the Tenth's armor, the road was called "rolling bahn", or bowling alley, by German war prisoners.

"For the second successive day, correspondents tried to get down this road and failed. The best instructions General Morris' men were able to give was to "start like a bat out of hell and keep going faster."

"But the Germans kept up an incessant slamming, and the path had been liberally sprinkled with German mines last night. Along with the artillery coming in liberal quantities, there are the steel fingers of snipers' bullets searching out every moving thing along that road.

"Despite this murderous fire, a convoy plunged through from Mergentheim to Crailsheim at 6 o'clock this morning to bring gasoline and ammunition to the armor. Later in the day 100 C-47 cargo planes landed at the Crailsheim airbase.

"With cool confidence, General Morris studied the situation map this afternoon, watching the crayoned tentacles probing into German positions. He knew he had the enemy guessing his intentions.

"He launched this attack against fully experienced and well trained German troops who used this area for replacement training. But the audacity and speed of the Tenth's drive seemed to have confused the enemy, who, despite his strength and cunning, has been unable to nip off the swiftly advancing armor or figure out General Morris' next move.

"The Supreme effort being made by the Germans to retake Crailsheim, as well as sever its supply route, indicates that the Germans have taken alarm at the Seventh Army's advantage of sitting astride axial line running westward to Nuremburg.

"In an effort to find out what is going on, the Luftwaffe tried during the day to be everywhere at the same time.

GROUND GUNNERS BAG PLANE

"Into the area of a forward command post roared three Messerschmitt-109's strafing from a height of 74 feet. Anti-aircraft crews and machine gunners scored hits on one plane, which crashed within yards of a point where four correspondents were holding a conversation.

" 'Get the pilot's name and address,' said one gunner, 'while we get you another.'

"Twelfth Tactical Air Command bombers maintained a protective cover for the American forces and the battle presented the odd spectacle of two opposing air-ground contests going on simultaneously.

"But our superiority weakened the German effort, forcing the Luftwaffe to give up the battle and flee from the area.

"West of Crailsheim Lieut. Col. John R. Riley of Danville, Va., forged ahead to take Croffelbach, ten miles from Crailsheim, and tonight elements of his forces were less than fourteen miles from a junction with the 63rd Infantry Division driving down from the Bad Mergentheim area.

"To keep open the Bad Mergentheim-Crailsheim road, Col.

B. G. Thayer of Cleveland, Ohio, commanding Combat Command B, has divided his forces into two units and is covering the supply route."

BEACHHEAD NEWS
Wednesday, April 11, 1945
CRAILSHEIM SUPPLIED FROM AIR

"In one of the closest front line air supply missions ever attempted on the Western Front or any other front three missions totalling 50 C-47 planes yesterday and the day before landed supplies of gasoline and ammunition for elements of the 10th Armored Division at Crailsheim within 1,000 yards of the front lines.

"The planes, flown by pilots of the 9th Troop Carrier Command, were heavily escorted by P-47's of the 6th Fighter Wing and landed on a strip marked with panels by the 10th Armored. A check later showed that not a single plane was lost in the spectacular mission.

"Besides gas and ammunition supplied by air, five cub planes flew in a medical team and medical supplies with equal success and evacuated a seriously wounded man.

10th Armored Beats Off Kraut Attacks

"Elements of the 10th Armored Division yesterday successfully repulsed German counterattacks on Crailsheim and Ilshofen designed to bite off the nose of the salient punched into the enemy lines several days ago.

"Shortly before dawn 600 troops of an Alpine Regiment attacked Crailsheim from the south and southeast. Some managed to infiltrate into the town and occupy a few buildings. Within a few hours, however, these buildings were burned out by our troops and the situation restored.

"Soon after the attack on Crailsheim started, another force of Germans, estimated at 600 and supported by self-propelled guns, attacked Ilshofen from the northwest. Before noon 50 Krauts had been killed, including a company commander, and another 50 taken prisoner.

"Airmen of XII TAC flew 90 missions of 900 sorties in support of Seventh Army on Monday. The enemy's rolling stock was further depleted, bullets and bombs rendering over 500 railroad cars and locomotives unserviceable.

"In an effort at defense the Luftwaffe again appeared, only to lose 26 planes in the ensuing dogfights. In addition the American pilots accounted for another 40 planes on the ground.

"Medium bombers succeeded in blowing up another ammunition dump, the explosion being felt at 15,000 feet, and the town of Neustadt was bombed and left in flames.

"Tabulated results yesterday disclosed that the Luftwaffe's record flying against VI Corps troops on Monday cost it heavily. Corps AA units shot down 7 planes and were credited with another possible."

NEW YORK TIMES
By Richard J. H. Johnston
WITH THE UNITED STATES SEVENTH ARMY, GERMANY, April 8—"The Tenth Armored Division, under the command of Maj. Gen. William H. H. Morris, sent a spearhead today to Crailsheim to catch the Germans completely off balance, and with swift deployment the armor turned sharply westward from that town to threaten an estimated 5000 to 7000 German troops with encirclement.

"Under the command of Maj. T. F. Hankins, a stubby, fiery, red-headed tank commander, 'Task Force Hankins' roared into the town and swung sharp right to begin the plunge westward. Along the Crailsheim-Heilbronn road near Crailsheim another armored column, commanded by Lieut. Col. John R. Reilly of Danville, Va., captured intact an enemy supply train that was puffing along a track in the opposite direction."

10th ARMORED SWEATS IT OUT
By A. I. Goldberg

CRAILSHEIM, Germany, April 9 (Associated Press)

"The heavy tanks, artillery and infantry components of the Tenth Armored division lay in this battered junction on the road to Munich today waiting for their third major German counter-attack in three days.

"The Americans reached Crailsheim Friday after slicing twenty-five miles in less than ten hours and cutting the 17th German SS division in half.

" 'Let 'em come,' said Major Curtis Hankins, Pine Bluff, Ark., who commands the daring task force which slashed south in a maneuver that may spoil any German defense line along the upper Danube.

CAN DO IT AGAIN

" 'We fought them off twice and we can fight 'em off again.'

"There were reports that three thousand Germans were massing in a woods southeast of Crailsheim. The Germans were pouring six-barrel mortar fire into the town and Nazi fighter planes repeatedly strafed it. Jet-planes swooped over at intervals, dropping bombs.

"Just east of the town fifteen C-47 transport planes were taking off after delivering a load of ammunition and gasoline to the American unit. From the north, supplies kept rolling down through German anti-tank gun fire and sniper bullets which took a heavy toll of truck and jeep drivers. By dusk, infantry reinforcements fifteen miles away were slowly clearing a salient toward the town.

" 'If we had had that infantry with us we'd have been half way to Munich by now,' Hankins said.

"Hankins' task force is forty-two miles from the Danube and ninety-five miles from Munich. A red-faced, red-haired Arkansas farmer, Hankins made his reputation first when his task force took Kastel.

"This correspondent reached Crailsheim with Captain Lester Nichols, Division Public Relations Officer, after a dash down the highway known to the Tankers as the "Rollerbahn".

"At the command post was Lt. John Hill of Greenville, N. C., who rode the third tank into the town. He is a combat infantryman who wears the Silver Star and got a battlefield promotion for action covering the withdrawal from Burdorf a month ago.

"Hill was in a hurry to 'get down there and place my men.'

SWEATING IT OUT

" 'We are sweating this out now,' said Lt. Max Schoenberg of Seymour, Conn., who said he had been bombed out of two command posts in the last three days.

" 'If they don't throw any more at us than they have the last two nights, I think we have enough to hold them,' Hankins declared. 'They have been attacking in at least six company strength and they are tough SS babies of all ages, but mostly twenty to twenty-five. They want this town awfully bad.'

"The Germans have been showing strong air activity against the force, sending as many as thirty-eight planes at a time over the town. Several planes have been knocked down.

"German fighters attempted to get a Cub observation plane but an ack-ack outfit including Pfc. Clarence Daniels, Salisbury, N. C., chased them off.

" 'The first supply truck to reach the town got here Sunday,' said supply officer Captain George Signius of Kingstree, S. C., who is a graduate of The Citadel.

"Eight miles north of Crailsheim, a German anti-tank gun in a house forced a bunch of us to jump from our seats, take to a ditch. A tankbuster outfit was called up and with two well-placed shots silenced the gun."

XII

DIVIDE AND CONQUER

FROM THE KOCHER RIVER TO THE DANUBE

AFTER PROCESSING the two thousand German prisoners captured in the Crailsheim fighting and sending them to the rear, the
Tenth, on April 11, turned its attention to new battle assignments.
VI Corps' revised plans now called for the Tiger Division to shift
its combat power in the direction of Heilbronn where the 100th Infantry Division continued to batter that stronghold. East of Heilbronn was Oehringen, ordinarily a set-up for the Tigers, but now
a strong point for the tiring enemy. Task Forces led by Lieut. Col.
Riley and Major Ulrich, thwarted in their efforts to find a bridge
to cross the Kocher, finally found a place to ford that river and
shoved out toward Kirchensall to the south at 1320 on April 11.
Earlier, the entire Division had moved out from the Crailsheim
area to assemble north of the Kocher River. At this time, General
Morris directed Combat Command A to seize Oehringen and continue its movement to the west to meet up with the 100th Infantry
which was at the same time, now driving to the east. At the same
time, the Reserve Command was ordered to back up Combat Command A, while Combat Command B was placed in VI Corps reserve on a two-hour alert basis. Now, Brig. Gen. Edwin W. Piburn's troops barreled ahead, as its three task forces in a power-
packed drive, converged on Bavarian Prince Hohenlohe-Oehr-
ingen's castle-dominated town. When the Command's Riley, Ulrich and Hankins forces entered Oehringen on April 12, they were
met by a hail of panzerfaust, bazooka and burp gun fire. Nazi
fanaticism was slow to die as Wehrmacht and civilians alike resisted with renewed determination. To deal effectively with the
town's defenders, "time on target" fire was ordered by CC A to
"soften up" the enemy. As a result, 52 cannons of the Division's

Major General Edward H. Brooks, VI Corps commander indicates direction of attack to Oehringen to Tiger commanders Lieut. Col. McChristian (left), General Morris and General Piburn.

Artillery were timed to send simultaneous bursts on a carefully pinpointed area over the town.

The Tigers' persistent efforts against the enemy at Oehringen prevailed and the town was captured on April 13. But it took Riley's and the Reserve Command's Thackston forces who had re-entered Oehringen at 2100 the night before to smash resistance amid the burning buildings. Meanwhile, the 90th Recon screened the left flank of Task Forces Ulrich and Hankins as they darted south of Oehringen to continue the attack westward. By mid-afternoon, the last resistance at Oehringen was crushed by the Armor-raiders of Thackston and Riley permitting both forces to roll on toward Heilbronn. At 2130 the Tigers linked up with the 100th Infantry's doughs at a point six miles east of the fortress city of Heilbronn. Then, while Riley maintained contact with the infantry and patrolled the road to swallow up by-passed enemy, Ulrich drove west through several towns to Dimbach where his forces also joined the 100th's doughs. At Windischenbach, the Reserve Command aided Ulrich in eliminating strong small arms fire coming from the left flank. At this time, Task Force Hankins was relieved by the 63rd Infantry and hurried to an assembly area near Oehringen.

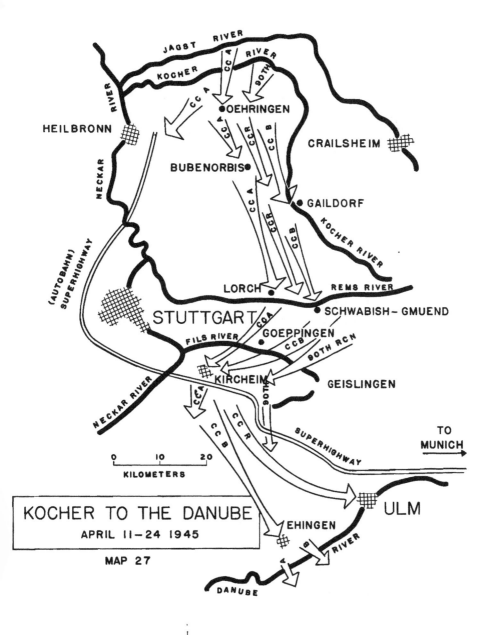

KOCHER TO THE DANUBE

APRIL 11—24 1945

MAP 27

MISSION COMPLETED

The Tenth's meeting with the doughs of the 100th and 63rd Infantry just east of Heilbronn signalled the end of its mission. Now supported by the two crack infantry outfits, the Tiger Division was ready to spring southward to the Danube River. Bavaria's rugged terrain lay ahead, in addition to the Rems and Fils Rivers. These obstacles were to cause great difficulty in tank and track mobility later. On April 16, the Tenth was removed from VI Corps' reserve and passed through the left flank of the 63rd Infantry. For two days, Colonel Thayer's Combat Command B, aided by the Second Battalion of the 254th Infantry Regiment, fought to capture Schwabisch Hall. Hidden allies of the enemy were minefields, roadblocks and blown bridges, which strained the already overworked Tiger engineers' efforts to clear a path for continued advance. By April 18, however, the VI Corps push blossomed into a major drive as CC A larruped through the 100th Infantry's right flank and joined CC B and the Reserve Command to bolt ahead nine miles through crumbling enemy lines. A formidable array of six armored columns belonging to the three combat commands streaked ahead to grab Schwabisch Hall, Wielandsweiler, Gaildorf, Goeppingen, Lorch and Kircheim. During this period, Brig. Gen. Edwin W. Piburn, one of the Army's most highly-decorated general officers, was seriously wounded and was evacuated to a rear area field hospital. Two days later, the author accompanied General Morris to the hospital where the latter pinned the Silver Star medal on Piburn's blood-stained shirt. His face and hands were burned and his leg was shattered but eventually, he recovered sufficiently to be assigned to active duty again. Later, he served with distinction in Korea as did a few other Tiger commanders. Colonel Thomas Brinkley replaced General Piburn when the latter was wounded and Colonel Cornelius A. Lichirie became Trains commander. Then too, Major Richard Scott was named 90th Recon commander.

On April 19, the 44th Infantry Division was attached to

VI Corps and wheeled through the 63rd Infantry to back up the Tenth's drive. At the same time, VI Corps' General Brooks ordered the 103rd Infantry Division to attack in the area between the Tenth Armored and the 100th Infantry. Two days earlier, Task Force Hankins had taken Schupach, as Task Forces Riley and Ulrich overran Bubenorbis and Gailsbach. The Reserve Command led by Colonel Wade C. Gatchell ran into a minefield at Raibach but overcame this problem and forged ahead as Major Richard Scott's 90th Recon worked ahead quietly and efficiently along the east flank. Combat Command B's units commanded by Chamberlain and Richardson skirted Schwabish Hall in their push southward and sped ten miles further into the Fatherland. On April 18, too, Hankins' forces to the west drilled ahead, clearing hundreds of yards of the enemy's tree-felled abatis, as it battled its way through Sittenhardt to Hauten. Riley's forces at the time took possession of Oberrot and Schobrunn. During the morning of April 19, the Division's advance was slowed by steep hills and deep valleys but later in the day the Tigers triumphed over the unfavorable terrain to forge ahead 17 miles to the Rems River. The approach to the Schwabish Albe, a high plateau, could have been

Brig. Gen. Edwin W. Piburn is decorated with Silver Star by General Morris in field hospital

271

Tigers'water supply is assured
by Armoraiders of 55th
Armored Engineer Battalion

easily defended by the enemy. But he was certain that the American attack would come from the west. When it rolled in from the north instead, the Germans were unable to halt the Armoraiders.

Combat Command B which had been dominating the Lowenstein hills to the south, seized two intact bridges across the Rems River west of Schwabisch Gmuend. After by-passing that town, it crossed the river to continue the advance. CC A, to the west, hit a 40 MPH pace as a result of its quick-thinking Tigers, who carried a power saw to rip through the roadblocks. Later in the day, CC A grabbed another bridge over the Rems River at Lorch which was about 5 miles west of Gmuend. Here, an enemy plane was scared off as it was about to land and an enemy train, instead of making a stop, got up steam and raced away as both plane and train were surprised by Tiger armored units in the town. Left behind were the enemy's Volksturm who were quickly dumped into the Tenth's PW cages. Leading CC A's rapid pace was Task Force Hankins which hurdled both the Rems and Fils Rivers in a drive that consumed 19 miles. Other units of CC A pushed on to capture another bridge at Feurndau, near Goeppingen, the same day. On April 20, the Reserve Command, supported by the 114th Infantry of the 44th Division, mopped up in the by-passed Gmuend area as CC A and CC B crossed the Fils River and slammed southwest to Kircheim, which fell quickly to the two Commands. Task Force Hankins again led the atack which covered 32 miles in two days to Kircheim. By April 22, Chamberlain and Richardson closed in on the same target and then burst ahead to the Danube

272

River at Ehingen. At the same time, the Reserve Command had cut the autobahn just south of Kircheim and in so doing, reached the Division's first objective in its flight to the south.

STUTTGART ENCIRCLED

On April 22, the Tenth was ordered by VI Corps to swing southeast and continue to harrass the fleeing enemy. Mopping up and guarding our flanks were the alert doughs of the 44th Infantry Division. When the Armoraiders captured Kircheim, they were only 15 miles north of French forces which, by this time, had prodded southeast from Reutlingen below Hitler's famed autobahn. The Germans' key city of Stuttgart was now virtually surrounded and the escape corridor was considerably narrowed. The enemy was harrassed even more in the corridor by our Air Corps which teamed up with ground forces to plaster that area with fire. The Tenth Armored's breakthrough, greatly aided by its infantry support, helped to form a giant pocket from which the 19th German Army struggled desperately to escape. Their efforts to avoid capture were further minimized by the effectiveness of the 103rd Infantry on the right and the 100th Infantry on the left of the spearheading Tigers who squeezed against the corridor. When the Division's final objective was reached at Kircheim, it signalled the end of Hitler's remaining die-hard army units in that sector. For at last, the enemy's line of resistance was shattered at both flanks and in the center. In just one day, on April 21, more than 400 prisoners were taken, including a German major general. More important was the fact that the Stuttgart-Munich Reich autobahn had been cut and thousands of the enemy were trapped as they attempted to defend Stuttgart against the French who knifed in from the west. The Division's situation was considerably improved on April 21, when five of its task forces ground out 12 miles in the direction of the Danube and took 1,000 additional prisoners to swell its PW cages far beyond capacity. Killed at Kircheim was the Tenth's much-decorated Lieut. Col. Jack J. Richardson. He was replaced by Major James B. Duncan.

One of the most important days in the Tenth's memorable history was April 22, the day Chamberlain's forces steamrollered to the Danube. By midnight they succeeded in capturing a bridge at Ehingen. Then, on April 23, while Task Force Duncan probed along the Danube's north bank to locate two more bridges, Chamberlain destroyed a German supply column north of Ehingen. Further downstream, Combat Command A's Riley rumbled across another bridge as Duncan's tanks and tracks crossed the Danube at 2200. On April 24 Hankins was attached to the Reserve Command. The same day his force sped across the river and headed for Ulm. Upon arrival there, Hankins and his Tigers joined the 44th Infantry in wiping out waning resistance while Task Force Thackston blocked outside Ulm. At this juncture, the Tigers were further south than any other American Army unit, and were ready to claw at the heart of Germany's highly touted National Redoubt area. The Third Reich was almost a dead government now, as allied armies to the north were inflicting terrific punishment on the beaten enemy. The Tenth Armored was now poised above the great National Redoubt, an area which the Germans claimed could never be captured by the Americans. However, this claim, along with their hopes for a "Thousand Year Reich" died when the Tiger's mailed fist hit them again and for the last time to end the war in the first week of May of 1945.

Wartime landscape. Enemy forces are driven from buildings set afire by tankers south of Oehringen

XIII

THE LAST KILOMETER

FROM THE DANUBE TO THE ALPS

THE FINAL MISSION of the United States Seventh Army was to block the passes into Austria and to seize the Brenner Pass-Innsbruck area. In the closing days of the war, the Germans retreated without hope before the Army's relentless advance. Their 19th Army was almost destroyed and their 1st and 7th Armies had been ripped to shreds by rampaging American tank and infantry divisions. Enemy troops, caught in vast pockets, were issued "discharges" by the hundreds by their commanders. On April 23, Hitler's southern armies were on the verge of collapse as General Alexander S. Patch's United States Seventh Army drove into the heart of the Tyrol and Bavaria. On the right flank was Major General Edward H. Brooks' VI Corps, in the center was Major General Frank W. Milburn's XXI Corps and on the left flank was Major General Wade H. Haislip's XV Corps.

Forty-eight hours after the Tenth Armored broke through the enemy's lines near Lorch, the VI Corps' offensive assumed major proportions. Now, the Division's combat commands were running wild, as they raced through town after town, leaving the 44th and 103rd Infantry Divisions to mop up after them. "To hell with the enemy's strongpoints", General Brooks told the Tigers and added, "Don't fight with the resistors—there will be plenty of infantry backing you up." Following Corps' directive, General Morris sent his armored units out to search for all available bridges at the Danube between Ulm and Ehingen. Intelligence reports indicated that General Foertch's 1st German Army planned to make a stand at Ulm. This information was gleaned from captured enemy who told of new troop concentrations readied for the defense of Ulm. Despite a known German high command directive that, "Cities are situated at important traffic junctions. Therefore, they must be held at all costs. Should battle commanders fail to defend every town and village, they will be put to death as will all civilians who try to prevent battle commanders from doing their duty," the Seventh Army decided to attack Ulm. VI Corps, which had been driving southwest, was now forced to shift its direction to southeast to carry out Army's newest orders. For this reason too, the 44th Division was placed in support of the Tenth as the Tigers raced to Ehingen at the Danube. By April 23, the First French Army and the American Seventh Army reached the Danube at the same time to deliver a final knockout blow to the enemy's southernmost armies. Now too, as a result of the Germans' very inadequate distribution of forces and scarcity of transportation, they were forced to defend quickly-organized strongpoints as best they could, leaving other and often more important areas unprotected. For these reasons, the Tenth Armored spearheads were able to slash deep into the enemy's rear. Always, this rapid penetration was characterized by mopping up operations of by-passed enemy units by infantry riding on Tiger tanks and more infantry behind our armor. At the time, Tenth Armored reports told of, "consecutive front overlays which had the appearance of an irresistable molten mass spreading southward over the maps. Armored rivulets moved ahead suddenly—were slowed and outdistanced by other rivulets which they joined. Pockets of resistance were left in the armored wake and overrun . . .".

END IN SIGHT

On April 23, 1945, the Tenth Armored Division was spread along the north bank of the Danube River southwest of Ulm. After hurried probing by Combat Commands A and B, three bridges were captured intact and before midnight, crossings were made. Three miles southwest of Ehingen, Tiger forces, at 2200, crossed the river, leaving Chamberlain to finish the clean-up in that town. Forty minutes later, Task Force Riley streamed across

the Danube at a point east of Ehingen. Finally, Ulrich passed
through the Reserve Command's bridgehead and at the same
time, Chamberlain's Tigers crossed. Then all the columns pow-
ered their way eastward. In the meantime, Task Force Hankins
joined Thackston's unit and both were assigned to the Reserve
Command, which was now pushing northeast to assist the 44th
Infantry Division at Ulm. During the morning of April 24, Red
Hankins and his force battled their way into Ulm, a city noted
for its great cathedral and steeple—highest in the world. In 1377,
Ulm was regarded as one of the world's great trading centers but
in the ensuing centuries its trade and power dwindled. Nevertheless, its exquisite gothic spire, rising 528 feet, still stands. The
Tigers had little time for sight-seeing, however, as they battled
an enemy regiment there.

CLOBBERED BY CONNOLLY

Ulm was the most important remaining objective in Wurt-
tenberg. Assigned to lead Task Force Hankins into the city was
Team Connolly, who jumped off in the attack from Blaubeuren
at 2200 on December 24. This Team was strengthened when 55
doughs of the Forty-Fourth joined it to aid in the assault. At
0700 on April 25, Connolly abruptly altered his direction of
attack when he was informed that four other attacking columns,
including part of a French Armored Division, had been stopped
by strong enemy anti-tank fire, and proceeded to Grittelfinger,
located less than two miles from Ulm. Here he was able to survey
the city from a high hill. In less than an hour he outlined a bold
plan of action and then struck out through an enemy-defended
mine field. Once safely through it, the Team went into wedge
formation and charged down into Ulm. In front were five Mediums which gunned aside all opposition as the Team swept ahead
into the western part of the city. In the process, Connolly's
Tigers bagged 600 Germans. Shortly afterwards, an enemy company commander notified Connolly that his battalion commander
wished to surrender. When the two officers returned, they brought

half of an engineer battalion with them. In one day alone, the Team accounted for 1500 prisoners and Connolly, for his imaginative attack, was dubbed "No Road Connolly". While the Reserve Command was busily occupied at Ulm, Combat Command A on the north flank, and Combat Command B on the south, ploughed ahead 23 miles to the Iller Canal where both were stopped for lack of bridges. However, CC B's engineers erected a floating bridge across the river at Dietenheim and a trestle treadway across the canal during the night of April 24. But construction of a bridge for CC A was slowed by persistent enemy fire.

CALCULATED RISK

At this time, an enemy column trapped behind our lines, attempted to escape across CC B's treadway near Dietenheim. Under cover of darkness and led by an American truck, the column rolled on past Tenth Armored units and would have made good its escape were it not for the fact that their own countrymen had blown the bridge across the river which forced the lead vehicle to stop there. A Tiger guard challenged the halted column. He was answered by, "Vas is dat?" from the truck's cab which started a wild fire fight in pitch darkness. In the ensuing struggle, the enemy was routed and a towed 88 captured intact, along with two smaller anti-tank weapons. At the same time, one of Major Geiler's engineer bulldozer operators cut an enemy lieutenant down with his blade.

"MARCHING NORTH, SOUTH, EAST AND WEST"

Resistance in the western part of Ulm had been crushed by Hankins' Armoraiders by late afternoon on April 25 and the force bucked on south of the Danube River beyond the city. At 1400, Chamberlain scooted across the Iller and wheeled south towards Memmingen. He was followed by Task Force Ulrich which prodded north to shut off Ulm's southern escape routes. Riley's command thrust eastward and Duncan turned south

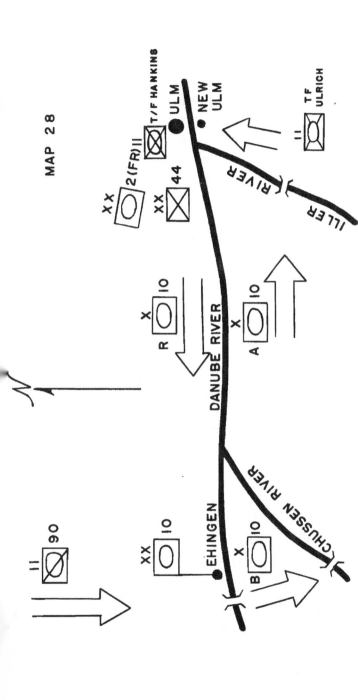

MAP 28

SITUATION ON AFTERNOON 24 APRIL 45
DIVISION WAS MOVING: NORTH – T/F ULRICH
SOUTH – CC B & 90TH RCN.
EAST – CC A
WEST – RES. COMMAND

to back up Chamberlain. At the same time, Lichirie's 90th Recon mopped up by-passed enemy pockets west of the Iller. When Lieut. Gen. Alexander S. Patch, commander of the Seventh Army visited Tiger Headquarters on April 24, he collared Lieut. Col. John W. Sheffield and asked, "Sheffield, what is the Division doing now?" The G-3 answered, "Sir, the Division is marching north, south, east and west!". Then, as the scholarly commander watched with a kind of "show me" attitude, Sheffield described the unusual four-directional movements of Tiger task forces on the war room's maps.

Two days after Patch visited the Tenth Armored's CP, American and French forces in Ulm were disentangled and the bulk of VI Corps troops were shuttled across the Danube to begin the mad dash into the Tyrolean Alps all the way to the Brenner Pass at Innsbruck, Austria. From the River line south, Tenth Armored units spearheaded into the passes and the mountains. Following the armor were the 44th and 103rd Infantry Divisions who protected the Tenth's left and right flanks. The three powerful Divisions roared along at will, smashing the last remnants of General Brandenberg's 19th German Army in the south. The Third Reich was now in a state of collapse as the British closed in on Hamburg, the U. S. First and Ninth Armies neared the Elbe facing Berlin and Patton's Third Army penetrated Czechoslovakia.

PRESS COMMUNIQUE

April 25, 1945

"The fighting Tenth Armored Division in the past 48 hours has captured an estimated 1200 prisoners and taken 40 towns.

"The big news of the day comes from Task Force Hankins, currently 'reducing' resistance in the city of Ulm. Hankins reports that it was Team Connolly who first entered Ulm yesterday morning at 0854. Lt. Bernard Connolly was leading in the point of the task force and banged his way thru the woods west of the city, thereby earning the name of 'No Road' Connolly. At 1400 today, Hankins and elements of the 324 Regiment of the 44th

Division cleared everything to the Danube in Ulm—thus leaving Neu Ulm still to be taken. Incidentally, the nattily-uniformed police force of Ulm was captured intact and with it many pistols were acquired by Pfc. John Stumpf of the 61st Armd. Inf. Bn. of the Tenth Armored. Stumpf decided to play Santa Claus and went back to his CP giving pistols to everyone in sight.

"Among the larger cities the crack Tenth Armored took are Laupheim and Schwendi and, with elements of the 44th Div., Ulm.

"When the Tenth captured Ehingen a few days ago, they sealed off a 1,500 square mile pocket comprising most of Wurtenberg.

"Today, the shortest tour of duty on record for a Jerry was reported by Task Force Chamberlain. This outfit captured a Nazi soldier exactly 15 minutes after he had put on his uniform and reported for duty in the vicinity of Ulm."
Authenticated by G-3.

—Nichols

Men of the 796 Anti-Aircraft Artillery Battalion protect Tiger engineers rebuilding span over Iller Canal.

ARMOR RAMPANT

On April 26, the 44th Infantry took charge of the situation at Ulm permitting Task Forces Hankins, Thackston and Ulrich to join the chase to the south and east. Pushing ahead with violent effectiveness now were the Tenth's three major battle commands. As they streamed southward to the Memmingen-Mindelheim-Landsberg line they were egged on by Major General Edward H. Brooks of VI Corps who declared, "Push on and push hard, this is a pursuit not an attack." The Tigers reached fantastic speeds of more than 30 miles a day during the rout and at the same time managed to gobble up 9,000 prisoners. Along the way, under-manned strong points were destroyed by fire and the enemy's vehicles wrecked. Huge enemy groups were shipped to the rear in never-ending truck loads. During this period, the Tigers of Task Force Hankins overran a carefully camouflaged airfield and sharpened their aim as they picked off German jets as they attempted to take off.

Following the Iller River banks southward, both Chamberlain and Duncan slammed all the way to Memmingen on April 26. The author and Howard Byrnes of "Stars and Stripes" trailed behind Task Force Chamberlain as the latter captured Memmingen. Here we picked up an RAF pilot who had just escaped from an outlying prison camp. Asked if he would be willing to guide us there, he answered in the affirmative and hopped into our vehicle. In less than ten minutes we pulled up at the main gate where we were greeted by about 5,000 gleeful, howling Allied prisoners. The camp commandant ordered the big gate swung open and then lined up all the prison guards at the entrance where their weapons were taken from them. In the next hour the author experienced the moment of a lifetime as he drove through the milling, happy throng, hearing excited shouts of welcome in French, Belgium, Serbian, English and Russian languages. Most gratifying of all, was the experience of being recognized there by four Tenth Armored tankers who had been captured at Bastogne.

When they saw his Tenth Armored sleeve patch, in their uncontrollable joy, they surged out of the crowd and pulled him to the ground. Lest anyone regard the liberation of the camp a matter of heroics, not a shot was fired as the guards surrendered meekly in the knowledge that the war was now past history for them. About an hour later, a Tiger tank platoon arrived to take over, but not before Howard Byrnes had written another great story for "Stars and Stripes".

In the meantime, Combat Command A's Task Force Riley rolled on to Mindelheim as the Reserve Command, on the left, lunged towards Landsberg. Leading the latter's drive was Task Force Thackston who swept by the city on April 26. Few were aware of the fact that Hitler was confined here in Landsberg's prison from November 11, 1923 until December 20, 1934 as a result of his ill-fated Munich beer hall Putsch and that he had written "Mein Kampf" at that time. It might be said too, that few Tigers cared. In the north, Lichirie's cavalrymen provided flank protection as CC A's attack veered south from Mindelheim. On April 27, the three commands spurted 30 miles closer to the Austro-German border and bagged a record 1,800 prisoners. Although the Germans had been committed to hold the line west of the Iller, they were unable to do so in the face of armored columns plunging at them from three directions. These troops were swept up by the supporting infantry which mopped up behind the Tenth. East of the Iller, the enemy's opposition consisted of small arms, anti-tank and occasional artillery fire.

Lt. John Mayhew and 55th Armored Engineer Commander, Lt. Col. William R. Geiler, inspect captured "88" at Dietenheim.

Faces of the Free! Captured American and Allied prisoners of war are liberated from Stalag 7 at Memmingen,
Germany

PSYCHOLOGICAL WARFARE

For a brief moment, each town became a strong point as the
Germans employed panzerfaust and artillery fire which found
their mark against Combat Command B's tanks. This enemy action
resulted in the employment of new devices, when town burgo-
meisters were sent in front of Tiger units armed with ultimatum
notices. Memmingen was one of the towns captured without a
fight as a result of the "messenger" service idea. However, balky
fanatics often insisted on fighting for a losing cause and had to
be rounded up by their own countrymen. Colonel Basil G. Thayer

of CC B, irritated by the delay, sent the following message to the officials in Memmingen, "My troops will march into the town immediately. Display white flags. There will be no firing of any kind. If opposition is received, our tanks, artillery and bombers will destroy the town." The directive was heeded within an hour. No resistance was encountered when Lieut. Col. Thomas C. Chamberlain's Armoraiders entered. A bit of humor unfolded here when a German lieutenant was picked up. He told the Tigers that he had been stopped only a short time before by an SS general who handed him 60 bedraggled Volksturm. "Defend this area to the last man," he was ordered. The general then jumped into his car and left in a cloud of dust.

Without pause, the assault continued as Seventh Army troops controlled successive approaches to the enemy's mountain Redoubt area. The Germans' own blitzkrieg tactics were utilized as one town after another was swallowed up in the rush. Colonel Wade C. Gatchell's Reserve Command on the extreme left flank, made contact with reconnaissance units of the Twelfth Armored Division at the Lech River south of Landsberg, while thirteen miles upstream, Task Forces Riley and Hankins were slowed by a knocked-out bridge at Schongau. Elsewhere, Chamberlain and Duncan, advancing on parallel routes, closed on Kempten which was captured by the Armoraiders of Task Force Chamberlain on April 27. During the same day, this force swept across the Austrian border and captured Imst. The next day Schongau fell to Hankins' fighters. Then Kaufbeuren, Immenstadt and Fuessen all were taken by the Tenth. On April 28, Combat Command A was busily occupied at Schongau where the Fifty-Fifth Engineers sweated in bridging the Lech River. Fortunately, the abutments of a partially destroyed railway bridge were still standing. They were strengthened by the engineers who built a Bailey bridge across the narrow top to permit continued advance. At times, there were grave doubts that the structure would continue to bear heavy traffic which further added to the strain. Luck continued to favor the Tigers however, as CC A traversed the wobbly bridge and pushed south and east. At Riedhausen, Riley's troops met stiff resistance and were temporarily stopped but Hankins' force barreled 23 miles to take Oberammergau, scene of the world-famous Passion Play. Not pausing, this unit pushed on to within 5 miles of Garmisch-Partenkirchen where it was halted by a huge crater.

Damaged railway bridge at Schongau is readied for tanks, track and truck crossing to continue attack into southern Bavaria

VITAL ASSIGNMENT

This phase provided one of the most dramatic episodes in the Tenth Armored's distinguished battle campaign. For it contributed in no small measure to shattering the hope of remaining die-hard Nazis for a last ditch stand in the western sector of their National Redoubt. The vital Echlesbacher Bridge connecting the lowlands of southern Bavaria with the German Alpine country had to be seized intact if the Tigers were to be permitted to continue their attack. The important mission fell to Troop C of the 90th Cavalry Reconnaissance Squadron commanded by Captain John J. D'Orazio. At midnight on April 28, the Troop wheeled out of Schongau with the mission of penetrating some 15 kilometers behind enemy lines to seize and hold the great bridge which was 1,000 feet long and spanned a 250 foot gorge. The Troop closed in on the structure and in quiet darkness Lieut. Eugene C. Patterson called for volunteers to accompany him on the last and most dangerous phase of the assignment. Immediately, Corporal Dennis F. Burke, Pfc. Thomas H. Scurlock, and Pvt. Herbert W. Biles, Jr., stepped forward. The four Tigers then crept cautiously to the northern approach to the bridge and overpowered the guards who were found snoozing peacefully. Though they were certain that the bridge was rigged for demolition, they raced to the other side to silence the other guards there. Thus, at 0300 on April 29 an important new bridgehead was established across the Ammer River. Troop C had carried out its duties with absolute perfection.

During "Red" Hankins' rapid movement south from Schongau, it was necessary to by-pass an enemy airfield. At about dusk on April 29, three light German planes took off from the field and flew over the column, dropping panzerfaust as bombs. One hit dangerously near "Red" Hankins' vehicle and blew off his right rear tire. Fortunately, none of the occupants were injured when they were thrown from the jeep.

ARTFUL ENEMY

On the same day, General Brooks contacted General Morris to discuss the problem of getting around blown craters in the roads which effectively slowed the Tigers. As a result of the conference, the infantry was brought up to clarify the situation. Of particular irritation were the enemy who perched on the high ground overlooking the roads. Using panzerfaust, they succeeded in wrecking some of our Mediums but in short order, they were knocked off the hills by the rugged infantry called up to do just that kind of a job. On April 29, General Brooks told both armor and infantry, "I want speed today. The tanks will take care of the roads and the infantry will take care of the hills." The Tenth cooperated fully as its units drove deeper into the Alps. Combat Command B, after grabbing Fuessen, sent Task Forces Chamberlain and Duncan south along the Lech River to career across the Austrian border and become the first units of the United States Seventh Army to enter Austria. Entrenched German infantry blocked CC B s way for awhile but were brushed aside as the attack proceeded. The last kilometer however, was recorded when CC B's tanks ran into an absolute impasse. The only two available routes remaining for these Tigers were effectively plugged by the artful enemy who utilized a concrete roadblock on one highway and blew a giant crater on another. No longer was it possible to by-pass in the Alps. On April 30, the Tenth Armored Division bagged 2,500 prisoners and in just five days had negotiated more than 100 miles of difficult terrain. Only a few more kilometers were left now, for the remainder of the Division's fighting Tigers.

Tiger infantry enter Ehingen

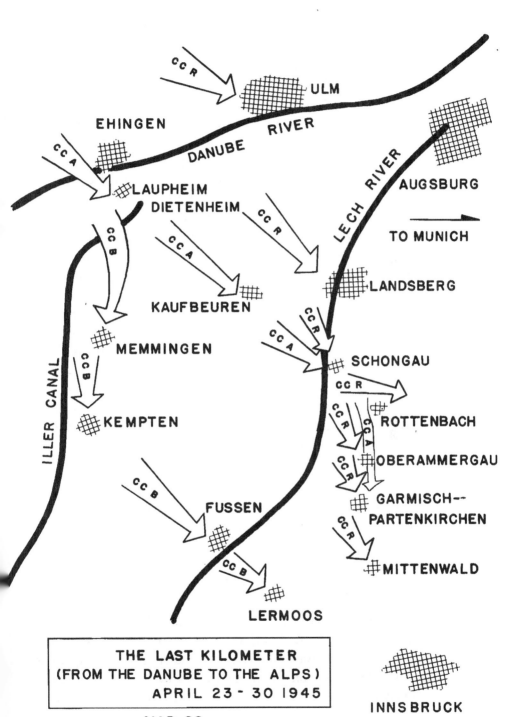

THE LAST KILOMETER
(FROM THE DANUBE TO THE ALPS)
APRIL 23 - 30 1945

MAP 29

Task Force Hankins, driving southeast, shoved enemy opposition aside at Oberammergau and rolled on to Garmisch-Partenkirchen, scene of the 1936 Winter Olympics. Here, a stiff-necked German colonel drove up to Hankins and offered to surrender the city. He was quickly accommodated. During the first few days in Garmisch-Partenkirchen, the Division took a German field marshal and five generals. Lieut. Kurt Meyer was surprised to hear his German telephone ring one morning. Answering it, he heard a pompous voice ask, "Are you ready to pick up the general tomorrow?". He answered, "Sure, just tell me where to meet you." With address in hand, Meyer and his men proceeded to the rendezvous the next day. When he arrived there, he found in addition to the general, 7 staff officers and 150 men. Before they departed, the general had one more request. "I have three other colonels here", he said, "may they come along too?" Lieut. Meyer obliged. The same day, a platoon headed by Lieut. Edward Gurocky uncovered a cache of 100 American and Canadian Red Cross parcels. While destroying a German ammunition dump, Sergeant Bert Treadwell and his squad noticed that the earth was loose. Investigating, they found a log covering a trench full of parcels. This was one of many instances in which the Germans had diverted Red Cross parcels for their own use.

ACHTUNG!

Prize catch of the day was that of Field Marshal Wilhelm List by Lieut. Warren P. Moss. Along with the author who accompanied Moss, an intensive search was made for the much-wanted List. He was found in mid-afternoon on April 30 hiding in the outskirts of Garmisch and delivered to the Tenth's stockade. In typical militaristic style, the other prisoners there clicked to immediate attention when he entered the PW cage. During the same day, he was hustled to Corps and then to Army headquarters and later, was shuttled to SHAEF. Finally, he was imprisoned in Nuremberg's prison where he resides even now. In 1942, he commanded Army Group A in Russia. In September, 1942, he

For German troops too, it was The Last Kilometer deep
in the heart of the Bavarian Alps

was ousted from his command by Hitler for refusing to make a
suicidal attack on Stalingrad. Before that he commanded the
14th German Army in Poland in 1939, the 12th German Army
in France in 1940 and in Greece in 1941.

On April 30, too, Task Force Duncan pushed to within 35
miles of the Italian border and was also stopped because of road
craters. Earlier, a final Tenth Armored Division Field Order was
issued which called for the capture of Innsbruck, Austria. However, the Germans had already blown out great chunks of the road
just south of Mittenwald to prevent further armored advance and
the Innsbruck Field Order had to be scrapped. At this juncture,
the steady doughs of the 44th Division came to the fore and

291

penetrated for a short distance, through the narrow mountain passes. So intent were the Tigers in grinding out the last mile, that they even tried to roll their tanks over the railroad tracks. The going was extremely difficult however, as the steel rails did not match the width of the tank tracks. Furthermore, signal block devices along the railroad completely prevented the tankers from making any further headway. The last kilometer was now a matter of record anyway. The big fight was over. And Garmisch-Partenkirchen, in the opinion of the Armoraiders, was a fine place to end the war on this, the last day of April of 1945. The final major battle operation of the Tiger Division consumed seven weeks. This period was marked with continuous combat, sleepless days and nights, sizzling speed, strained nerves, rain, snow, mud and cold. But at last, the ordeal was over.

THE PRICE FOR PEACE

General Paul W. Newgarden's careful pre-battle training paid huge dividends and General Morris' leadership propelled the Division through every battle with distinction. The price paid for victory was dear. Tigers losses were heavy. Almost 5,000 were killed or wounded. The Tigers' combat achievements are a matter of record. More than 56,000 enemy were taken prisoner and 650 towns and cities were captured. More important, the Tigers played a key role in many of the war's greatest battles. The epic stand at Bastogne will never be forgotten nor will the spectacular successes in the Saar-Moselle Triangle be overlooked by military historians. The capture of Trier was most important in the U. S. Third Army's effort to pierce the vaunted German West Wall. And finally, every step of the way from Cherbourg to the Brenner Pass, a distance of 600 miles, was made possible by the Tigers' courage, initiative and persistence. They had met and defeated the enemy's best. Hitler's earlier boast that American soldiers would never stand and fight must have provided slim comfort to the Nazi commanders who, one by one, capitulated in late April of 1945.

XIV

THE OCCUPATION

A LANKY CORPORAL from Harlan County, Kentucky, scooped up a handful of snow and slipped it down the back of a pretty fraulein in a bathing suit. She squealed and then took off down the slope on her skis. "This is the first time", he said, "that I ever realized snow was fit for anything." With that, he too pushed off with his ski poles and promptly fell flat on his face. The time was May, 1945, the place was the Zugspitz, where most Tigers played in their off-hours at one time or another during the Occupation period.

Whether Occupation days were pleasant, as in the case of the young Tiger corporal, or otherwise, was a matter of individual experience. No one could deny, however, that this phase of life in the European Theater of Operations was in vivid contrast to the days of combat which ended only a few short weeks before. The not-so-strenuous duties of Occupation began on May 9, 1945. For the first time, the lights were turned on, ending the hated blackout. On V-E day, the Tenth Armored staged a full-dress Review on the main street in Garmisch. Many Tigers suspected at the time, that higher headquarters had ordered the parade to give the Germans a good look at the men and machines which had helped to destroy Hitler's Nazi legions. For the author, it was a fascinating experience to watch the Germans turn out en masse to admire Tiger warriors and their equipment. The intense spectator interest indicated once again the military-minded type of philosophy of the Germans.

The Division's tanks, tracks and trucks were given a hurried bath for the big show to remove all signs of combat-accumulated mud. In the reviewing stand were Major General H. Edward Brooks, commander of the VI Corps, and Major General William

H. H. Morris, Jr., commander of the Tenth Armored. The weather was perfect, the spirit of the troops high, and everyone agreed that the Review was a huge success. There was much speculation in the next few days as to the Division's next assignment. To the great satisfaction of all, uncertainty was removed by the announcement that the Tenth would occupy the area. The Tigers of the Tenth were fortunate indeed in being assigned to one of the most strikingly beautiful areas in all Europe.

Dress parade: Germans get a good look at men and machines who defeated them in Partenkirchen on V-E Day

AT HOME ABROAD

Two weeks later, General Morris was elevated to the command of VI Corps, a promotion richly deserved. The General had earned the respect and admiration of everyone during the hectic days of battle across Europe. His place in the Tenth was taken by Major General Fay Brink Prickett, former commander of the 75th Infantry Division. And, after an absence of nine months, the "Tigers' Tale" returned to print. A commandeered local newspaper plant served as both printer and home to the Division newspaper. It was no small task to get rolling again, what with language and mechanical difficulties. Problems would have been increased, however, were it not for Lauren MacDaniel, who set type for fifteen subsequent issues during the occupation of Garmisch. Under the talented editorship of Richard S. Henry, the Division paper maintained a high quality from the start. Many editors at home rated "Tigers' Tale" an outstanding publication. Contributing also was Loren "Nero" Wolfe, who produced all the sports news that was fit to print. Eugene Dutchack and Carroll M. Rines collaborated in bringing to the Tigers additional sports coverage. A never-ending flow of good pictures came from ace photographer Ray Lutz. The Division was blessed with the artistic talents of Louis J. Short and Paul Kinnear. Their cartoons provided great GI humor for everyone. Adding zip to the "Tale" were the subtle, interesting and witty columns of Robert Murray.

Scenic Alps provide background for Tenth Armored Review

SUPER SPECIAL SERVICES

Later in May, the first large contingent of high-pointers left for the States and took with them the envy of the remaining Tigers. Soon new faces were appearing in the Division's units to await orders for shipment home, along with the Tigers. In the meantime, every one settled down to the business of Occupation. The billets were good, the food improved, duties were anything but strenuous and the opportunity for play had no limits. In early June of 1945, Special Service Units under the capable direction of Captain Harry Steigelman were hard at work setting up extensive facilities for the benefit of the Tigers. On June 4, the 55th Armored Engineers completed the "Tigers' Lair" at Lake Eibsee, which nestled under the towering 10,000 foot high Zugspitz peak. The "Tigers' Lair" provided every comfort and convenience imaginable for the Tigers. In short, this place was paradise recovered. At this time too, a major sports program was launched. The Tiger Softball Team annexed the championships of the XX Corps, Third Army and southern Germany. They went all the way to the final championship game of the European Theater of Operations where they were beaten by the Com Z All Stars. The world of the theater appeared at the Olympic Stadium in Garmisch, too. Jack Benny, Martha Tilton and Larry Adler entertained the appreciative Tigers. They were followed by "Information Please", Billy Rose's "Diamond Horseshoe Show", the USO's "Flying High", Eugene List, violinist, and the program concluded with German soprano Erna Sachs.

Not to be forgotten is the outstanding work of the girls of the Red Cross. Eighteen in number, they effectively cared for the Tigers all through the war. Their two clubmobiles were to be found everywhere, including up front. It was not an unusual sight to see one of the pretty girls, after having brought them hot coffee and doughnuts, holding her hands over her ears to lessen the shock of the booming guns of the artillerymen. Their faithful service to the Division may be illustrated by just one of many hardships they faced when they stood for eight consecutive hours in the pouring rain giving out 15,000 cups of coffee and 30,000 doughnuts when the Division passed through two checkpoints on its way to its first bivouac area after debarking at Cherbourg in September of 1944.

The SSO had its troubles too, in the early days overseas. Though it had 14 projectors, it was given only 1 film which had to be rotated through the Division units. Often the projectors would break down or the generator would conk out, making life difficult for the men of the SSO who did their best to provide efficient service. They were blamed for almost every snafu that occurred, despite the fact that the fault often belonged elsewhere. Two days after Metz was liberated, the theaters were functioning under SSO, and the Crystal Ballroom was reopened. At Trier, only hours after its capture, Roscoe Ates stuttered through a

Stars and Stripes are displayed at Partenkirchen's city hall

hilarious comedy routine in an auditorium which seated, or rather floored, 800 Tigers. A gaping hole in the roof and shattered walls did not deter the Tigers' fun there. Later, during the Occupation, the SSO got the aerial tramways, the cog railroad and other facilities operating for the benefit of the armoraiders. Plush hotels were opened, nightclubs functioned again and luxurious living became almost commonplace. Golfing, riding, fishing, swimming, skiing, sailing, hunting and every sport imaginable was made available for the conquerors, who behaved more like contented tourists, much to the satisfaction of the Bavarians. So perfect was the greater Garmisch area that it became the Third Army recreation area and later, it served the entire European Theater of Operations.

Carbine-carrying Tigers stroll along Midway at Olympic Stadium

The Tenth's Third Anniversary celebration, arranged by Lieut. Col. Joseph A. McChristian and the Special Service Office, easily surpassed all other events. For two days, beginning on July 14, the Tigers gorged themselves on 30,000 hotdogs, drank numerous barrels of fine Munich beer and strolled endless hours along the immense midway built in record time by the Second

Platoon, B Company of the 55th Engineers. During the celebration, they watched the largest circus in Europe perform in the hockey rink at the Olympic Stadium. Thanks to the efforts of Lieut. Scotty Rogers and the 132nd Ordnance Battalion which, among other things, transported the elephants, the circus proved to be a great success.

German circus performs for Armoraiders in Olympic hockey rink

Sightseeing tours and skiing were among the primary interests of many Tigers. They utilized the excellent slopes atop the Zugspitz all summer. They examined the breathtaking Bavarian alpine countryside from Munich all the way to Innsbruck, Austria, located at the northern approaches to the Brenner Pass. Nothing escaped the wandering eyes of the Tigers as they toured centuries-old castles, religious shrines, sports centers, wine-making establishments and entertainment meccas. Visited often were Oberammergau, home of the world-famous Passion Play, and Schloss Linderhof, summer palace of former King Ludwig of Bavaria. The final visit to Garmisch-Partenkirchen by General Patton came on July 15 in connection with the Division Review staged in his

Linderhof palace's 100 foot-high fountain adds to nature's splendor in Bavarian Alps

honor and in celebration of the Tigers' Third anniversary. His speech then holds true now. He said, "The enemy's only chance for victory in another war would be to try and knock us out in the first round." He added, "American military preparedness is of utmost importance," and concluded, "fire drills in our schools are not the cause of fires."

Luxury hotel on Lake Eibsee provides "summer home" for battle-weary troops during Occupation

On Saturday, June 30, 1945, the Armoraiders were startled to read in "Tigers Tale" that 450 top V-2 German scientists were harbored in Garmisch. They had been brought there from Peenemuende where, earlier, 12,000 Germans had toiled to develop rockets for eventual targets in America. Fortunately, their efforts met with failure. The war ended before they could complete their project of destruction. Two weeks before, the 55th Armored Engineers announced with dramatic impact the finding of ten tons of German gold at Walchensee, near Garmisch. Using mine detectors in a search for mines, the engineers instead found gold, a cool ten million dollars' worth which had been removed from the Reichsbank at Munich in the closing days of the war. Near

301

Oberau, another $400,000 in American currency was uncovered and turned over to Captain Noel Hinrichs and Captain Henry Knight of Division Headquarters, for processing and delivery to the proper authorities.

By mid-September, the Tigers had become familiar with both the countryside and the people who inhabited it and they liked what they saw. Even more, they liked the orders which had just been issued and meant departing for home at last. The advance party had already left on September 8. The remainder of the Division made hurried preparations to leave. GI watches and other materials were recaptured from the Tigers by Lieut. Col. James T. Phillips, the Division's Inspector General. Records were boxed, orders issued, equipment packed, farewells made and low-pointers were brought into the area to take over.

Tigers are entertained by Bavarian folk dancers during celebration of Tenth's Third Anniversary

Schneefernerhouse atop the Zugspitz, Germany's highest mountain provides Occupation troops with rare opportunity for winter sports

General George S. Patton, flanked by Major Generals Morris and Prickett, leave Olympic Stadium after USO performance of Billy Rose's Diamond Horseshoe Show

Outspoken Patton: "Fire drills are not the cause of fires"

Generals Patton, Morris and Prickett prepare to review entire Division assembled near Garmisch for Third Anniversary celebration

Vacationing Tiger troops at Eibsee are hosts to General Patton. Giant telescope permits excellent view of mountain climbers attempting to scale vertical walls of Zugspitz

Mother nature transforms area into winter wonderland

132nd Ordnance's Sergeant Bert Tradewell uncovers 100 Red Cross boxes meant for Allies but diverted and hidden by Germans

$400,000 in American currency found in barn near Oberau is checked by Sergeant Leroy Batson, Captain Noel Hinrichs and Captain James H. Knight at Tiger Headquarters

Occupation headquarters in Garmisch-Partenkirchen, Germany

For GI's only: The Tigers' lair at Eibsee is paradise recovered

GOING HOME

For many, going home meant an uncomfortable ride in the infamous "40 and 8" railroad cars. But this time, the "8 horses" did not make the trip, making room for more Tigers in the car—room that didn't exist in the first place. However, no one complained, for this was the one trip that everyone wanted to make, regardless of conditions. For those who travelled by motor convoy, the going was just as rough. Enroute, two stops were made. One was at a desolate airfield near Ulm, and the other at a super GI tourist camp at Nancy, France. There was little time to enjoy the facilities at either camp since the "hosts" insisted on an early morning departure to make room for other incoming convoys. The next stop signalled the half-way mark, the Rheims assembly area. Here, at Camp Norfolk, movies were provided, along with good stage shows. Facilities of all kinds were made available to the Tigers but most of the time here was spent repacking, remark-

Pfc. John Berberian, Company C, 55th Armored Engineers holds one of 728 bars of gold taken from mountain cache near Walchensee. Each bar worth almost $15,000

ing, exchanging money, turning in clothing, and completing tons of paper work. After a few days, and several shot injections, the Tigers were shipped by train to Marseilles on September 22, with the exception of a small motor convoy which had been sent ahead to prepare for the main group's arrival there.

The Calais staging area, 15 miles north of Marseilles, became our next and final assembly point. Processing was completed here, including pay in American currency. And finally, after a few days wait, the Tigers were loaded aboard the "Breckinridge," a Navy transport making its first return trip to America. This was a new ship. It was spanking clean and provided excellent food and reasonably good quarters for the happy home-bound Tigers.

Jack Benny is assisted by two Tigers in carrying singer Martha Tilton off stage during big show at Olympic Stadium

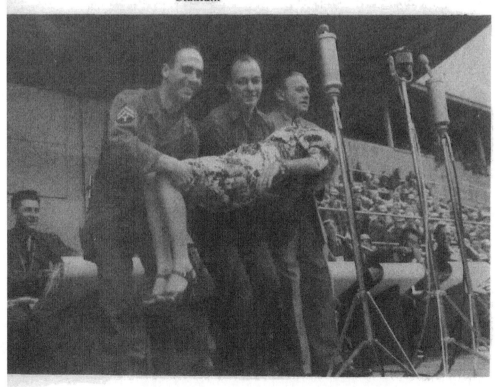

Combat Command B's units get Bastogne battle streamers
from General Morris as General McAuliffe and General
Prickett watch ceremony

Nine days later, at noon on October 13, 1945, the big transport
nosed alongside the dock at Newport News and unloaded its cargo
of war-weary veterans. By mid-afternoon the Tigers were all
transported to Camp Patrick Henry where its most important facil-
ity, the telephone, immediately became the center of attraction.
Virtually every Tiger placed a long distance call to his wife, fam-
ily, sweetheart or friend. A day later, almost everyone was enroute
home. Forgotten for the moment were the ordeals of war, the
buddies left behind, the magnificent achievements of the Division
and almost everything that followed when the Tiger left for
overseas the year before. It is hoped that IMPACT will serve to
recall to the reader, the day by day actions of the Tenth Armored
Division throughout its distinguished history. For the Division
owes its great fighting reputation to each of the valiant men who
served it and America so well.

311

Lucky Tiger "high pointers" assemble at Partenkirchen prior to entraining for home

USO performers wave goodbye to departing Armoraiders at Marseilles, France

STAFF AND UNIT COMMANDERS

(From July 15, 1942 to September 15, 1945)

Commanding General   * MAJOR GENERAL PAUL W. NEWGARDEN
LIEUT. GENERAL WILLIAM H. H. MORRIS, JR.
MAJOR GENERAL FAY BRINK PRICKETT
BRIGADIER GENERAL H. B. CHEADLE

Chief of Staff   COLONEL JULIAN E. RAYMOND
*** COLONEL BASIL G. THAYER
LIEUT. COL. JOSEPH A. McCHRISTIAN
COLONEL RICHARD STEINBACH
LIEUT. COL. JOSEPH A. McCHRISTIAN
COLONEL CORNELIUS A. LICHIRIE
LIEUT. COL. JOHN F. LAUDIG

G-1   LIEUT. COL. JOHN F. LAUDIG

G-2   LIEUT. COL. ROBERT M. BLANCHARD
LIEUT. COL. WILLIAM E. ECKLES

G-3   LIEUT. COL. THOMAS H. ALLEN
COLONEL FRANK E. BRITTON
LIEUT. COL. JOHN W. SHEFFIELD
LIEUT. COL. JOSEPH A. McCHRISTIAN
LIEUT. COL. JOHN W. SHEFFIELD

G-4   LIEUT. COL. DONALD A. POORMAN
LIEUT. COL. CLARK WEBBER

G-5   CAPTAIN LEIGH S. PLUMMER

G-3 Air   MAJOR RICHARD STANFIELD
** MAJOR RANDOLPH C. JORDAN
MAJOR RICHARD CRERIE

Division Artillery   COLONEL MAURICE W. DANIEL
LIEUT. COL. JOHN O. TAYLOR
COLONEL J. J. B. WILLIAMS

** COLONEL BERNARD F. LUEBBERMANN
COLONEL EDWARD H. METZGER
COLONEL HUGH S. McLEOD

Combat Command A

BRIG. GEN. ROBERT W. GROW
BRIG. GEN. KENNETH G. ALTHAUS
*** BRIG. GEN. EDWIN W. PIBURN
COLONEL BASIL G. THAYER
COLONEL THOMAS M. BRINKLEY
COLONEL FRED H. KELLY

Combat Command B

BRIG. GEN. MORRILL ROSS
* COLONEL RENN LAWRENCE
COLONEL WILLIAM L. ROBERTS
BRIG. GEN. EDWIN W. PIBURN
COLONEL BASIL G. THAYER
COLONEL THOMAS M. BRINKLEY
LIEUT. COL. ROBERT W. BLACK

Reserve Command

COLONEL JOHN A. LAMBERT
COLONEL NUMA A. WATSON
COLONEL WILLIAM L. ROBERTS
COLONEL WADE C. GATCHELL
LIEUT. COL. JOHN C. GOLDEN

Division Trains

COLONEL THOMAS M. BRINKLEY
COLONEL CORNELIUS A. LICHIRIE
MAJOR R. F. WALTERS

Inspector General

LIEUT. COL. JAMES T. PHILLIPS

Adjutant General

* LIEUT. COL. FRANCIS S. MALLON
LIEUT. COL. RALPH R. CARLIN

Division Surgeon

COLONEL PAUL G. HANSEN
LIEUT. COL. MICHAEL D. BUSCEMI
LIEUT. COL. E. S. WALLACE

Judge Advocate General

MAJOR J. H. SARGENT
LIEUT. COL. ALEXANDER A. LaFLEUR

Division Chaplain	LIEUT. COL. PAUL MADDOX LIEUT. COL. MITCHELL W. PHILLIPS
Division Ordnance Officer	LIEUT. COL. MERTON K. HEIMSTEAD
Provost Marshal	LIEUT. COL. JOHN W. SHEFFIELD MAJOR CARL P. CRONINGER MAJOR ROBERT W. BROWN MAJOR ROBERT J. McPEAK
Division Signal Officer	CAPTAIN WILLIAM SHULTZ LIEUT. COL. RILEY A. GRAHAM
Division Finance Officer	LIEUT. COL. RAYMOND M. ST. CLAIR
Chemical Warfare Officer	LIEUT. COL. HARRY B. FELDMAN
Division Quartermaster	MAJOR FRANKLIN R. SIBERT LIEUT. COL. VALENTINE SEEGER
Division Engineer	LIEUT. COL. WILLIAM SPANGLER LIEUT. COL. WILLIAM H. LEWIS ** LIEUT. COL. WADSWORTH P. CLAPP LIEUT. COL. WILLIAM R. GEILER
Headquarters Commandant	LIEUT. COL. JOHN W. SHEFFIELD ** MAJOR WALTER S. BARNES CAPTAIN JAMES H. KNIGHT
Division Motor Officer	LIEUT. COL. ROBERT S. DEMITZ
Special Service Officer	CAPTAIN RUSSELL C. HINOTE MAJOR COURTLAND A. BASSETT CAPTAIN HARRY A. STEIGELMAN
Public Relations Officer	CAPTAIN WAYNE C. JACKSON CAPTAIN LESTER M. NICHOLS
Aides to General Newgarden	LIEUT. COL. JOHN W. SHEFFIELD MAJOR ROGER RAWLEY

315

MAJOR R. F. WALTERS
CAPTAIN HENRY J. KNIGHT

Aides to General Morris MAJOR R. C. JORDAN
MAJOR JOHN E. FINCH
CAPTAIN D. M. CHAPMAN

Third Armored Regiment COLONEL THOMAS M. BRINKLEY

Third Tank Battalion *** LIEUT. COL. HENRY T. CHERRY, JR.
MAJOR WHEELER M. THACKSTON
LIEUT. COL. HENRY T. CHERRY, JR.

Eleventh Armored Regiment COLONEL BERTRAM MORROW
BRIG. GENERAL KENNETH G. ALTHAUS

Eleventh Tank Battalion COLONEL WHITSIDE MILLER
LIEUT. COL. THOMAS C. CHAMBERLAIN

Twenty-First Tank Battalion LIEUT. COL. JOHN R. RILEY

*Twentieth Armored Infantry
Battalion* LIEUT. COL. NELSON A. BUTLER
LIEUT. COL. THOMAS H. ALLEN
LIEUT. COL. HENRY H. HESTER
*** MAJOR STANLEY WEINER
*** LIEUT. COL. WILLIAM R. DESOBRY
MAJOR CHARLES L. HUSTEAD
** LIEUT. COL. JACK J. RICHARDSON
MAJOR JAMES B. DUNCAN

Fifty-Fourth Armored Regiment COLONEL THOMAS ELY
COLONEL NUMA A. WATSON

*Fifty-Fourth Armored Infantry
Battalion* *** LIEUT. COL. JAMES O'HARA
** LIEUT. COL. WILLIAM T. S. ROBERTS
LIEUT. COL. JAMES O'HARA
MAJOR RICHARD W. ULRICH

*Sixty-First Armored Infantry
Battalion* *** LIEUT. COL. HENRY R. HESTER
** LIEUT. COL. MILES L. STANDISH

316

LIEUT. COL. CURTISS L. HANKINS

Four-Nineteenth Armored Field	LIEUT. COL. ROBERT C. McCABE
Artillery Battalion	
Four-Twentieth Armored Field	LIEUT. COL. MASON H. LUCAS
Artillery Battalion	** LIEUT. COL. BARRY D. BROWNE
	LIEUT. COL. WILLIS D. CRITTENBERGER, JR.

Four-Twenty Third Armored LIEUT. COL. WILLIAM W. BEVERLY
Field Artillery Battalion
Fifty-Fifth Armored Engineer ** LIEUT. COL. WILLIAM SPANGLER
Battalion LIEUT. COL. WILLIAM H. LEWIS
** LIEUT. COL. WADSWORTH P. CLAPP
LIEUT. COL. WILLIAM R. GEILER

Eightieth Armored Medical LIEUT. COL. MICHAEL D. BUSCEMI
Battalion LIEUT. COL. EDWIN S. WALLACE

Ninetieth Cavalry Reconnais- COLONEL CORNELIUS A. LICHIRIE
sance Squadron LIEUT. COL. RICHARD P. SCOTT

One Thirty-Second Ordnance LIEUT. COL. MERTON K. HEIMSTEAD
Maintenance Battalion
609th Tank Destroyer Battalion LIEUT. COL. ROWLAND A. BROWNE
MAJOR WILLIAM F .SHOTOLA

796 AAA AW (SP) Battalion LIEUT. COL. ORMAND K. WILLIAMS

THE PRICE FOR PEACE

Killed In Action	642
Died From Wounds	132
Died After Capture	10
Wounded In Action	3,247
	TOTAL 4,031

DECORATIONS AND AWARDS

TOTAL AWARDS AND DECORATIONS	3,086
ORIGINAL	2,844
OAK LEAF CLUSTERS	242
DISTINGUISHED SERVICE CROSS	19
DITINGUISHED SERVICE MEDAL	1
SILVER STAR	412
LEGION OF MERIT	20
DISTINGUISHED FLYING CROSS	2
SOLDIER'S MEDAL	25
BRONZE STAR MEDAL	2,578
AIR MEDAL	29
PURPLE HEART MEDAL	4,031
ALL OTHER AWARDS (except foreign decorations)	3,086
DECORATIONS AND AWARDS · Grand Total	7,117

(plus 320 Certificates of Merit)

UNIT DECORATIONS AND CITATIONS

DISTINGUISHED UNIT CITATION: COMBAT COMMAND B

HIGHER HEADQUARTERS ASSIGNMENTS
OVERSEAS

5 SEPTEMBER 44	III CORPS, NINTH ARMY, TWELFTH ARMY GROUP
10 OCTOBER	THIRD ARMY, TWELFTH ARMY GROUP
23 OCTOBER	XX CORPS, THIRD ARMY, TWELFTH ARMY GROUP
16 DECEMBER	XX CORPS, THIRD ARMY BUT ATTACHED TO FIRST ARMY
17 DECEMBER	ATTACHED TO VIII CORPS, FIRST ARMY
20 DECEMBER	III CORPS, THIRD ARMY, TWELFTH ARMY GROUP
21 DECEMBER	XII CORPS, THIRD ARMY, TWELFTH ARMY GROUP

26 DECEMBER	XX CORPS, THIRD ARMY, TWELFTH ARMY GROUP
17 JANUARY 45	ATTACHED TO XXI CORPS, SEVENTH ARMY, SIXTH ARMY GROUP
25 JANUARY	XV CORPS, THIRD ARMY, TWELFTH ARMY GROUP
10 FEBRUARY	XX CORPS, THIRD ARMY, TWELFTH ARMY GROUP
23 MARCH	ATTACHED TO XXI CORPS, SEVENTH ARMY, SIXTH ARMY GROUP
1 APRIL	VI CORPS, SEVENTH ARMY, SIXTH ARMY GROUP
9 MAY	THIRD ARMY, TWELFTH ARMY GROUP (OCCUPATION)

TENTH ARMORED DIVISION CHRONOLOGY

15 JULY 42—Tenth Armored Division Activated at Fort Benning, Georgia. (Major General Paul W. Newgarden assumed command)

5 SEPTEMBER 43—Division moved to Camp Gordon, Georgia.

14 JULY 44—Maj. Gen. Newgarden and Col. Renn Lawrence killed in plane crash near Chattanooga, Tennessee.

15 JULY 44—Division Review in honor of Gen. Newgarden and Col. Lawrence.

25 JULY 44—Maj. Gen. William H. H. Morris, Jr., named commanding general of the Division.

31 AUGUST 44—Division entrained for New York Port of Embarkation at Camp Shanks, New York.

13 SEPTEMBER 44—Division sailed for overseas assignment.

23 SEPTEMBER 44—Arrived at Cherbourg, France.

2 NOVEMBER 44—First combat at 0926 at Mars La Tours, France.

15 NOVEMBER 44—First major offensive. Support of XX Corps at Metz.

19 NOVEMBER 44—First U. S. Third Army Division to enter Germany.

17 DECEMBER 44—First Division rushed north to help stop German Bulge.

19 DECEMBER 44—Combat Command B begins epic defense of Bastogne.

20 FEBRUARY 45—Tenth overruns Saar-Moselle Triangle.

2 MARCH 45—Trier, first major Third Army city captured.

28 MARCH 45—Crossed Rhine River near Worms, Germany.

23 APRIL 45—Crossed Danube River at Ehingen, Germany.

27 APRIL 45—First U. S. Seventh Army Division to enter Austria.

30 APRIL 45—Captured Garmisch-Partenkirchen in southern Bavaria.

9 MAY 45—End of hostilities at 0001.

10 MAY 45—Occupation duties began.

23 MAY 45—Maj. Gen. Morris named Commanding General of VI Corps. Maj. Gen. F. B. Prickett named Tenth Armored C. G.

12 SEPTEMBER 45—Ended Occupation. Left for embarkation at Marseilles.

3 OCTOBER 45—Sailed from Marseilles, France.

13 OCTOBER 45—Arrived at Camp Patrick Henry, Newport News, Virginia.

15 OCTOBER 45—Inactivation of Tenth Armored Division.

COMMAND POSTS ADVANCE DETAIL

Left Camp Gordon, Georgia	21 August	1944
Arrived Fort Hamilton, New York	22 August	
Left New York	28 August	
Arrived Scotland (Gurock)	3 September	
Arrived England (Winchester)	4 September	
Left England (Southampton)	7 September	
Arrived Omaha Beach, France	7 September	
Arrived Valogne, France	8 September	

Left Valogne	14 September
Arrived Teurtheville, France	14 September

DIVISION HEADQUARTERS

Left Camp Gordon, Georgia	31 August	1944
Arrived Camp Shank, New York	1 September	
Left New York	13 September	
Arrived Cherbourg, France	23 September	
Left Teurtheville, France	24 October	
Arrived Mars-la-Tour	29 October	
Division's first actual contact with enemy Time: 0926.	2 November	1944
Left Mars-la-Tour	9 November	
Arrived Ottange	9 November	
Left Ottange	14 November	
Arrived Petite Hettange	15 November	
Arrived Laumesfeld	19 November	
Left Laumesfeld	21 November	
Arrived Apach	21 November	
Left Apach	17 December	
Arrived Luxembourg	17 December	
Left Luxembourg	23 December	
Arrived Mersch	23 December	
Left Mersch	27 December	
Arrived Metz	27 December	
Arrived Dieuze	17 January	1945
Left Dieuze	22 January	1945
Arrived Falquemont	22 January	
Left Falquemont	10 February	
Arrived Metz	10 February	
Left Metz	19 February	
Arrived Apach	19 February	
Left Apach	22 February	
Arrived Wincheringen	22 February	

Left Wincheringen	22 February 1945
Arrived Ayl	22 February
Left Ayl	2 March
Arrived Trier	2 March
Left Trier	17 March
Arrived Mitlosheim	17 March
Left Mitlosheim	18 March
Arrived Wadern	18 March
Left Wadern	19 March
Arrived St. Wendel	19 March
Left St. Wendel	20 March
Arrived Kaiserslautern	20 March
Left Kaiserslauten	21 March
Arrived Edenkoben	24 March
Went Under Seventh Army 241800B March 45	
Left Edenkoben	28 March
Arrived Manheim (Waldhoff)	
Crossed Rhine R 1925B	28 March
Left Manheim	31 March
Arrived Hiedelbourg	2 April
Left Hiedelbourg	2 April
Arrived Hoffenheim	2 April
Left Hoffenheim	4 April
Arrived Bad Rappeneau	4 April
Left Bad Rappeneau	6 April
Arrived Merchingen	6 April
Left Merchingen Crossed Neckar River	7 April
Arrived Assamstadt	7 April
Left Assamstadt	12 April
Arrived Ingelfingen	12 April
Left Ingelfingen	14 April
Arrived Ohringen	14 April
Left Ohringen	18 April
Arrived Bubenorbis	18 April

Left Bubenorbis	19 April	1945
Arrived Fichtenberg	19 April	
Left Fichtenberg	20 April	
Arrived Lorch	20 April	
Left Lorch	21 April	
Arrived Goppingen	21 April	
Left Goppingen	23 April	
Arrived Laichingen	23 April	
Left Laichingen	23 April	
Arrived Ehingen	23 April	
Left Ehingen	24 April	
Arrived Laupheim	24 April	
Left Laupheim	25 April	
Arrived Dietenheim	25 April	
Left Dietenheim	26 April	
Arrived Baben Hausen	26 April	
Left Baben Hausen	27 April	
Arrived Mindelheim 1130	27 April	
Left Mindelheim 1830	27 April	
Arrived Kaufbeuren 2000	27 April	
Left Kaufbeuren	28 April	
Arrived Schongau	28 April	
Left Schongau	29 April	
Arrived Steingarden	29 April	
Left Steingarden	30 April	
Arrived Garmisch, Partenkirchen	30 April	

All hostilities in the ETO ceased 0001, 9 May 1945

DIVISION HIGHLIGHTS

First American armored division to debark on French soil directly from America. Landed at Cherbourg, France on September 23, 1944.

Fought with distinction in France, Luxembourg, Belgium, Germany and Austria.

Captured 56,000 German prisoners and 650 towns and cities.

Served in four United States operational armies overseas: First, Third, Seventh and Ninth armies.

Fought with III, VI, VIII, XII, XV, XX and XXI Corps.

Captured first major Third Army City . . . Trier. March 2, 1945

Overran Saar-Moselle Triangle in one of the war's most audacious operations on February 20, 1945.

Dubbed the "Ghost Division" by Germans. Reappeared several times in different U. S. Army sectors against same German units.

Was first U. S. Third Army Division to cross German border. Eft, November 19, 1944.

Was first U. S. Seventh Army Division to cross Austrian border. Fuessen, April 27, 1945.

Spearheaded attack of U. S. Third Army to the Rhine and U. S. Seventh Army to the Alps.

Participated in capture of Metz. First time Metz fortress captured in 1500 years. November 15, 1944.

Played major role in epic defense of Bastogne. Was first to stem German attack east of that city. December 19, 1944.

Was first Division to be rushed north by Eisenhower to help stop German winter blitz which became known as "The Battle of the Bulge". December 17, 1944.

Received Distinguished Unit Citation for Combat Command B's stand at Bastogne.

Captured vital Echlesbacher bridge which connected lowlands of southern Bavaria with Alpine country. This action speeded war's end in the south. April 28, 1945.

Aided materially in preventing Germans from capturing city of Luxembourg. December 17, 1945.

GENERAL DWIGHT D. EISENHOWER

MAJOR GENERAL PAUL W. NEWGARDEN

LIEUT. GEN. WILLIAM H. H. MORRIS, Jr.

MAJOR GENERAL FAY BRINK PRICKETT

After reviewing French Second Armored Division during rainstorm at Metz, General De Gaulle receives Brig. Gen. Edwin W. Pilburn at City Hall

Brigadier General Kenneth G. Althaus

Before capture of Metz: Lieut. Gen. George S. Patton, Maj. Gen. Walton H. Walker, Maj. Gen. William H. H. Morris and Brig. Gen. Kenneth G. Althaus

Lieut. Col. Henry T. Cherry awards Silver Stars to men
of the crack Third Tank Battalion

CC A's mascot, M-1, is cared for by Sergeant Leslie K.
Reynolds. Pup was smuggled from America

Armoraiders enjoy rest center at Lake Eibsee

General Prickett bestows blue upon "Ace" ridden by
Private Thomas Willingham of CC A at Tiger horse show

At Camp Gordon Georgia: Major General and Mrs. Paul
W. Newgarden

"Admiral" Patton on Lake Eibsee. With him are General
Prickett and Colonel Cornelius A. Lichirie

At Garmisch: Lieut. Gen. Alexander S. Patch, center,
Maj. Gen. Edward H. Brooks, left, and Maj. Gen. William
H. H. Morris

Tiger Baseball Team: Champions of Southern Germany

At Innsbruck: Lieut. Gen. Devers pins Distinguished Service Medal on General Morris. Awaiting same award is General Anthony McAuliffe

Captain "Bud" Billet, third from left, poses with his platoon leaders of Company B, 20th Armored Infantry near Metz

Silver Star recipients of Third Tank Battalion

Lt. Col.'s Phillips and Seeger

Lt. Col. Ralph R. Carlin

Lt. Col. Curtiss L. Hankins

Lt. Col. Henry T. Cherry

Lt. Col. Jack J. Richardson

Lt. Col. Thomas C. Chambe

Col. Julian E. Raymond

Col. Renn Lawrence

Col. Wade C. Gatchell

Lt. Col. John R. Riley

Lt. Col. William W. Beverly

Major Bill Taylor

Col. Richard P. Scott

Col. Cornelius A. Lichirie

Lt. Col. Riley A. Graham

Major Cortland A. Bassett

Capt. Harry A. Steigelman

Lt. Col. Joseph A. McChristian

Col. Basil G. Thayer

Lt. Col. William E. Eckles

Lt. Col. John F. Laudig

Col. Thomas M. Brinkley

Lt. Col. William T. S. Roberts

Lt. Col. Miles L. Standish

Train Headquarters Company bakes cake for Sergeant
George Rathey, center, prior to his departure for the
States

Armoraiders celebrate end of war at unit's private milk
bar

Staff NCO's stage
"Nazi" party at Metz

Brig. Gen. William L. Roberts at Midway in Partenkirchen

General Morris awards Bronze Star to Lieut. Col. John W. Sheffield

Former heavyweight champion Billy Conn atop the Zugspitz with the Author

Best Band in the Land: Tiger Division Orchestra

Hail and fairwell: Tiger officers line up to greet General Morris prior to his departure for VI Corps

Tiger staff officers enjoy brief interlude near Saar River

Generals Morris, Prickett and McAuliffe and Tiger staff stand in review at Olympic Stadium, Garmisch-Partenkirchen as Bastogne colors are awarded Combat Command B

Division public relations staff at Garmisch Headquarters

"Commandant" Jerry Bluestein poses at Murnau, Germany

Hate to see you go pal: Hilarious send off for departing Tiger Cub

Excited exodus: Occupation duties are over for these happy Tigers

End of the Line

CPSIA information can be obtained at www.ICGtesting.com
Printed in the USA
LVOW011852161212

311891LV00024B/1022/P